Mastering Cloud Development using Microsoft Azure

Master the art of efficiently composing Azure services
and implement them in real-world scenarios

Roberto Freato

Marco Parenzan

BIRMINGHAM - MUMBAI

Mastering Cloud Development using Microsoft Azure

First published: June 2016

Production reference: 1220616

Published by Packt Publishing Ltd.
Livery Place
35 Livery Street
Birmingham B3 2PB, UK.

ISBN 978-1-78217-333-5

www.packtpub.com

Credits

Authors
Roberto Freato
Marco Parenzan

Reviewer
Florian Klaffenbach

Commissioning Editor
Amarabha Banerjee

Acquisition Editor
Tushar Gupta

Content Development Editor
Viranchi Shetty

Technical Editor
Ravikiran Pise

Copy Editors
Safis Editing
Karuna Narayanan
Stuti Srivastava

Project Coordinator
Izzat Contractor

Proofreader
Safis Editing

Indexer
Mariammal Chettiyar

Graphics
Jason Monteiro

Production Coordinator
Aparna Bhagat

Cover Work
Aparna Bhagat

About the Authors

Roberto Freato has been an independent IT consultant since he started to work. Working for small software factories while he was studying, after his M.Sc. in Computer Science Engineering with his thesis on *Consumer Cloud Computing*, he got specialization in Cloud and Azure. Today, he works as a freelance consultant for major companies in Italy, helping clients design and kick off their distributed software solutions. He trains the developer community in his free time, speaking at many conferences. He has been a Microsoft MVP since 2010.

> I would like to thank Simona, Mom, and Dad.

Marco Parenzan is an experienced .NET developer, now also a Cloud Computing and Azure trainer. A Microsoft MVP on Azure since 2014, he is curious about the IoT business and architectures. He loves retrogaming, and he tries programming little games in his spare time. He is a community lead for 1nn0va, a local Microsoft community in Pordenone, Italy, and he likes training developers in companies and university.

> First, I'm grateful to Roberto for involving me writing this great book. One of my dreams was sharing my knowledge of technology, which started many years ago when my friend Marco Pozzan involved me in 1nn0va, our local Microsoft community in Pordenone. This book helped me achieve this dream.
>
> Finally, I want to thank my wife, Paola, and our two beloved children for supporting me and giving me the large amount of time I needed to complete this book.

About the Reviewer

Florian Klaffenbach started his IT carrier in 2004 as the first and second level IT support technician and IT salesman trainee for a B2B online shop. After this, he moved to a small company, working as IT project manager, involved in planning, implementing, and integrating industrial plants and laundries into enterprise IT. After spending some years there, he joined Dell Germany. Here, he started from scratch as an Enterprise technical support analyst and later worked on a project to start Dell Technical Communities and support over social media in Europe and outside the U.S. Currently, he works as a solutions architect and consultant for Microsoft Infrastructure and Cloud specialized on Microsoft Hyper-V, fileservices, System Center Virtual Machine Manager, and Microsoft Azure IaaS.

Additionally to his job engagement, he is active as a Microsoft blogger and lecturer. He blogs at his own page, `Datacenter-Flo.de`, or Azure Germany Community. Together with a very good friend, he founded the Windows Server User Group Berlin to create a network of Microsoft ITPros in Berlin. Florian maintains a very tight network for many vendors such as Cisco, Dell, Microsoft, and communities. This helps him increase his experience and get the best solution for his customers. Since 2016, he is also co-chairman of the Azure Community Germany. In April 2016, Microsoft awarded Florian as Microsoft's Most Valuable Professional for Cloud and Datacenter Management.

Florian worked for several companies, such as Dell Germany, CGI Germany, and his first employer TACK GmbH. Currently, he works at msg service ag as Senior Consultant Microsoft Cloud Infrastructure.

He has worked on the books *Taking Control with System Center App Controller*, *Microsoft Azure Storage Essentials*, *Mastering Microsoft Azure Development*, and *Mastering Microsoft Deployment Toolkit 2013* for Packt Publishing before working on this book.

I want to thank Packt Publishing for giving me the chance to review the book. I would also like to thank my employer. I especially want to thank my girlfriend for not killing me because I spend so much of my spare time on the community and work.

www.PacktPub.com

eBooks, discount offers, and more

Did you know that Packt offers eBook versions of every book published, with PDF and ePub files available? You can upgrade to the eBook version at www.PacktPub.com and as a print book customer, you are entitled to a discount on the eBook copy. Get in touch with us at customercare@packtpub.com for more details.

At www.PacktPub.com, you can also read a collection of free technical articles, sign up for a range of free newsletters and receive exclusive discounts and offers on Packt books and eBooks.

https://www2.packtpub.com/books/subscription/packtlib

Do you need instant solutions to your IT questions? PacktLib is Packt's online digital book library. Here, you can search, access, and read Packt's entire library of books.

Why subscribe?

- Fully searchable across every book published by Packt
- Copy and paste, print, and bookmark content
- On demand and accessible via a web browser

Instant updates on new Packt books

Get notified! Find out when new books are published by following @PacktEnterprise on Twitter or the *Packt Enterprise* Facebook page.

Table of Contents

Preface	**v**
Chapter 1: Building Basic Services	**1**
CloudMakers.XYZ	**2**
Scenario 1 – Bootstrapping the company	3
Setting up the development environment	**4**
Where is my data center?	7
Building a development machine	8
Generalizing the VM	13
Implementing the development process	**16**
Creating a new VSO environment	18
Integrating Visual Studio	21
Integrating third-party services	23
Provisioning development environments for mobility	**25**
Azure Active Directory	27
Azure RemoteApp	29
Automating repetitive operations	**33**
Azure Automation	34
Azure Scheduler	40
Summary	**42**
Chapter 2: Enhancing the Hybrid Process	**43**
CloudMakers.XYZ	**43**
Service Manager (classic) mode versus Resource Manager mode	**44**
Configuring a Resource mode Virtual Network for the frontend servers	**47**
Configuring a Service mode (classic) Virtual Network for the backend servers	**52**
Connecting two virtual networks with site-to-site connection	**56**

Configuring Office connectivity with a point-to-site VPN	59
Deploy a Windows Azure Virtual Machine in an ARM Virtual Network	61
Managing virtual networks with Operational Insight	65
System Update Assessment	71
SQL Assessment	73
Malware Assessment	76
Summary	78
Chapter 3: Building the Frontend	**79**
It's all about data	79
Polyglot Persistence	82
Scenario	84
Writing catalogs into Azure DocumentDB	87
Building up your web frontend with Microsoft ASP.NET MVC	102
Searching in catalogs via Azure Search	107
Storing unstructured data in Azure Storage	115
Speeding up data access with caching and Azure Redis	123
Persisting a shopping cart with Azure Table Storage	126
Publishing your application into Azure web apps	131
Configuring a web application with a Custom Domain Name	138
Summary	140
Chapter 4: Building the Backend	**141**
CloudMakers.XYZ scenario evolution	142
Handling orders	144
Decoupling user actions from SQL sinking	145
Producing denormalized data for analysis	152
Extracting, transforming, and loading data into a data warehouse	155
Predicting valuable information with machine learning	164
Outsourcing Identity and Access Management	172
Azure AD and claims-based authentication	174
Azure Active Directory B2C	176
Advanced features	181
Summary	184
Chapter 5: Building the Mobile Experience	**185**
The technical community case study	185
Writing mobile applications	187
Building a mobile app with Visual Studio Tools for Apache Cordova	190
The need for a fast and easy solution	200
Introduction to mobile apps	202
Getting data from the service	209

Sending data to the service   **213**
Azure and Node.js   **217**
Summary   **223**

Chapter 6: Building the API Layer   225

CloudMakers.XYZ scenario evolution   **226**
Building the API   **228**
   Using the ASP.NET Web API   229
   ServiceStack   233
   Documenting the API with the Swagger/OpenAPI   235
Deploying the API   **237**
   Advanced App Service features   238
     App Settings management   239
     Slots and traffic routing   240
     Continuous deployment   241
     Hybrid connections   242
     Application logs   243
     Backup and restore   244
   API Gateway   245
Using Azure API Management   **246**
   Creating an API   248
   Using policies   251
   Identity and Access Management   255
   Advanced APIM Management   256
Debugging complex API workflows   **257**
   Debugging App Service with remote debugging   259
   Using a Service Bus relay to debug REST services   260
Summary   **263**

Chapter 7: Working with Messages   265

Dealing the future with commands   **266**
Messages and queues   **267**
The scenario   **269**
Sending messages with queues   **270**
Processing messages with workers   **275**
Dealing the past with events   **280**
Per-message event handling   **281**
Per-stream event handling   **288**
   Collecting events with Azure Event Hubs   290
   Processing event streams with Azure Stream Analytics   291
Summary   **298**

Chapter 8: Deploying Solutions in Azure   299
Azure Resource Manager   300
Writing the template   302
Programming the template   312
Organizing deployment tasks with the Deploy to Azure button   317
Summary   322
Index   325

Preface

This is a book for you, the developer, who lives in his/her comfort zone. This book is made up of the experience gained during the evolution of the Web from its inception (the nineties) to the present. Earlier, you used a single reference architecture and reused it as many times as possible. This is because you grew up in an object-oriented development era with a focus on tools and languages. Therefore, you are used to developing web and applications in the same manner using the same tools. You find moving away from a monolithic, three tier, strongly-coupled, SQL-based, on-premise, web-only development environment uncomfortable.

This is a book for you, the developer, who does not know why you should move away from your comfort zone, or you do not find real value evolving your skills and embrace the cloud.

You are not alone; many other developers over the world feel the same way we did just quite some time ago.

Facing new challenges

Software complexity is increasing over time and we need to concentrate on the functional aspects of domain problem, coding domain logic, and presentation. If possible, we would reuse as many functionalities that we could if they respected common patterns that were accepted, solved, and shared by developer community.

Development is different to Operations, as the developer has a different role from an IT professional. While developing solutions, we cannot really avoid any knowledge about operations, deployment, security, and authentication issues.

On-premise, many solutions are avoided because of lack of business view and no clearance from the management. We need to move our business costs from capital expenses to operation expenses. This lowers acquisition barriers as every company, single professionals, or small independent teams can access the same cloud power. We can also view this as a democratization of the web.

We now live in a global village, and we need to deploy our solutions worldwide, minimizing latency and give the users better responses without moving away from our company and country.

We need a self-service approach to turn services on and off, instantiating and destroying appliances, which allow us to control costs and invites experimenting, new technologies, platforms, and architectures.

The cloud democratizes access to advanced deployment scenarios such as clustering and high availability, backup, and operational management.

This is a book for you, the developer, who feels uncomfortable and needs to improve your skills and embrace the cloud. This book is all about real-world scenarios where you can train new skills and the start mapping your daily projects in this new and exciting world.

Let's move on, together.

What this book covers

Chapter 1, Building Basic Services, shows you how to start approaching the basic concepts of cloud computing in Azure and how to move some basic on-premise functionalities to the cloud.

Chapter 2, Enhancing the Hybrid Process, shows you how to integrate services to your local environment and processes and how to move virtual machine and networking concepts to the cloud.

Chapter 3, Building the Frontend, shows you how to build a comprehensive frontend composed of Azure services and approach the Platform-as-a-Service model to reduce costs.

Chapter 4, Building the Backend, explains how to use polyglot persistence to build a tailored-data platform, where each logical application block has its corresponding optimal technology and evaluate some new technologies to embrace new challenges.

Chapter 5, Building the Mobile Experience, covers the world of mobile apps development from the hybrid apps point of view and how a mobile-focused developer can approach building a backend Azure service.

Chapter 6, Building the API Layer, shows you how to handle real world API development, deployment, and long-term management.

Chapter 7, Working with Messages, shows you how you can build solutions composed by different blocks and explains the services that need to communicate in an asynchronous a decoupled manner.

Chapter 8, Deploying Solutions in Azure, shows you how to handle Azure service and to proceed with deployment in a formal, repeatable, and modern way.

What you need for this book

You need a good spec machine with any version of Windows from Window 7 to Windows 10 installed on it.

Visual Studio 2015 is the development environment that you require for this book, and all features required for this book are available from the free Community edition (https://www.visualstudio.com/en-us/products/visual-studio-community-vs.aspx).

Azure SDK for Visual Studio 2015 is required, and you can download it at https://azure.microsoft.com/en-us/downloads/.

You will sign up for a Microsoft Azure subscription at the start of the book if you have not already got one: there are various paid options, but a one-month trial is available.

There is also the Visual Studio Dev Essentials initiative (https://www.visualstudio.com/en-us/products/visual-studio-dev-essentials-vs.aspx), which gives us access to many benefits, such as an Azure subscription with $25 prepaid monthly credit.

Who this book is for

This book is for developers who want to improve their development skills in terms of development style and patterns with the cloud using some real-world, end-to-end scenarios, inspiring them to map their real projects at home.

This book is for Windows and .NET developers, as examples are mainly displayed as ASP.NET and C# code.

Conventions

In this book, you will find a number of text styles that distinguish between different kinds of information. Here are some examples of these styles and an explanation of their meaning.

Code words in text, database table names, folder names, filenames, file extensions, pathnames, dummy URLs, user input, and Twitter handles are shown as follows: "First, deallocate the VM by invoking the `deallocate` command."

A block of code is set as follows:

```
<AddressSpace>
  <AddressPrefix>10.1.0.0/16</AddressPrefix>
</AddressSpace>
<Subnets>
  <Subnet name="DataServer">
  <AddressPrefix>10.1.2.0/24</AddressPrefix>
</Subnet>
```

Any command-line input or output is written as follows:

```
$vn = Get-AzureRmVirtualNetwork
  -ResourceGroupName "CloudMakers" -Name "CloudMakers"
```

New terms and important words are shown in bold. Words that you see on the screen, for example, in menus or dialog boxes, appear in the text like this: "Locate the **New** action and choose **Data + Storage** (or another semantically equivalent group)."

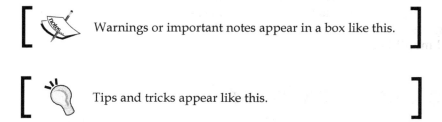

Warnings or important notes appear in a box like this.

Tips and tricks appear like this.

Reader feedback

Feedback from our readers is always welcome. Let us know what you think about this book—what you liked or disliked. Reader feedback is important for us as it helps us develop titles that you will really get the most out of.

To send us general feedback, simply e-mail `feedback@packtpub.com`, and mention the book's title in the subject of your message.

If there is a topic that you have expertise in and you are interested in either writing or contributing to a book, see our author guide at www.packtpub.com/authors.

Customer support

Now that you are the proud owner of a Packt book, we have a number of things to help you to get the most from your purchase.

Downloading the example code

You can download the example code files for this book from your account at http://www.packtpub.com. If you purchased this book elsewhere, you can visit http://www.packtpub.com/support and register to have the files e-mailed directly to you.

You can download the code files by following these steps:

1. Log in or register to our website using your e-mail address and password.
2. Hover the mouse pointer on the **SUPPORT** tab at the top.
3. Click on **Code Downloads & Errata**.
4. Enter the name of the book in the **Search** box.
5. Select the book for which you're looking to download the code files.
6. Choose from the drop-down menu where you purchased this book from.
7. Click on **Code Download**.

You can also download the code files by clicking on the **Code Files** button on the book's webpage at the Packt Publishing website. This page can be accessed by entering the book's name in the **Search** box. Please note that you need to be logged in to your Packt account.

Once the file is downloaded, please make sure that you unzip or extract the folder using the latest version of:

- WinRAR / 7-Zip for Windows
- Zipeg / iZip / UnRarX for Mac
- 7-Zip / PeaZip for Linux

The code bundle for the book is also hosted on GitHub at https://github.com/PacktPublishing/Mastering-Cloud-Development-using-Microsoft-Azure. We also have other code bundles from our rich catalog of books and videos available at https://github.com/PacktPublishing/. Check them out!

Downloading the color images of this book

We also provide you with a PDF file that has color images of the screenshots/diagrams used in this book. The color images will help you better understand the changes in the output. You can download this file from `https://www.packtpub.com/sites/default/files/downloads/MasteringCloudDevelopmentusingMicrosoftAzure_ColorImages.pdf`.

Errata

Although we have taken every care to ensure the accuracy of our content, mistakes do happen. If you find a mistake in one of our books — maybe a mistake in the text or the code — we would be grateful if you could report this to us. By doing so, you can save other readers from frustration and help us improve subsequent versions of this book. If you find any errata, please report them by visiting `http://www.packtpub.com/submit-errata`, selecting your book, clicking on the **Errata Submission Form** link, and entering the details of your errata. Once your errata are verified, your submission will be accepted and the errata will be uploaded to our website or added to any list of existing errata under the Errata section of that title.

To view the previously submitted errata, go to `https://www.packtpub.com/books/content/support` and enter the name of the book in the search field. The required information will appear under the **Errata** section.

Piracy

Piracy of copyrighted material on the Internet is an ongoing problem across all media. At Packt, we take the protection of our copyright and licenses very seriously. If you come across any illegal copies of our works in any form on the Internet, please provide us with the location address or website name immediately so that we can pursue a remedy.

Please contact us at `copyright@packtpub.com` with a link to the suspected pirated material.

We appreciate your help in protecting our authors and our ability to bring you valuable content.

Questions

If you have a problem with any aspect of this book, you can contact us at `questions@packtpub.com`, and we will do our best to address the problem.

1

Building Basic Services

Platform-as-a-Service (**PaaS**) is probably the next (or current) big thing in computing that is here to stay in the future of software and services. With PaaS, companies can abstract their services from the underlying IT infrastructure, investing the majority of the effort in the core business instead of managing several building blocks, often with repetitive actions and operations.

However, Azure is not just PaaS, and in this chapter, we are going to use IaaS instead. **Infrastructure-as-a-Service** (**IaaS**) is a model-provisioning IT low-level infrastructure (such as virtual machines) that works without having to manage the entire stack as it takes place on-premise.

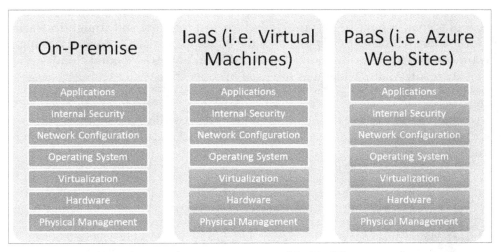

A figure showing what customers manage (blue) in different scenarios.

In this chapter, we present the first scenario of the book, where a fictional company wants to start up, minimizing the initial IT investment as well as the time to market. We learn how several Azure building blocks (such as virtual machines, Visual Studio Online, Azure Resource Manager, RemoteApp, Azure Storage, among others) can be combined in order to provide a set of foundation platforms for a software development company.

CloudMakers.XYZ

As mentioned in the preface, in order to better understand the key points of this book, we decided to translate them into practical situations, using scenarios taken from a fictional company named "Cloud Makers XYZ" (hereafter mentioned as just "CloudMakers" or "CM").

The entire book is divided into four main scenarios, which explore the company's assets in a step-by-step manner, focusing on how Microsoft Azure has been used to provide foundation services:

- **Scenario 1**: Bootstrapping the company
- **Scenario 2**: Building the e-commerce product
- **Scenario 3**: Building the GeoProvider product
- **Scenario 4**: Enhancing the company

These four scenarios have been conceived to create a coherent and straightforward path for readers who are already aware of the issues to be managed when dealing with software and services. Furthermore, it is useful in order to understand cloud services, such as Microsoft Azure, while they are used in connection with existing processes and workflows instead of having them deployed as is with "Hello World" samples.

Real-world experiences are the inspiration behind providing the samples shown in the scenarios; the majority of the tips, procedures, and code samples come from real production environments.

 As with many books claiming to represent a "best practice" or a "suggested usage" of a given service, this book does not have a complete understanding of what's going on in your specific company. We also know that each case is different and, finally, we strongly believe that architectures are not *good* or *bad* in an absolute sense and that they depend on specific use cases.

Hence, in this chapter and in the next one, we walk through the first scenario, where CM is bootstrapping itself.

Scenario 1 – Bootstrapping the company

CloudMakers is a newly founded company in Milano, Italy. The founders are as follows:

- Han, the CEO (chief executive officer), has a strong management background. His top qualities are leadership and commitment. He deeply understands technical inputs from the CTO and translates them into opportunities for the market. However, he demonstrated almost no real knowledge of how to build software.

- Luke, the CTO (chief technology officer), has a strong technical background. He prototypes new products, helps select candidate developers, and is responsible for the quality of the software produced by CM in general.

- Leila, the CFO (chief financial officer) and main project manager, is responsible for the financial strategy of CM and is in charge of managing and monitoring the projects delivered by CM.

In addition to these three key people, who have been getting along for many years before founding CM, there are a couple of additional, IT-related people:

- Owen, a senior IT professional, has a strong background in managing IT infrastructure. Before joining CM, he was responsible for the entire physical infrastructure of his old workplace.

- Flint, a full-stack developer, has previous experience in a failed start-up. He has been hired to develop the main products with Luke and learn everything about cloud computing and Microsoft Azure from him.

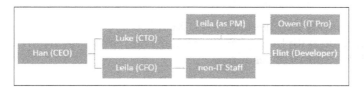

A summary of the most relevant resources of CloudMakers

CM has been founded with a very limited budget, and the board has taken the decision to minimize the IT investment in order to prioritize their marketing and advertisement efforts until they break even. Under this constraint, every initial investment should be evaluated and approved while pay-per-use services are welcomed.

Luke planned to build the new core infrastructure on Microsoft Azure, using the cloud to quickly deliver new services as well as the development environments required for the entire company and the technical team.

He planned to implement a BYOD (Bring Your Own Device) policy to reduce the governance of physical assets; so, the employees are invited to use their personal laptops and mobile phones for the purpose of work while they're at home or in the office.

Luke's plan is to build a consistent development environment entirely on the cloud, where employees can connect through **Remote Desktop Protocol** (**RDP**) to do their work (refer to the *Setting up the development environment* section).

Since the majority of the code is going to be written using Visual Studio and Luke has had strong experience in using **Team Foundation Server** (**TFS**) for **Application Lifecycle Management** (**ALM**), CM is going to use Visual Studio Online to store the company's code base as well as to help Leila keep track of the actual activities of the technical team (refer to the *Implementing the development process* section).

Since Luke is often out of the office due to several business events with Han and due to his participation in international meetings about start-ups and technical conferences and as a consequence of the ability of the entire staff to work from home, CM planned to introduce a way to let employees have a complete workplace even from their mobile devices: smartphones, tablets, and non-Windows PCs (refer to the *Provisioning development environments for mobility* section).

After a demand made by Owen, overwhelmed by growing requests from Flint to prepare a complex **Test/Prod Deployment Environment**, Han asks Luke to find an appropriate solution to simplify and automate the process of the creation and maintenance of these environments since they are used to provide clients with demo products. In addition, they should be online in minutes with minimal administrative effort (refer to the *Automating repetitive operations* section)

In *Chapter 2, Enhancing the Hybrid Process*, we'll learn how CM enhances the process it's just been created with by paying particular attention to security, disaster recovery, and the control of resources.

Setting up the development environment

In this book, we started with the assumption that the right cloud computing vendor has been chosen already. But, in general, when planning a cloud approach, these are useful questions to answer before you start working:

- What do I need from the cloud vendor?
- Which vendors have the stuff I need?
- What does it cost, compared to other major cloud vendors?
- Are there some pros/cons of one platform over another?

- Where is my business located (in conjunction with the cloud vendor data centers) and, more importantly, where are my services going to be consumed by users?

These are just a few of the initial questions we need to answer before we go ahead with making any plans. To answer these questions, a little bit of foresight is required.

Some of the most relevant players in the cloud computing market of IaaS and PaaS are listed as follows:

IaaS	PaaS
Amazon Web Service	Salesforce
Microsoft Azure	Microsoft Azure
Rackspace	Google Cloud Platform
CenturyLink	Red Hat
Google Cloud Platform	Progess
VMware	IBM SoftLayer
IBM SoftLayer	SAP

IaaS might suffice for putting a development infrastructure in the cloud is something. However, as the scenario evolves into a more complex cloud positioning made of services for the customer base, the answer is not something as simple as "We need just VMs."

These other questions can help identify which services are required:

- Is my company planning to sell **Software-as-a-Service (SaaS)**?
  - ° Building SaaS products on a PaaS can be effective in terms of pros versus cons. It is proven that a minor focus on managing the infrastructure can reduce costs but also improve the overall focus a company has on its core business.
  - ° A PaaS pricing model can also be translated into a SaaS pricing model, helping companies find out the right price for an elastic service, avoiding the complexity of the CAPEX approach.
- Does my company have dedicated IT staff capable of maintaining infrastructures?
  - ° If the answer is *no*, you should probably take into consideration *only* PaaS, avoiding the use of IaaS, which, however small, introduces some administrative effort.

- Does my company have a preference between *make* or *buy* choices?

  ○ If *make* choices are always preferred (although the term *always* is a per-se limitation), PaaS can be avoided and IaaS should be enough to build end-to-end services.

  ○ If *buy* is the choice, PaaS should be optimal. There are ready-to-go PaaS services where users just have to deploy some custom preexistent code in order to go live. But of course, since it is a value-added service, it costs more.

  ○ If the correct balance between *make* and *buy* choices has been made, both IaaS and PaaS are useful depending on the specific situation.

 This is the preferable approach, since there is no an absolute *best* between IaaS and PaaS. PaaS is probably growing much faster due to being a natural fit in this business, but companies often need IaaS to manage specific business areas, so we think both are here to stay for a long time.

This is not the right place to perform a comparison between cloud vendors—first, because it is really hard to do, and second, because it is beyond the scope of this book. However, everybody knows the following vendors, beyond among the most important players in the Public Cloud market (in alphabetical order):

- Amazon Web Services
- Google Cloud Platform
- Microsoft Azure

At the time of writing, each of the three platform has an almost comparable cloud offer, so the choice has to be taken with some in-depth analysis.

If we need IaaS, these can be valid questions:

- Does the platform provide virtual machines?

  ○ Of which sizes?

- Can the VM environment (network, attached disks, or balancer) be customizable?

  ○ How is it customizable and does it fit the needs?

- Is there any appliance we need (or should need) in order to work better with the chosen public cloud?

  ○ Is that a mandatory choice or is it up to the user?

If, instead, we need PaaS, these can be valid questions:

- Do we have an existing product to deploy? In which language has it been written? Does it have constraints for deployment?
    - Does the cloud vendor PaaS fit this product?
- Does the provided PaaS accelerate our existing development process?
    - Does it propose a new one?
- Is there good integration between services of the same cloud vendor?
    - Is there good integration from/to other cloud vendors (that is, to enable multicloud solutions)?
- Is there a lock-in while choosing a given PaaS product?
    - How much could it cost in the case of an outside migration?
- Does is have a learning curve to go live?
    - How much could it cost in the case of adoption?

We always prefer to exploit questions to analyze problems, since we should never take a decision without evaluating the pros and cons.

Finally, we should look at an aspect that seems to be secondary (but isn't): the data center location.

Where is my data center?

In the public cloud, there is often no private data center, so resources are almost always shared between different customers from around the world. This points to several potential issues about security, isolation, and more, but it is up to the cloud vendor to solve these issues.

Anyway, there comes a time when we need to decide where to place our data, our code, and our VMs. If the business is primarily located in the US and we choose a cloud vendor that has a single data center in Australia, this is probably not the better choice in terms of latency.

Latency is a term that indicates the time between input arriving to the other side of the communication channel. If we send a signal to a satellite, an average latency could be around 600 ms, which means that more than a second is required to make a round-trip (that is, an HTTP request). Latency depends on the physical constraints of the channel plus the distance, so the second is of primary importance while evaluating a data center location.

Again, if we decided for a cloud vendor that has a data center near us (the company) but far from the customers (that is, a company located in the UK with the data center in the UK but users in the US), this is, again, not a good choice. The best idea is a cloud vendor that provides different locations for a service, where companies can choose appropriately where to place (or replicate) services.

Content Delivery Networks (**CDNs**), covered later on in the book, represent a solution to shorten the distance between content and the end users. While Data Centers (DCs) are few, a CDN has hundreds of nodes distributed in regions even outside the Azure perimeter. For instance, a web application serving photos for users throughout the whole planet can have this topology:

- The deployment of the web application code into a few DCs (or even just one)
- The replication of the contents (the photos) all around the globe with a CDN

The intention of the user is to gain access to resources faster, since the content is served from the nearest CDN location while the page is served by the central DC.

Building a development machine

A good point to start building the company's development environment is to build a development machine for employees. In the last few years, developing through a well-configured virtual machine (either on-premise or in the cloud) has been a growing trend that has had consistent advantages:

- It reduces the need to maintain several pieces of hardware in order to comply with performance needs
- It enables the use of legacy hardware (thin clients and netbooks, among others) to act as a workstation proxy
- It centralizes the governance of the involved VMs into a single place where it should be easier to provide support
- It provides an efficient method to build a new workstation, with the required software, to let a new employee work immediately

In Microsoft Azure, VMs are basically provided in two main operating systems: Windows and Linux. The requirements a VM has are as follows:

- An underlying storage account where the VMs disks are saved
- A containing **Virtual Network (VN)**
- A public IP if the VM should be accessed from outside the VN
- A **Network Security Group (NSG)**, which defines the firewall/security rules between VMs and VNs in Azure

Since VNs, NSGs, and IPs will be covered in the next chapters, we'll now introduce the concept of a **storage account**. For this account, the other requirements discussed earlier can be met even during VM provisioning, but it is better to plan this in advance according to requirement analysis:

- How many storage accounts should we create?
    - One per VM? One per division? Just one?
- What are the constraints of the storage account service?
    - Can I create an indefinite number of accounts?
    - Does each account have its own limits in terms of capacity and bandwidth?
    - Is there a different type of storage we can use?

These questions should help you understand how it is very important to stop and think before creating a new resource in the cloud. It is true that one of the main pillars of cloud computing is to be "elastic" (and in fact you can create/destroy almost everything in a few seconds/clicks); however, since different services are often interdependent, it is very important to avoid the use of a blind **Next | Next** approach.

Let's start with creating a new storage account:

1. Go to `https://portal.azure.com` (the new portal) and locate your desired directory/subscription in the upper-right corner.

2. Locate the **New** action and choose **Data + Storage** (or another semantically equivalent group).

 As the Portal can change its layout and/or internal links frequently, a good advice is to abstract from the exact steps you need to do in order to complete an action. Since the Azure Portal can change frequently, it is useless to imprint solid step-by-step guidance where a reasoning-based approach is more efficient.

3. Look up the **Storage account** item (with the green icon) and follow the steps required to create it. Ensure that you specify **Resource Manager** and **Deployment model** before starting with the creation process.

> Azure started transitioning from the original deployment model (**classic**) to a new one (**Resource Manager**) a few years ago. This new deployment model is almost complete, but we are still in an intermediate phase. Later in the chapter and in the book, always use the Resource Manager model (as well as the new portal) when available.

During the creation process, some inputs are required:

- **Name**: This is the account name as well as the DNS prefix of the root service domain (`*.core.windows.net`). Choose it according to the requirements (`https://msdn.microsoft.com/en-us/library/azure/dd135715.aspx`) and know that we cannot change it after the creation process.

- **Type/pricing**: This is the type of offer (and consequently, the feature set) of the storage account. It is primarily divided into two areas:

  ◦ **Premium**: This is made just to host the disks of the virtual machine, and it has great performances since it is an SSD-based service. Of course, it is more expensive.

  ◦ **Standard**: This is a general-purpose service to host disks as well as generic resources, plus it has three other services (**Queues**, **Tables**, and **Files**) that we will explain later.

A group of three service types with prices (valid at the time of writing) with a different feature set

- **The resource group**: For now, think about this as a logical group of resources. So, depending on the planned life cycle of the storage account, choose the appropriate existing group, or, if new, name it appropriately (that is, `TestResourceGroup`, `CM_Storage`, or `CM_Development`).

In the next few steps, we provide a fresh Windows Server environment to later configure the applications required for the reference workstation:

1. Locate the **New** action and navigate to **Compute | Visual Studio**.

2. Select the appropriate image type for your needs (like in the following screenshot):

This provides the latest Windows Server image with Visual Studio preinstalled

3. Again, ensure that you choose **Resource Manager** as the deployment model before clicking on the **Create** button.

Following the creation steps, you will be prompted with some input requests, such as the following:

- **Basics**: This includes information about the administrator username and password, location, and the resource group.

- **Size**: This includes the actual size of the VM. There are several options since the available sizes span small machines to very large ones. Some instance types are named DSX (where X is a number), indicating that they support the usage of **Premium Storage** and provisioned IOPS.

  As for the storage account (and for every single Azure service, actually), we can choose the service type, which maps the feature set of the service. In the case of VMs, the differences between them are as follows:

    ○ **Cores, memory, and data disks**: Primarily, these are metrics that define the performance

    ○ **Load balancing**: This provides the support of a load balancer on top of the VMs in the same set (in the case of just one VM, this option is useless)

    ○ **Auto scaling**: This is the capability to dynamically create new VM instances based on some triggers

○ **Advanced features**: Provisioned IOPS, SSD local disks, and RDMA support are included in some of the most powerful (and often, the most expensive) pricing tiers

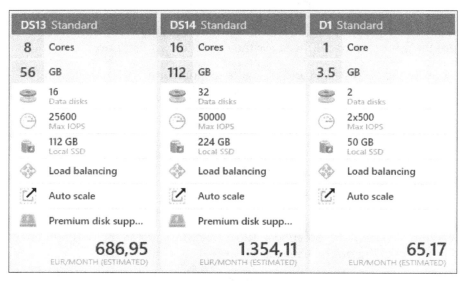

Some DS instance types and **D1**, a good choice for a simple remote development environment.

- **Settings**: As mentioned earlier in this chapter, we use default settings for VNs, IPs, and NSGs, covering them in further detail later in the chapter.

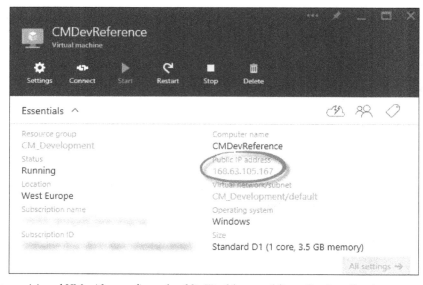

This is the provisioned VM with a configured public IP address and firewall rules, allowing us to connect to it

Generalizing the VM

The creation of a VM also implies the creation of one (or more) **Virtual Hard Disks** (**VHDs**) in order to store the operating system and the data of the running instance. It is possible to look at the contents of a storage account (containing the VHDs of the VMs) in the vhds container of **Blob service** directly from **Portal**, as shown in the following figures:

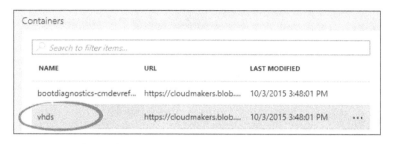

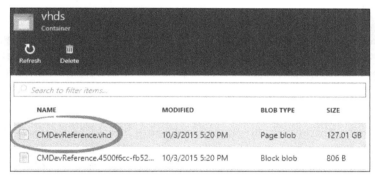

This is the storage account blade, where it is possible to inspect storage services and perform basic operations

When the VM is ready for use, it is possible to connect through RDP to customize it by deploying local software, such as SDKs, development tools, productivity suites, and so on. This is not in the scope of the book, so we assume it has already been done. What we want to do, instead, is create a generalized image of the VM in order to enable further image-based VM creation with minimal administrative effort.

In Windows-based operating systems, the sysprep command is used to generalize the operating system instance, removing specialized details, such as users, keys, and profiles. In Linux, we need to use the Azure Agent with the waagent command.

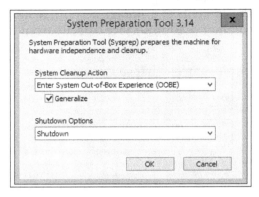

You can just launch the sysprep command to open this window.
Then, specify the **Generalize** and **Shutdown** options.

Earlier in this chapter, we used a portal to perform various administrative activities. However, Azure has a fully featured REST management API. In addition, Microsoft provides a .NET management library wrapped by PowerShell in order to perform almost every operation from the command line. We will properly use PowerShell later in the book.

But now, we use a third option to operate on Azure, the ARM Explorer. During the creation of the storage account, we briefly went over the concept of resource groups, the logical container for a group of service instances. The ARM Explorer (available here in preview: https://resources.azure.com/) is a lightweight tool used to inspect and administer Microsoft Azure using the Resource Manager deployment model (which is actually JSON-based).

The ARM Explorer tool is a great tool to learn what's under the hood of the ARM model. For example, for the given VM created previously, this is what the explorer shows:

The output shown by ARM Explorer while selecting a resource from the resources tree

As we can see in the preceding image, ARM Explorer lets us explore the various objects in the Azure subscriptions, also providing a PowerShell sample code to perform basic contextual operations.

In the previous figure, we selected the **virtualMachines** node. However, if we select the specific VM (in the preceding case, the **CMDevReference** tree node), the **Action** tab becomes available with a series of options. To perform the capture of the VM's image, we can proceed as follows:

1. First, deallocate the VM by invoking the `deallocate` command.

 Note that the ARM Explorer must run in read/write mode in order to perform many configuration actions. Also, keep in mind that the tool just invokes the REST Management API on your behalf.

2. After the status of the VM has passed from **Stopped** to **Stopped (deallocated)** (you can even check this in the ARM Explorer itself or in the portal), launch the `generalize` action.

3. Now the VM is ready to be captured, while the `capture` operation needs some arguments for it to be executed, as specified here:

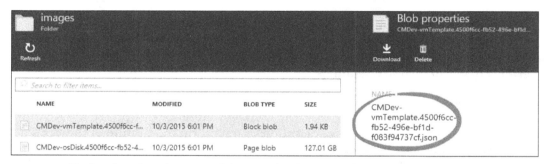

```
capture    POST https://management.azure.com/subscriptions/...

1 ▾ {
2      "vhdPrefix": "CMDev",
3      "destinationContainerName": "images",
4      "overwriteVhds": "true"
5   }
```

The `capture` operation with its argument to be executed properly. At the time of writing, `destinationContainerName` may have been ignored from the platform during the capturing process

We can check out the image that has been properly created by navigating the storage account, looking for the VHD we just created. Along with the VHD, Azure created a JSON representing the command to be used with ARM in order to create a fresh VM based on the captured image.

The location where Azure stored the generalized images with the corresponding ARM-ready JSON template to create new VMs

CloudMakers now has a generalized Windows-based image for development machines. In the *Automating repetitive operations* section, we'll learn how to automate many of these related activities.

Implementing the development process

Instead of teaching you how to manage the development process at its best, this is an overview of how to integrate services in order to reduce the complexity of the deployment and the administration of a popular **Team Foundation Server** (**TFS**) infrastructure.

TFS is a comprehensive product providing source code control, automated testing, an automated build platform, reporting, project management, and counting. On the other hand, the new kid on the block (over the last few years) is called **Visual Studio Online (VSO)**, which is the Azure-hosted version of TFS, missing just some advanced features (such as SQL Reporting/BI).

There are a lot of connected products and services around TFS/VSO, designed to integrate and develop the even more complex scenarios of **Application Lifecycle Management (ALM)**. The advantage of using VSO is that, as SaaS, it requires zero maintenance (it is all up by Microsoft) and a very short provisioning time: this is why it is useful in many contexts where a ready-to-go solution is required with a minimal set of customization points.

CM primarily needs to save/control its code base by adopting a source code repository service. As usual, some questions can help while choosing the appropriate vendor/service:

- Where is the code repository located?
- Which protocols (a.k.a. source control engines) is CM using?
- Does the service integrate with third-party services? Which ones?

We know that real questions can be many more than just these, but always try to stop and write down the requirements before jumping into a new service.

SaaS and PaaS maintenance

We are repeating the power of Platform-as-a-Service (and, consequently, also the power of SaaS) as a prayer in reducing the overall governance of a company by focusing just on its core businesses without dealing with the management and maintenance of the IT infrastructure. All true and all beautiful, but do not confuse this with the capability of raising the number of services indefinitely and without any real scope.

Even PaaS services require, as far as possible, some maintenance effort; once created, they need attention. Try to introduce a new service only if the existing services in place do not cover the requirements and only if the new service can be correctly investigated before building strong dependencies on it.

Creating a new VSO environment

CloudMakers developers (which are actually two in number, Luke and Flint, at the time of beginning the start-up) come with different kinds of experience. Among the differences between them, Luke has always used TFS in his project, and he is accustomed to its native, centralized source control engine. On the other hand, Flint has been a full stack developer, using distributed source control engines, such as Mercurial and Git.

As we see later, since every team project has its own source control engine, we can create personal workspaces (workspaces under the control of a single developer to test, play, and prototype) according to the developers' preference, while the company's workspaces (those containing the actual code base) can use a single, shared, and different engine.

 Using different source control engines can be very fair in organizations where several languages and technologies are put in place. However, some operations (such as collection-level branching and merging) are not allowed, making the integration between projects managed with different engines harder.

We can create a brand new VSO account by directly going to `https://go.microsoft.com/fwlink/?LinkId=307137&clcid=0x409`. Or, we can use the Azure Portal by creating our first team project.

In the TFS/VSO ecosystem, a single deployment can have this tree structure:

- **Project collections**: These can be 1 to *n* in number. A project collection is a high-level collection of folders named `Team Projects`.

- **Team Projects**: These can be 1 to *n* in number. A Team Project is a collection of code, no matter how many real software solutions there may be. The term "project" should refer to a business project, which, of course, is a collection of multiple software packages/solutions/projects itself.

In VSO, there is just one collection (`DefaultCollection`) with many (to be created by users) Team Projects.

 For more information on what a team project is (or should be), go to `https://msdn.microsoft.com/en-us/library/ms181234(v=vs.90).aspx`.

From within the Azure Portal, we can find the **New Team Project** wizard to open this blade:

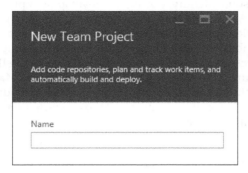

This is where we can create new Team Projects

Contextually, if not already created/owned, we need to create a new VSO account.

The creation of the CM account within `DefaultCollection`

The first team project we create can be a test, so play with the configuration settings:

- **Version control**: We can choose between **TFVC** (the standard engine of TFS) and **Git** (the well-known open and distributed engine)
- **Process Template**: We can choose how the development process should be set in order to organize the frontend experience as well as part of the implicit ALM (the current options are **Scrum 2013**, **Agile 2013** and **CMMI 2013**)

VSO can integrate users with personal identities (Microsoft accounts) or organizations' identities (Azure AD). We'll learn how Azure AD works in the next sections, but remember that it is a good practice to bind a VSO account with an Azure AD tenant in order to implement better control of who has access to resources.

In fact, try to imagine a contributor using the company's VSO with their personal identity: during the development process, even if it lasts years, they can gain access to multiple resources by adding their ID to various projects/folders. When they decide to leave (or when the contribution ends), an administrator has to manually check all the projects and resources involved and disable the ID from access. With Azure AD, which is an **Identity and Access Management (IAM)** solution, an administrator can just centrally disable the access of the single account, disabling all the connected services' entry points with a single action.

After provisioning a VSO account, when the billing and some minor configuration details are summarized in the Azure Portal, its management console is available here:

```
https://<<name_of_account>>.visualstudio.com
```

Each team project is available at this link, as shown here:

```
https://<<name_of_account>>.visualstudio.com/
DefaultCollection/<<name_of_project>>
```

The management console of the portal looks similar to the one shown in the following screenshot:

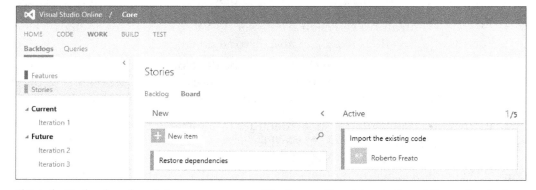

This is the Kanban board created as a consequence of the **Process Template** selection while creating the team project. We can define tasks, assign people, create items (such as **Stories**, **Iterations**, and **Features**) and also manage other aspects of the development process (using the **Code/Build/Test** menus).

Integrating Visual Studio

Visual Studio automatically recognizes VSO/TFS based on the endpoint URL we give to it. In the case of VSO, a web-based sign-in is asked from the user in order to perform a claims-based authentication for the correct provider (a Microsoft account or Azure AD). If a standard TFS is detected, even basic authentication will be available.

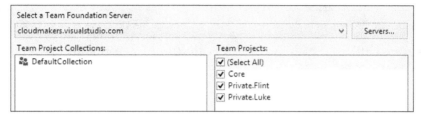

This is the `DefaultCollection` collection of the Team Project of the VSO account along with three Team Projects

Visual Studio 2013/2015 natively supports both Git and TFS as backend source control engines, but only one at time can be the default, as shown in the following screenshot:

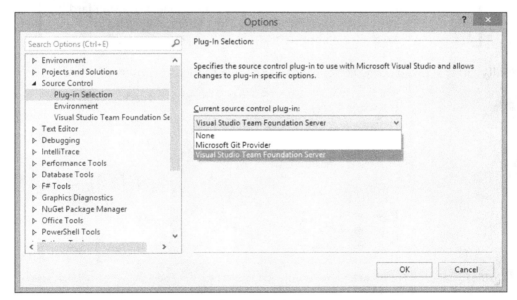

This is where we can choose the default source control engine

In the case of TFVC-based Team Projects, we can map and get the entire project collection in a base local folder, as follows:

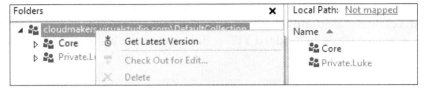

This is the source control explorer, the place where we can manage the TFVC-based projects of the collection

In the case of a Git-based team project, we can start by just cloning the repository.

We are now cloning the Git-based repo into a local folder

 The Git backend of VSO has been implemented in a standard way in order to enable the majority of the existing clients to connect to it and push the code.

Finally, after writing some code, we can save our work as follows:

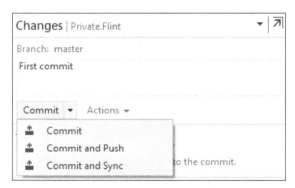

In this example, we both Commit (save locally) and Push (align the remote Git repo) in a single action. For further information regarding Git, refer to the Git documentation

Integrating third-party services

As mentioned at the beginning of this section, VSO is a complete solution for ALM, and it's not just another source control environment. It can automatically deploy the build result to connected services, and more generally, it can react to specific triggers with custom actions even against third-party services.

A webhook is a method to notify decoupled systems in a standard way based on HTTP and public endpoints. In VSO, there are several predefined service hooks, whose purpose is to trigger events against third-party services in the case of a specific VSO event that has occurred. At the time of writing, the events supported by VSO (which VSO can listen to) are as follows:

- **Build completed**: This triggers if a build is completed (in the case of failure, success, and other supported statuses)

- **Code checked-in/pushed**: This triggers when someone saves their code

- **Team room message posted**: This is self-explanatory

- **Work item actions (creation/comment/update)**: This triggers in the event of one of the supported actions on work items

 This last one is particularly useful for the purpose of integrating with a company chat service in order to create real-time engagement on the progress of the overall work.

In fact, among the built-in supported third-party services, we have the following:

- **Azure Service Bus and Storage**: Supported actions are related to sending a message on a queue, a topic, a notification hub, or a storage queue. It's useful in building some logic applications in response to these events.

- **Jenkins**: Supported actions are related to triggering a build into Jenkins since it is a popular (and open source) **Continuous Integration (CI)** service.

- **MyGet**: This is a **NuGet-as-a-Service** solution with great features. The most useful supported action is to automatically publish a NuGet package into the MyGet repository if a build occurs on the VSO side.

- **Slack**: Since this is one of the most popular messaging systems, the obvious supported action is to post a message on a specific channel in the case of an event on the VSO side.

- **ZenDesk**: This is one of the most popular ticketing systems in the world. A nice use case for integration shows that users from Visual Studio can comment on a work item, triggering a private comment in a ticket on the ZenDesk side.

In fact, there are a lot more built-in integrations, and there is also a provider, Zapier, that acts as a simple orchestrator itself. On the Zapier side, we can react to webhooks by triggering a lot (hundreds) of different services, even the ones mentioned earlier.

 Take a look at Zapier's capabilities here: `https://zapier.com/app/use-cases` in order to get an idea about the possible integration scenarios.

Finally, if you want to trigger a custom HTTP listener, there is a simple webhooks provider, letting you decide what to notify and how to do it as long as it's understood that the target should be an HTTP endpoint.

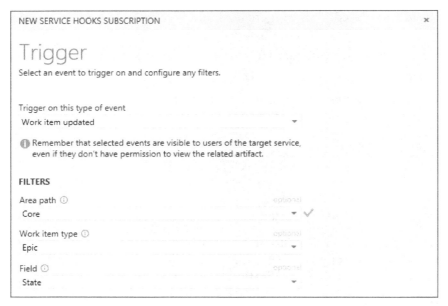

In this hook, we listen to the **Work item updated** event in case the event occurred in the **Core** area for an **Epic** work item type and when someone change the **State** field

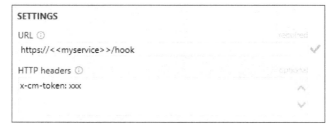

These are some of the invocation settings in custom webhooks. We can also specify an optional basic authentication and the details of what to send in the body of the POST request.

Provisioning development environments for mobility

In the *Setting up the development environment* section, we saw how much value resides in off-shoring the development environment (later called **DevEnv**) in the cloud by building VMs with development tools instead of using the local computer.

This pattern also highlights some hidden advantages:

- If the connectivity between the remote development environment and the company deployments is low-latency and high-speed, then every operation between them can be easier and the productivity witnesses a boost compared to local environments.

- If you are in the middle of a complicated debugging session just before the office closes, you can disconnect from the remote VM and continue debugging from anywhere else (even from your home computer).

- Your data is generally more secure in terms of availability than a personal workstation. A remote VM can obviously be accessed from the Internet (directly or through a VPN), along with the potential issues related, but a personal computer can also be stolen or damaged (backups are always our best friends in such scenarios).

This pattern leads to a consideration: "Do we still need powerful IT stuff to run development environments?". Since the DevEnv is remote, we can use any device supporting the RDP protocol (for Windows VMs) or the SSH protocol (for Linux ones). The next step is to use a mobile phone, a tablet, or a thin client.

 Microsoft Thin PC, for example, is a reduced Windows 7-based OS project with minimal functions and a RDP client. The purpose of this OS is to run on legacy computers with outdated hardware, enabling the consumption of even complex applications through the Internet and the remote desktop. For more information, refer to the deployment guide here: `https://www.microsoft.com/en-us/download/details.aspx?id=26676`.

Under this hypothesis, we can build a workstation with almost any device connected to the Internet.

Nobody really wants to develop with Visual Studio and multiple open windows on a smartphone display. However, Project Continuum by Microsoft lets users use their continuum-enabled devices as workstations by connecting them to a TV or a PC monitor. The idea behind this is the thin client pattern, where services or applications are available on the Internet through HTTP or RDP. At this link, there is an accessory for Windows Phone devices that makes the magic happen: `http://www.microsoft.com/en-us/mobile/accessory/hd-500/`.

That said, CloudMakers wants to enable its workers to have the same facilities that they have in their office while on the move. Luke also has a Surface 2 RT tablet, which is very useful for basic office usage and for Internet usage/e-mail and less useful for development due to its ARM-based processor architecture (Surface RT has a specific version of Windows compiled for ARM).

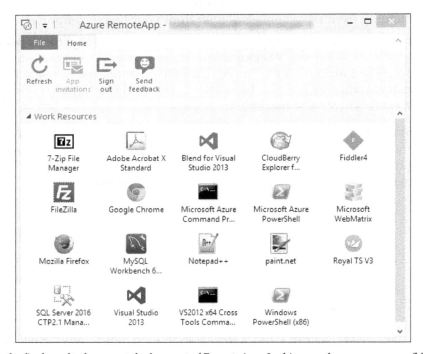

This is the final result of a correct deployment of **RemoteApp**. In this case, the company user (blurred) has access to a bunch of applications, which are not running from its local environment but are provided through an abstraction on Remote Desktop Protocol instead.

Until this point, the remote development environment requirement can be easily fitted by the VMs created in the previous part of the chapter: Luke just has to connect to them from the Surface, and that's it! However, as a CTO, he identifies some drawbacks in the previous approach, as follows:

- As the provisioning is one VM per user, with each new employee Owen needs to:

    ○ Run the scripts to build the VM (we'll learn later which kind of scripts)

    ○ Tell new users the appropriate credentials

- In the case of reimaging, Owen has to set up an appropriate backup-restore solution for the personal archives on the remote machine

- Users need to maintain (at least) two different accounts: one for the company and one for the newly created VM

- In the case of software updates, each user has to manually update their VM

Finally, and this is both an advantage and a disadvantage, each user is the administrator of the remote VM, with these two main categories of possible consequences:

- **Advantage**: The user needs to install other tools to customize their environment

- **Disadvantage**: The user can compromise the health of the VM by misusing it or installing malware inadvertently

As Luke plans to extend this pattern to the whole company, it emerges that it is not really sustainable in terms of the management effort (the time spent to activate/deactivate or support people), consistency (some VMs are different from others), and security.

Azure Active Directory

Let's introduce Azure AD before explaining RemoteApp, and let's start identifying what Azure AD is not. It is not the managed version of the Windows Server Active Directory. Despite its resemblance in name, Azure AD is *just* an IAM service managed and hosted by Microsoft in Azure. We should not even try to make a comparison because they have different scopes and different features. It is true that we can link Azure AD with an on-premise Active Directory, but that will be just for the purpose of extending the on-premise AD functionalities to work with Internet-based applications.

Azure Active Directory is a growing **Identity and Access Management (IAM)** service (now with B2C features), with great integration options for custom applications; different applications (and the various services of Azure itself) can use Azure AD as their IAM solution in order to provide authentication/authorization.

 It is a good practice to group multiple subscriptions (related to the same organization or logic group) into the same Azure Active Directory (AD).

To create a new Azure AD tenant, we need to move to the old portal (`https://manage.windowsazure.com`) and proceed as follows:

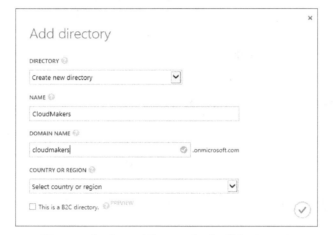

We create the Azure AD tenant for the CM company.

This directory will host the users of the company in order to provide them with authentication/authorization of services.

If we plan to centralize the access rules for online resources, Azure AD can help us by providing a single identity for our users, created one by one (or through REST APIs), as follows:

This creates a new user

Complete coverage of the capabilities of Azure AD is beyond the scope of this book. However, some advanced topics can be found in the next chapters.

Azure RemoteApp

Microsoft tries to solve the issues of the scenario mentioned earlier, implementing a layer of abstraction between the user and the actual VM performing the work. RemoteApp is this layer, completely based on existing technologies (such as RDP), and enables users to connect to applications instead of VMs.

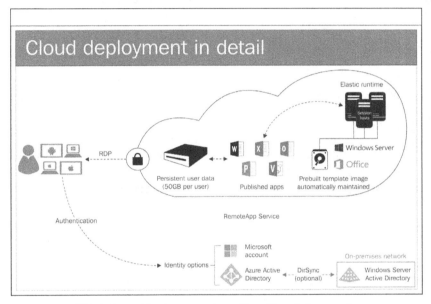

This is the architecture overview of how RemoteApp works

To start from the beginning, we should:

1. Create an Azure Active Directory tenant for the organization (we did this in the previous section).

2. Create a custom VM image with the complete development environment (we can use the previously created one).

3. Activate RemoteApp and assign users.

A pricing note

RemoteApp has an elastic pricing model, just like many cloud services. However, it has a strong requirement: a minimum of 20 users (at the time of writing). This is due to how the service is internally provisioned; if you have less than 20 users, you would still be billed for 20. If you compare the service to a medium-sized instance (or even a small one) per user, it is probably still more convenient. However, this is an aspect that should be considered before implementation.

As for the Azure AD tenant, even the RemoteApp collection can be created only from the old portal (`https://manage.windowsazure.com`).

Classic versus Resource Manager: the hidden issue

Earlier in this chapter, we recommended that you create new resources by always using the Resource Manager mode and not the classic one. This is because the Resource Manager mode is the new one, and hosts new features and investments. However, there is a strong separation between these two areas: so strong that, for example in the old portal (which is based on the classic model), there is no way to reuse components created in the new way.

As an example of this, try to look at storage accounts or custom VM images in the old portal:

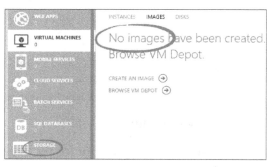

This screenshot has been taken in the same subscription where the storage account and the custom VM image were created previously. Remember this behavior and plan your deployments accordingly.

As a quick fix for the lack of the VM image in the old portal, proceed as follows:

1. Create a new storage account from the old portal.

2. Note the credentials for both the old and new storage accounts (the storage account name and one of the access keys).

3. Install this software: `http://www.cerebrata.com/products/azure-management-studio/introduction` in the trial mode.

4. Configure the two storage accounts (despite being created under different methods, they are equal from an API's perspective).

5. Copy the blob and paste it into the **Classic Storage Account** (the operation is almost immediate if accounts are in the same data center).

6. Create a **Custom Image** and, in order to enable RemoteApp using your image, import the VM image into the **TEMPLATE IMAGES** tab of the **RemoteApp** section of the old portal.

This creates a RemoteApp image based on the generalized VM image

Finally, to complete the creation process, go to **REMOTEAPP COLLECTIONS** and create a new collection based on the custom image you've just registered.

If all went well, you can now do the following:

- Publish individual programs.

Selecting RemoteApp programs

- Assign individual users to the RemoteApp collection (through the **USER ACCESS** tab)
- Create multiple collections to accommodate different types of users
- Update the VM image by simply running the **Update wizard** (custom user data is retained between sessions and between updates)

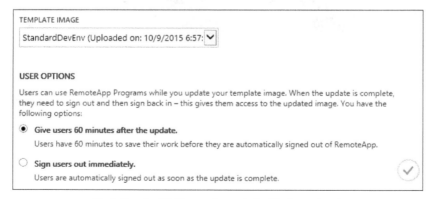

Updating the VM image through the Update wizard

- Connect from your iPad/iPhone through the dedicated RemoteApp application.

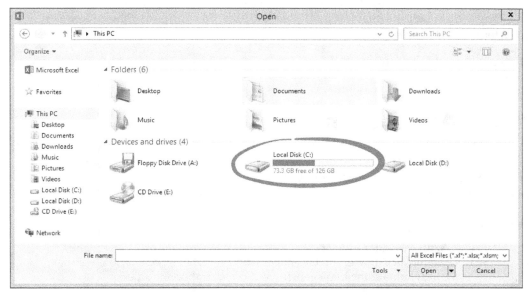

The file system seen by a RemoteApp application is the remote file system, which is persisted across different sessions and image updates

Automating repetitive operations

In IT, automation is often the key to improving the overall efficiency of a process while reducing the surface area of recurring exceptions due to human errors. Despite the intensive use of PaaS, which can reduce the amount of configuration effort required to set up complex environments by design, the provisioning process (even for those advanced PaaS solutions) is probably still a manual one.

Try to think about this scenario:

- CloudMakers.XYZ needs an HTTP proxy to simulate the web surfing activity coming in from the US despite the offices being located in Italy
- The proxy is used a few hours per day and only during working hours (9 to 18 or 9 A.M. to 6 P.M. +1 UTC)
- Luke says that it is a waste of money to keep the proxy running outside the boundary of the working hours mentioned

As per the preceding scenario, Owen must set up a process where he (or a colleague) has to switch off the VM at 6 PM and bring it back online at 9 AM. Needless to say, this process itself is a waste of time; if, for some reason, the person in charge of carrying it out is temporarily unavailable, employees cannot use the proxy as it may lead to bad consequences.

We approach this section with this scenario in mind using Azure Automation and Azure Scheduler.

Azure Automation

Azure Automation is a comprehensive set of features that provide automation over Azure resources as well as on-premise ones using PowerShell in conjunction with Azure APIs and other services. Think about Azure Automation as PowerShell-as-a-Service, since it provides an isolated execution engine for arbitrary PowerShell code.

 Currently, cmdLets modules supported out of the box are Azure, AzureRM (Compute and Profile only), PowerShell.Core, PowerShell. Diagnostics, PowerShell.Management, PowerShell.Security, PowerShell. Utility, plus some management and orchestration modules.

After creating an automation account, it is possible to import existing PowerShell modules by entering the **Assets** tile in the **Automation Account** blade and then selecting **Modules**.

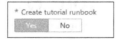

During the creation process, you can choose to create a sample **hello world**

A custom module can be added to the built-in ones by uploading the corresponding ZIP archive, as follows:

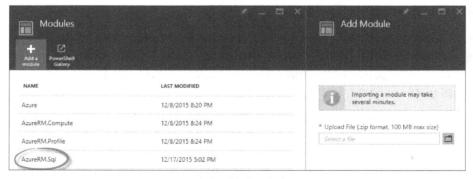

A custom module added to the built-in ones

To be able to write code against actual Azure resources, a valid credential or management certificate is required (in fact, there is no trust between the automation account and the subscription that hosts it).

It is strongly recommended that you create an Azure AD credential with specific permissions in order to place it in the automation code. Azure Automation provides an efficient mechanism to hide the actual credentials for the various **Runbooks** (scripts) by storing them in advance in the Assets folder.

The Assets folder actually contains resources, as follows:

- **Schedules**: This is the representation of an agnostic schedule without any information about what is to be scheduled.

- **Modules**: This refers to PowerShell modules, and contains built-in ones (global modules that cannot be deleted) as well as user-uploaded ones.

- **Certificates**: These are .cer or .pfx certificates that are to be used in the runbooks but securely stored as assets.

- **Variables**: These are the custom key-value pairs to be used as variables in the runbooks. The supported value types are String, Boolean, DateTime, and Integer.

- **Credentials**: The credentials set (just key pairs of username and password strings) to be used in runbooks. It is not necessary that they be related to Azure or Azure AD as they can also be custom credentials.

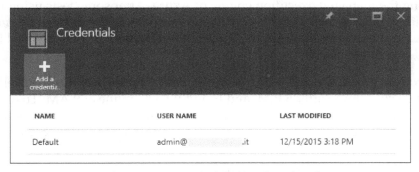

It is recommended that you provide default credentials with permissions to operate of the decider Azure subscriptions

When creating a new automation account, if specified during creation, a sample runbook (named `Get-AzureVMTutorial`) is added to the collection. The purpose of this runbook is to list the first 10 Azure VMs in the default subscription.

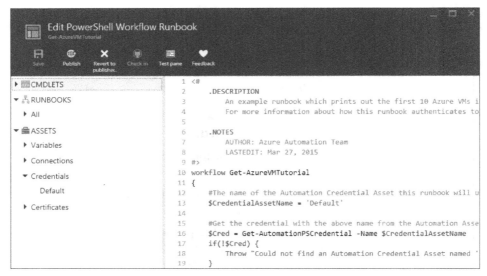

In this sample runbook, we edit $CredentialAssetName to reflect
the Credential asset that we have in the Assets folder

With automation, we can write PowerShell code directly into browser windows and test it using the managed execution engine of Azure. After some tests using the **Test pane** window (also shown in the preceding screenshot), a runbook can be *published*, which means that it is available in the **Runbooks** collection and can be used by other runbooks as a child activity.

In the next few pages, we set up the scenario mentioned earlier, where a well-known VM must be shut down after 6 P.M. and brought back online at 9 AM. To do this, we use a graphical runbook, which is, as the name suggests, a runbook created and edited completely with a GUI composer without touching a line of PowerShell code directly.

We start by creating the runbook, as follows:

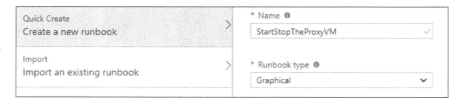

We specify the name and the **Graphical** type

We can now search for the `Add-AzureAccount` CmdLet and add it in the central canvas.

In the left-hand side pane, we search for CmdLets and add them in the right canvas

Each PowerShell CmdLet has its own set of parameters. The GUI of a Graphical runbook provides a complete and strongly typed mapping between these parameters and the user interface. In fact, for the `Add-AzureAccount` command, it recognizes the mandatory parameter as follows:

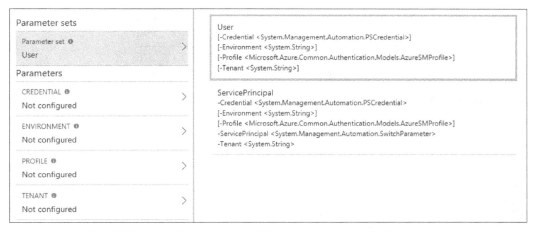

The GUI lets you choose between different parameter sets, and for each set,
it provides assistance in filling the expected values

In the preceding example, we just need to select **Credential** and specify that we need to pick it from the `Credentials` assets. We can find (if previously set up) the `Default` credential and use it for the sample.

Following this pattern, we can now add `Get-AzureVM`, `Start-AzureVM` and `Stop-AzureVM` to the canvas.

 Each of these activities can be joined by connecting the dots to each other. However, the connection itself has two different behaviors that can be controlled by clicking on the connection and editing its properties in the right-hand side pane.

The `Get-AzureVM` activity required at least the `ServiceName` parameter, but `VMName` can also be specified to get a specific VM instance. We provide this information without hardcoding it into the runbook in two ways:

- Defining variables in the `Assets` folder
- Defining inputs in the **Input and Output** pane of the runbook

Using the second method, we define two inputs with default values, as follows:

We specify both input parameters to keep the runbook implementation generic.
Default values are used in case no values are provided by the runbook executor.

We can now connect the dots to obtain the following structure:

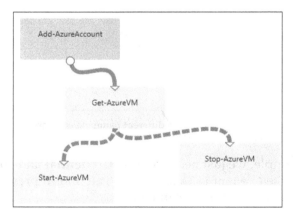

We linked the three activities in a single workflow. The connections between **Get-AzureVM**
and the lower nodes are different because they apply conditions

The connections from **Get-AzureVM** to the lower nodes are dashed because we specify a condition to navigate them. By clicking on the single connection, we can specify a set of parameters.

- **Type**: Choosing by `Pipeline` or `Sequence`, we can specify whether the target activity has to be run for each result of the source activity (`Pipeline`) or just once (`Sequence`)
- **Apply condition**: If specified `Yes`, a PowerShell expression can be specified in the **Condition expression** text area

The respective conditions for the two tasks are as follows:

- For **Start-AzureVM**, run the following code:

```
$ActivityOutput['Get-AzureVM'].Status -eq
  "StoppedDeallocated" -and ((Get-Date).Hour -lt 18 -or
  (Get-Date).Hour -gt 9)
```

- For **Stop-AzureVM**, run the following code:

```
$ActivityOutput['Get-AzureVM'].Status -ne
  "StoppedDeallocated" -and ((Get-Date).Hour -gt 18 -or
  (Get-Date).Hour -lt 9)
```

> Detailed steps to download the code bundle are mentioned in the Preface of this book. Please have a look.
>
> The code bundle for the book is also hosted on GitHub at https://github.com/ PacktPublishing/Mastering-Cloud-Development-using-Microsoft-Azure. We also have other code bundles from our rich catalog of books and videos available at https://github.com/PacktPublishing/. Check them out!

Each activity can have an output: in the preceding case, we check the `Status` property of the output of the `Get-AzureVM` activity, and in conjunction with a temporal condition, we activate the appropriate node.

For the `Start-AzureVM` and `Stop-AzureVM` activities, the VM can be specified by name using the runbook input, as mentioned earlier or using the activity output data source with one of the available sources for parameter values.

> The available data sources are runbook input, activity output, PowerShell expression, variable asset, credential asset, connection asset, and certificate asset.

The runbook can now be saved, published, or scheduled on an hourly basis. We can run a runbook in these three ways:

- **Using the Start button in the Runbook blade**: This command immediately puts a new job based on the runbook definition in the execution queue. There is some delay between the `Start` operation and the job execution, but that is completely normal.

- **Triggering a webhook by a remote location**: A webhook is a specific URL (it is often a hard-to-remind URL) which, called with an HTTP POST, triggers the execution of a new job. It requires no authentication, and it can be configured to have an expiration.

- **By setting up a schedule from inside the runbook blade**: This method can link an existing schedule (remember that it is created in the assets and is agnostic) to the runbook. The current options for the scheduling of a job are very limited, so it is often recommended that you use the Azure Scheduler service in connections to webhooks.

There are a lot of other advanced features in Azure Automation. It provides complete support in order to help you avoid mistakes during repetitive actions, while encouraging the IT staff to use Platform-as-a-service as the execution engine for their scripts.

Azure Scheduler

Azure Scheduler lets us create scheduled actions against an HTTP(s) endpoint as a storage queue. By implementing complex infrastructures, we often need to schedule some actions with specific recurrence: also, Windows Task Scheduler helps us run custom processes in a scheduled fashion. However, having a task scheduler running on a user-managed virtual machine involves maintenance and skills, not to mention that it is not a highly available solution, as the underlying VM represents a single point of failure.

Azure Scheduler, via the Azure Portal or the Management API, lets us submit jobs of two types:

- The HTTP endpoint call
- Message in Queue

In the former case, we can customize the request by appending custom headers and choosing the appropriate method (GET, POST, and so on); in the latter, we can place a message in a storage queue, assuming there is someone on the other side ready to process it before or later.

Azure Scheduler does not run custom code in .NET or other runtimes: triggered by Azure itself and following the recurrence rules, its purpose is to start a user process. It can be used, for example, in conjunction with Azure Automation webhooks to start specific runbook jobs on an advanced schedule basis.

From the old portal, in the **Scheduler** section, we can create a new job like this.
In this case, we call a plain **HTTP** endpoint with the **GET** method

Jobs are created in Job collections and stored in a specific region (the call will happen from this region to the target endpoint specified in the action).

As mentioned earlier, Azure Scheduler is more powerful than the Azure Automation built-in scheduler. In the following figure, we see an example of this:

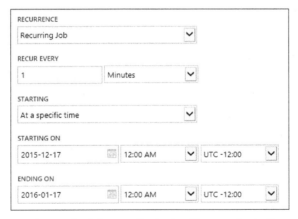

In this example, we set up a schedule every 1 minute with accurate starting and ending times

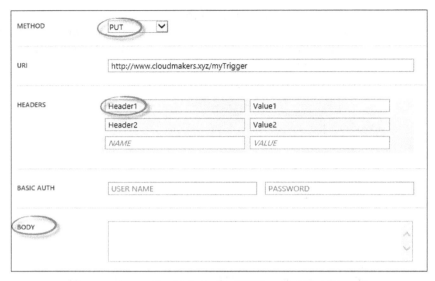

We can even specify a body for the HTTP method that allows it,
in addition to specific HTTP headers and basic authorization

Summary

In this chapter, we introduced the CloudMakers.XYZ scenario, highlighting some of the most important aspects a start-up has to cope with. We learned how to build a simple development environment, how to generalize it, and how to abstract it as just "Applications"-as-a-Service. We looked at how to create an ALM environment with VSO and what integration entry points are useful in various business contexts. Finally, we performed some automation using scripting technologies and we learned how to set up advanced schedules.

In the next chapter, we enhance the scenario with some hybrid options using networking and working with VMs.

2
Enhancing the Hybrid Process

In this chapter, you will learn how to integrate services to their local environment and processes. By integrating their local environment with the cloud, companies implement hybrid solutions to help themselves improve efficiency.

CloudMakers.XYZ

CloudMakers needs to manage some old software solutions already developed before this cloud experience. The migration in the cloud should be transparent, because there is not a specific activity for the customer. They need to recreate the same deployment environment for three-tier web applications to minimize the impact of the migration.

A frontend web server and a backend relational database make up the infrastructure for a typical three-tier, data-centric application. It was a common solution back in the last decade (and in some cases, a common solution today). This is due to some facts, which are mentioned here:

- The lack of affordable and performing alternatives to a relational database brought us to the typical "database-first" approach, best supported by tools that "scaffold" the database and automatically build the pages for CRUD operations.

- There was no culture for scalability, as all invocations were synchronous. So, one of the main topics was the correct sizing of the database machine, which had to support the maximum estimated number of calls from the frontend role.

- A support file server is necessary to store all the unstructured, filebase data that was generated internally or uploaded from pages.

- Modern cloud applications require some complex infrastructure and organizational skills, as these application models are quite faster to train.

Both the Windows and Linux environments support this architectural design. In the Windows world, the stack is composed of the following:

- Windows Server as the operating system

- Internet Information Services as the web server

- SQL Server as the relational database sever

- ASP.NET as the development platform

A typical representation of an infrastructure like this is shown here:

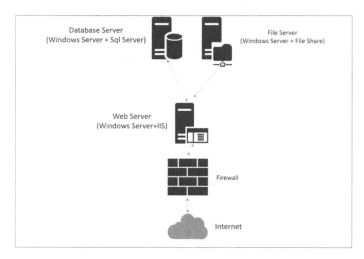

The objective of this chapter is to create an equivalent architecture in Azure, with the opportunity of making some infrastructural enhancements.

Service Manager (classic) mode versus Resource Manager mode

Azure has introduced **Azure Resource Manager (ARM)** to solve the challenges related to the way we manage projects in Azure. Most of the solutions deployed are a combination of two or more services. For example, running a virtual machine requires the deployment of three different services:

- A VM instance

- A storage account that contains the disk images

- A cloud service

A customer solution is more complex that this, and there are two main issues:

- Deploying a solution can be complex due to the number of services that needs to be created and configured
- Organizing and managing all these resources can become cumbersome if we cannot associate some metadata to describe why we have deployed every single resource and the solution it refers. If we can do this, we can then list, group, and filter services by solution and have a more clear and usable view of resources

ARM has changed the way we manage and deploy resources by including the following features:

- The entire solution can be described by a template that describes the resources, the dependencies, the parameters, and the variables of a deployable solution.
- Resources can be tagged to be easily organized and searched.
- Each resource is deployed inside a container called a **resource group**, a sort of **namespace**, that contains all the services deployed for that solution. The resource group resources are deployed as *a whole* in a repeatable way, after ensuring that they are deployed in a consistent state, as dependencies help deployment in the correct order. Deployment will be described in *Chapter 8, Deploying Solutions in Azure*.

The usage of the new ARM mode is a breaking change in the management of Azure resources. Services managed in the Resource Manager mode appear different from the corresponding services in the Service Manager mode.

At the time of writing this book, we can find these situations:

- New services that are ARM-only
- Some ASM services have equivalent new ARM services, but they are two distinct and different services
- Service that are ASM-only and not yet implemented as ARM
- ASM services that are not able to use other ARM services
- ARM services that are not able to use other ASM services

The migration to ARM is an opportunity for Azure to make enhancements to the service.

For example, in the ASM mode, VMs need an explicit, separated cloud service to make VMs addressable from the Internet. Virtual networks are an optional feature to organize our network in the cloud. In the ARM mode, a cloud service is not necessary to publish a VM. VM networking features are completely deployed to a **Virtual Network** (**VN**) associating a subnet, a network interface, a public IP address, and some security policies. In the ARM mode, VNs are mandatory to deploy VMs.

Future Azure services are ARM-based, that is, all new services will be based on resources. So, the investment needs to be done on ARM. Therefore, before deploying our first VM, it is necessary to understand how to explicitly manage a VN and how this relates to the current state.

At the time of writing this book, some limitations popped up. Listed as follows are some of them:

- The creation of a VPN is not allowed in VNet2, at the time of writing this book
- Recovery services for virtual machines work only with Classic VMs
- Classic VMs work only in Classic VNets
- ARM VNets with ARM VMs must connect with Classic VNet to access Classic VMs and VPNs

In summary, here is a diagram of what we want to create:

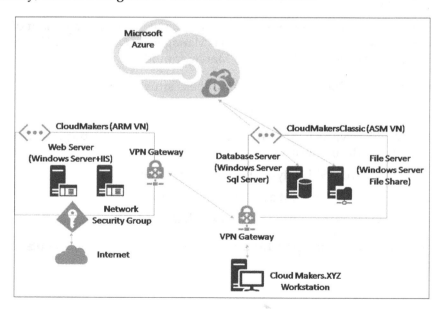

Configuring a Resource mode Virtual Network for the frontend servers

A VN is a representation of your own network in the cloud. It is a way to organize your VM. Three important aspects that need to be considered are:

- **Resource management**: Group and subdivide VMs in different VNs by internal security policies (some VMs cannot reach some others VMs).

- **Address spaces**: Different virtual networks can have different sets of addresses. A single address space can be subdivided into subnets.

- **Security**: While internal to a single VN, each VM can reach other VMs by default. You can control inbound and outbound traffic at subnet-level VMs with Network Security Groups.

VNs in an Azure account can be found in the **Ibiza** portal in two distinct containers by going to **Browse | Virtual Networks** or **Browse | Virtual Networks (Classic)**. From the **Classic** portal, you will find only Classic VNs.

You can create a VN by going to **New | Networking | Virtual Network**, by deciding whether you need a classic or a Resource Manager VN.

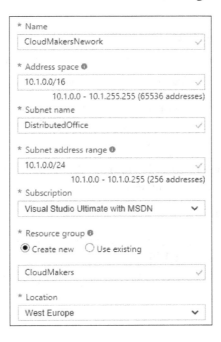

After clicking on **Create,** the main blade is opened, and general information can be inserted:

The name of the VN is a literal reference to the network:

A TCP/IP network is a set of connected and communicating nodes. Each node is identified by an IP address, which is assigned from a pool of addresses. An address space is identified by a base address that is the first address **physically** available (but generally not logically available) and a network mask that defines the size of the network itself. Depending on addressing (for simplicity, we choose IPv4), every address is theoretically available for our network. It is a common practice (and a general guideline in IP addressing) that a private network can have one of three main base addresses:

- `192.168.x.y` for up to 65536 (2^16) reservable addresses
- `172.16.x.y` for up to 1048576 (2^20) reservable addresses
- `10.x.y.z` for up to 16777216 (2^24) addresses

In each address space, the entire or a subset of that address can be used. The size of reservation is identified by a masking number in the CIDR notation (in the IP/mask notation), and the number of 1 bits contained in the mask.

A typical address space reservation is 16, from 255.255.0.0, which is 11111111.111111 11.00000000.00000000 in binary. This is exactly 16 1 bits.

Typical subnet reservations are:

- 24, from 255.255.255.0, which is 11111111.11111111.11111111.00000000 in binary, that is, exactly 24 1 bits
- 29, from 255.255.255.248, which is 11111111.11111111.11111111.11111000 in binary, that is, exactly 29 1 bits

If we perform this programmatically, via Azure PowerShell, this information is enough to create a new VN (given that Resource Group is already created):

```
New-AzureRmVirtualNetwork -ResourceGroupName "CloudMakers"
  -Name "CloudMakers" -AddressPrefix "192.168.0.0/16"
  -Location "NorthEurope"
```

Location is chosen by the opportunity.

The wizard continues, requiring the definition of the first subnetwork. As already discussed, a single VN is, by the number of addresses available, enough for CloudMakers' needs. In general, a unique, big address space is difficult to manage. Different resources, mixed in roles inside a single unique address space, have complicated security issues. This is where subnets are useful. A subnet is an internal partitioning of that single flat space.

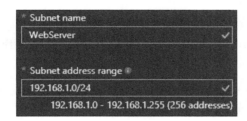

In PowerShell, you first get a reference to the VN:

```
$vn = Get-AzureRmVirtualNetwork
  -ResourceGroupName "CloudMakers" -Name "CloudMakers"
```

Then, you can add the new subnet configuration to the VN:

```
$webserverSN = Add-AzureRmVirtualNetworkSubnetConfig
  -Name "WebServer" -VirtualNetwork
  $vn -AddressPrefix "192.168.1.0/24"
```

Every update on elements that are part of the VN must be committed to make changes effective on your account:

```
Set-AzureRmVirtualNetwork -VirtualNetwork $vn
```

 If you execute PowerShell code interactively (for example, with PowerShell ISE), remember to refresh the $vn reference before executing any instruction that uses it.

To complete the creation, the resource group, subscription, and region have to be selected.

The address space of a VN is subdivided into logical subnets that assume the role of organizational containers of resources that share the same security requirements.

Organizational means that resources deployed to the cloud can have different roles. Here are some examples:

- **WebServer**: This is the server that implements services accessible by the cloud users
- **DataServer**: This is the server that can contain data or internal functionalities that are not exposed to the cloud users directly, but that should be accessible only from the web server or by company users or administrators
- **Gateway**: This is a special subnet that is useful for infrastructural issues, such as communication between different VNs

Each subnet, due to its role, needs different security policies. By default, these are as follows:

- Internally, each VM can reach other VMs without any limitation
- Any VM can access the outer networks
- From the outside, and this is the main issue, all access is denied, minimizing the attack surface of the subnet in the VN

Network security policies work at the IP port level. By default, access to all ports is denied. The typical prerequisites are:

Protocol	TCP/UDP	Port
HTTP	TCP	80
HTTPS	TCP	443
SQL Server	TCP	1433
RDP	TCP	3389
WinRM	TCP	5986

Publishing a web server needs port 80 open. The web server would need port 3389 to open a remote desktop access and port 5986 for remote PowerShell management via Windows Management Instrumentation.

Access to the SQL Server from outside needs port 1433 (or any equivalent port for corresponding generic database). These policies should be observed in a production environment:

- Sensitive data can be exposed directly in the cloud

- An application or an API should always be used in front of the data
- The SQL Server can authenticate probably only with SQL authentication and not with Windows authentication due to the lack of a domain service

Network Security Group (**NSG**) is the definition of a security policy. It has a meaning independent from any network and can be defined independently by any network. You can define any NSG you want and then apply it to the subnet(s) you need.

NSGs are automatically selected or created during the creation of the virtual machine. From the Azure portal, it is not possible to create a new NSG directly. By the way, we can manage the existing NSG and update the policy.

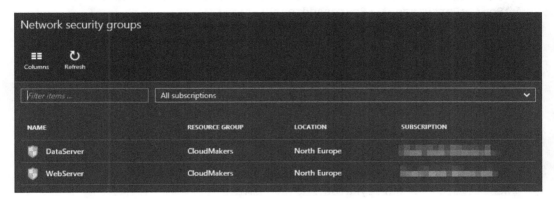

From PowerShell, the following information can be retrieved in the form of a command:

```
New-AzureRmNetworkSecurityGroup -Name "WebServer" location
  "NorthEurope" -ResourceGroupName "CloudMakers"
```

To get back a reference to the created NSG, we type:

```
$WebServerNSG = Get-AzureRmNetworkSecurityGroup -Name "WebServer"
  -ResourceGroupName "CloudMakers"
```

Any change to the NSG must be committed back with the following line:

```
Set-AzureRmNetworkSecurityGroup -NetworkSecurityGroup $WebServerNSG
```

To have a reference to a subnet to associate the NSG to the subnet, type the following line of code:

```
$webServerSN.NetworkSecurityGroup = $WebServerNSG
```

At this time, NSG is just a name, an empty container of inbound and outbound rules that are not already defined. For example, if *Web Server* means that we want to apply policy to make a web server accessible from the outside on port 80 from anywhere, this can be a new security rule:

```
$httpIn = New-AzureRmNetworkSecurityRuleConfig -Name HttpIn -
   DestinationPortRange 80 -Direction Inbound -Protocol Tcp -
   SourcePortRange * -SourceAddressPrefix * -
   DestinationAddressPrefix * -Access Allow -Priority 1000
```

If there are other rules that need to be added, define them accordingly:

```
$rdpIn = New-AzureRmNetworkSecurityRuleConfig -Name RdpIn -
   DestinationPortRange 3389 -Direction Inbound -Protocol Tcp -
   SourcePortRange * -SourceAddressPrefix * -
   DestinationAddressPrefix * -Access Allow -Priority 1100


$winRMIn = New-AzureRmNetworkSecurityRuleConfig -Name WinRMIn -
   DestinationPortRange 5985 -Direction Inbound -Protocol Tcp -
   SourcePortRange * -SourceAddressPrefix * -
   DestinationAddressPrefix * -Access Allow -Priority 1200
```

The rules must be associated to the NSG:

```
$WebServerNSG.SecurityRules.Add($httpIn)
$WebServerNSG.SecurityRules.Add($rdpIn )
$WebServerNSG.SecurityRules.Add($winrmIn)
```

The NSG must be committed in order for the change to be effective:

```
Set-AzureRmNetworkSecurityGroup -NetworkSecurityGroup $WebServerNSG
```

Configuring a Service mode (classic) Virtual Network for the backend servers

At the time of writing this book, not all virtual network features have been migrated to ARM virtual networks. VPN is one of these features. Therefore, it is necessary to create a VN in the Service Manager mode to configure a VPN to have safe access from the CloudMakers office. As we have two VNs, it is also necessary to have a safe and privileged access from the frontline ARM VN to this backend VN.

Configuring VN in the classic mode is quite different from ARM. The configuration in the service is XML-based (not JSON-based, like ARM), and it has no specific API. You need to write some XML to configure your VN. One issue is that you can change or create your VN only at the account level. There is only one network configuration XML that contains the network configuration of the entire account. Making changes to this configuration for a project can affect your other deployments.

 Make a copy of the downloaded VN XML configuration in a safe place to restore it in the case of configuration errors.

To download file configuration, type the following line of code:

```
Get-AzureVNetConfig -ExportToFile "<path to file>classicvnets.netcfg"
```

 If you have never created virtual networks from the portal (VN Classic, in the Ibiza portal), you need not download any configuration. So, there is no configuration file to download. The configuration file needs to be created manually.

You can edit the configuration with an XML editor. Choosing the address space is not arbitrary. As we need to connect via VPN, the network has to be on-premise with the network. The addresses must not overlap. Otherwise, problems routing from on premise to VN and vice versa will not work. Refer the following code for a better understanding:

```xml
<?xml version="1.0" encoding="utf-8"?>
<NetworkConfiguration xmlns:xsd="http://www.w3.org/2001/XMLSchema"
 xmlns:xsi="http://www.w3.org/2001/XMLSchema-instance"
 xmlns="http://schemas.microsoft.com/
ServiceHosting/2011/07/NetworkConfiguration">
  <VirtualNetworkConfiguration>
    <Dns />
    <VirtualNetworkSites>
      <VirtualNetworkSite name="Group CloudMakers
        CloudMakersClassic" Location="North Europe">
        <AddressSpace>
          <AddressPrefix>10.1.0.0/16</AddressPrefix>
        </AddressSpace>
        <Subnets>
          <Subnet name="DataServer">
            <AddressPrefix>10.1.2.0/24</AddressPrefix>
          </Subnet>
        </Subnets>
```

```
        </VirtualNetworkSite>
      </VirtualNetworkSites>
    </VirtualNetworkConfiguration>
  </NetworkConfiguration>
```

In this XML description, we find the configuration of networking for the entire Azure account. We can find the `VirtualNetworkSites` node that contains:

- **Address Space**: This is reserved for the entire VM
- **List of Subnets**: This is contained in `AddressSpace`, with a `Name` attribute to give it a role

After making changes to the file and saving it, it is necessary to update subscription configuration:

```
Set-AzureVNetConfig -ConfigurationPath "<path to
  file>classicvnets.netcfg"
```

Now, it is possible to configure VPN. From the portal, the classic virtual network shows the possibility of creating a VPN by clicking on it:

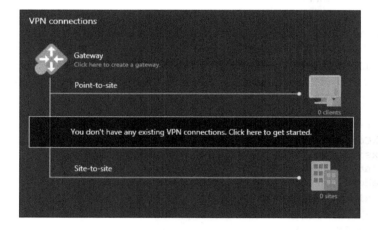

A VPN is defined into a VN with the existence of **Gateway**, that, as the name says, is an access from the outside:

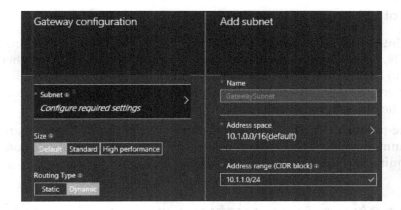

Some parameters have to be configured as follows:

- **Subnet**: In the VN address space, the gateway needs its own subnet. This will create another subnet with a reserved name `GatewaySubnet`.

- **Size**: This is the class of the gateway that implies the throughput of the connection, taking into account the number of concurrent users, the data traffic, and costs.

> Refer to `https://azure.microsoft.com/en-us/pricing/details/vpn-gateway/` for current pricing and performances of different VPN gateway configurations. Refer to `https://azure.microsoft.com/en-us/pricing/details/data-transfers/` for the current pricing of data transfer to and from VPNs.

- **Routing Type**: In general, **Dynamic Routing Type** is preferred. It is mandatory for point-to-site connections. However, some old VPN hardware can support only static routing for site-to-site connections.

After the creation, process the VN gateway has a public IP assigned to make it accessible. The IP address is accessible via PowerShell with the following command:

```
(Get-AzureVNetGateway -VNetName "Group CloudMakers
  CloudMakersClassic").VIPAddress
```

Two types of VPN that are available are as follows:

- **Point-to-site VPN**: This is useful to connect a single client machine to the VPN, when there is no need to share a common connection or when there is no hardware (router) capable to connect and share a compatible VPN to the entire LAN. This is a great solution for a single user who needs access to the office from home.

- **Site-to-site VPN**: This is useful to connect an entire LAN and share a single common connection between users. This is good for office solutions. It requires a router compatible with IPSec VPNs.

Connecting two virtual networks with site-to-site connection

We have created a Service Mode Classic VPN named **CloudMakersClassic** in order to access to VPNs. We have created another VPN in an ARM Virtual Network called **CloudMakers** to take advantage of the resource templates and resource groups. The two virtual networks are different by features and by roles, one being the VN for frontend servers and one for backend servers. Up to now, they don't communicate with each other. Up to now, they are two unrelated networks that could communicate only with public IP (but in our sample only ARM VN has one) and without any special privilege. In this situation we can have some security issues, that we need to avoid. So, we can configure a site-to-site connection to allow a privileged access to the classic VN. So, we can configure a site-to-site connection to allow access to the classic VN.

To start, we need to configure CloudMakers' ARM VN, the frontend ARM VN, or, in VPN terms, the local network.

As mentioned earlier, VPN support in ARM is missing (at the time of writing this book). Yet, accessing another VPN and implementing a VPN client is supported, but missing from the portal. Some code in PowerShell is needed. Switch to the Resource Manager mode.

At first, we need to create a local network gateway. This is useful to map the connection from ARM VN to ASM VN. Before that, configuring two pieces of information from ASM VN are necessary:

- `GatewayIpAddress`: This is the public IP assigned to the ASM VPN gateway (you can read it from the portal or via PowerShell in the ASM mode):

```
$CloudMakersClassicGWIp = (Get-AzureVNetGateway -VNetName
    "Group CloudMakers CloudMakersClassic").VIPAddress
```

- `AddressPrefix`: This was previously assigned to ASM VPN (`10.1.0.0/16`):

```
$CloudMakersClassicGW = New-AzureLocalNetworkGateway -
    ResourceGroupName CloudMakers
    -Name CloudMakersClassicGW -Location NorthEurope
    -GatewayIpAddress $CloudMakersClassicGWIp
    -AddressPrefix "10.1.0.0/16"
```

Now, we need to make the ARM VN accessible from outside. First, we create a subnet for a gateway in the virtual network, with a reserved name (`GatewaySubnet`, the same as the corresponding classic one):

```
$vn = Get-AzureRmVirtualNetwork -ResourceGroupName
  "CloudMakers" -Name "CloudMakers"

$GatewaySN = Add-AzureRmVirtualNetworkSubnetConfig -Name
  "GatewaySubnet" -VirtualNetwork $vn -AddressPrefix
  "192.168.0.0/24"

Set-AzureVirtualNetwork -VirtualNetwork $vn
```

 Look for the difference. `192.168.0.0/16` is the address space, and `192.168.0.0/24` is a subnet, if it is defined inside the address space.

The gateway needs a public IP to be reachable from the outside:

```
$GatewayIp = New-AzureRmPublicIpAddress -ResourceGroupName
  CloudMakers -Location NorthEurope -Name CloudMakersRMGW -
  AllocationMethod Dynamic
```

Then, this IP is necessary to configure the gateway. It maps the public IP to the gateway subnet we already created:

```
$CloudMakersGWIpConfig = New-AzureRmVirtualNetworkGatewayIpConfig
  -Name CloudMakersGWIpConfig
  -PublicIpAddressId $CloudMakersGWIp.Id
  -SubnetId $GatewaySubnetSN.Id
```

Now, the client gateway can be created on the configuration defined:

```
$CloudMakersGW = New-AzureRmVirtualNetworkGateway -
  ResourceGroupName CloudMakers -Location NorthEurope -Name
  CloudMakersGW -GatewayType Vpn -VpnType RouteBased -
  IpConfiguration $CloudMakersGWIpConfig
```

The last thing to do is establish the connection between the two VNs in the form of the local gateway and virtual gateway defined. The connection from the ASM to ARM network is based on the IPSec protocol. It cannot be established if there is not a shared secret defined to recognize each other. It's a string that, once defined from the ARM side, has to then be defined on the ASM side:

```
$sharedSecret = "..." #a string secret
$CloudMakersClassicConnection = New-AzureRmVirtualNetworkGatewayCo
nnection -ResourceGroupName CloudMakers -Location NorthEurope -Name
CloudMakersRMClassicConnection -VirtualNetworkGateway1
  $CloudMakersGW -LocalNetworkGateway2 $CloudMakersClassicGW -
  ConnectionType IPSec -RoutingWeight 10 -SharedKey $sharedSecret
```

The LocalNetwork is configured. We need to annotate the public IP assigned by Azure to the gateway (via PowerShell), the address space of the LocalNetwork (`192.168.0.0/16`), and the shared secret.

Now, let's go back to the VPN, the Classic VN, to complete the configuration.

From the virtual network (classic) in the portal, we need to configure a VPN site-to-site connection to a local network:

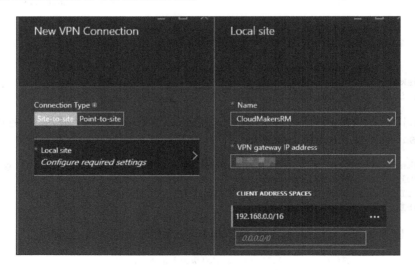

Name is a literal to recognize the specific local network. The VPN gateway is the public IP address we created and assigned to the ARM VN gateway. **Client Address Space** is the address space of the ARM VN.

Now, configure the shared key, from the ASM side, that relates the VPN with the local network:

```
Set-AzureVNetGatewayKey -VNetName "Group CloudMakers
  CloudMakersClassic" -LocalNetworkSiteName CloudMakersARM -
  SharedKey $sharedSecred -Verbose
```

Site-to-site connection is now ready, and the two VNs are connected and communicating.

Configuring Office connectivity with a point-to-site VPN

To connect to the VPN from Office, a point-to-site VPN connection is necessary. From the virtual network configuration, create a new VPN connection, selecting the type as **Point-to-site**:

Client Address Spaces is the client network assigned to the user's virtual adapter when they connect to the VPN.

The authorization in a point-to-site VPN is certificate-based. It is an asymmetric encryption algorithm that is used to sign the communication, where the keys are contained in certificates. A self-signed public key certificate means that the trust to the certificate is given by the fact that it was received by the VPN via an upload from an Azure account by the owner of the Azure subscription.

To create a self-signed certificate for a Windows developer with Visual Studio 2015, **Makecert.exe** is the tool necessary to generate it. In the **Developer Command Prompt** for Visual Studio 2015, type the following command:

```
makecert -sky exchange -r -n "CN= CloudMakersRoot" -pe -a sha1
  -len 2048 -ss My "CloudMakersRoot.cer"
```

The root certificate is safely stored in the private certificate store in the machine that generated it. In order to allow many users to access the VPN, the root certificate must be shared between the users so that they can generate their own client certificate.

> To export the root certificate, to protect it with a password, and to avoid the usage of the certificate by unattended users, follow the instructions at http://blogs.msdn.com/b/kaevans/archive/2015/06/05/configure-a-point-to-site-vpn-connection-to-an-azure-vnet.aspx.

After uploading the root certificate, the portal processes it and prepares the VPN accordingly. A client application is then downloadable (in 32- and 64-bit Windows versions) to configure VPN client access on the client machine.

Every user that needs to connect has to receive the client and the root certificate. The user has to install the client on their PC.

Then, they need to generate the certificate. First, the user has to install the certificate in their personal certificate store. Then, they can invoke the Makecert.exe tool to generate a client certificate from the root certificate using the following command:

```
makecert.exe -n "CN=OwenClientCloudMakers" -pe -sky exchange
  -m 96 -ss My -in "CloudMakersRoot" -is my -a sha256
```

Now, each user can install the client already downloaded from the portal and shared together with the root certificate. The client installs a new VPN, accessible like other connections, in the taskbar (shown in the following screenshot in Windows 10):

The same connection is available by going to **Control Panel** | **Network and Internet** | **Network Connections**. It opens the VPN window from which we can launch the client app for Windows Azure VPNs:

The connection is established if the client finds the client certificate in the personal certificate store. If the certificate is missing, an error can occur.

Deploy a Windows Azure Virtual Machine in an ARM Virtual Network

At this point, we have a network infrastructure over the cloud that is ready to accept new VMs:

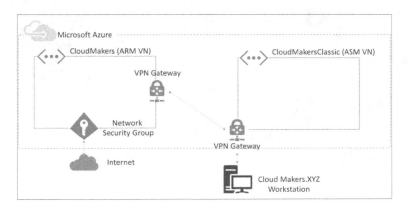

Now, we need to define a task to create a virtual machine in an ARM VN. It is a two-phase task:

1. Create a connection for a VM in an ARM VN.
2. Create the ARM VM.

Let's start from the connection to the VM. In general, any device that connects to a network has a network card, or a **Network Interface (NI)**. It has some characteristics:

- It has a private address that is from the address space of the subnet. The IP can be dynamic or static. Dynamic means that the IP address is dynamically assigned by a DHCP service because it is inside a subnet in a VN. Static means that the IP address is assigned during the creation or configuration of the NI. As a rule, an IP address should be used as dynamic. There is always name resolution through Azure DNS; that is, a VM can be reached by its name, and DNS automatically resolve its IP address. Choose a fixed private IP only if you have some legacy strategies that do not allow you to use naming resolution.

- It has a public address so that the interface is public and reachable by the outside world. Again, the address can be dynamic or static. The association of a public IP in an NI automatically updates Azure DNS when it is inside a VM. Therefore, in general, there is no need for a fixed IP for a VM. If you really need a static IP, for example, because you need to map that IP on an external DNS, remember that there is a cost to allocating a fixed IP address.

Refer to https://azure.microsoft.com/en-us/ pricing/details/ip-addresses/ to check the current IP address pricing. All IP addresses in the subscription can be seen on the portal.

- The network interface inherits the NSG from the subnet it relies on. However, a specific VM could override it by specific needs that can be satisfied by assigning a specific NSG to a specific NI. As a rule, an NSG should be somehow generic and reapplicable to many NIs or subnets, not just one NI.

From PowerShell, first we will create the public IP address, because we need to reach the VM from the outside:

```
$WebServer01PublicIp = New-AzureRmPublicIpAddress -Name
  WebServer01PublicIp -ResourceGroupName CloudMakers -Location
  NorthEurope -DomainNameLabel cloudmakerswebserver01 -
  AllocationMethod Dynamic
```

Then, we will create the NI. From the portal, navigate to **New | Network Interfaces**; or via PowerShell create it using the following command:

```
$WebServer01NI = New-AzureRmNetworkInterface -ResourceGroupName
  CloudMakers -Name WebServer01 -Subnet $webServerSN -Location
  NorthEurope -PublicIpAddress WebServer01PublicIp
```

The public IP assignment is explicit. If we do not explicit a private IP (that is implicitly static), DHCP dynamically assigns an IP.

Now, it is time to create the VM. The first argument to select is the size. The following code shows all the available zones in the selected location:

```
Get-AzureRmVMSize -Location NorthEurope | Select Name,
  NumberOfCores, MemoryInMb | Format-Table
```

Name is the value to use as an argument in configurations that follow (with only some reported):

Name	Number of cores	Memory (in MB)
Basic_A0	1	768
Basic_A1	1	1792
Basic_A2	2	3584
Basic_A3	4	7168
Basic_A4	8	14336

Now, we can define the first step by giving the VM a name and a size from the ones selected:

```
$vmConfig = New-AzureRmVMConfig -VMName CMWebServer01 -VMSize
  Basic_A1
```

Next, VM deployment depends on the specific family of operating systems that will be installed. Azure supports Windows and Linux. The provisioning of the VMAgent is necessary to inject Azure software at OS level that has knowledge of being inside an Azure Data Center. This allows the VM to execute accordingly, with deployment policies of the cloud. One example is to inject inside the VM some software that can be automatically installed after the deployment of the VM using the following code:

```
$vmOsConfig = $vmConfig | Set-AzureRmVMOperatingSystem -
  ComputerName CMWebServer01 -Windows -ProvisionVMAgent -
  Credential $adminCredential
```

Now, it is time to select the operating system. Azure deploys a new VM from an image, that is a .VHD image on which a preconfigured Windows (or Linux) is already installed and deployment is a *just* for it. Every operating system release image can be available in many versions, as they are distinguished and timely ordered by service pack or patches application. That current, most updated and patched version is indicated as the "latest" one.

```
$vmImageConfig = $vmOsConfig | Set-AzureRmVMSourceImage
  -PublisherName MicrosoftWindowsServer -Offer WindowsServer
  -Skus 2012-R2-Datacenter -Version "latest"
```

Now that the image is selected, we need to declare where to deploy the OS disk that will be created from the image. All VHDs are stored in a vhds folder in a blob storage in an Azure Storage Account (of which we need to get a reference):

```
$cloudmakersvms = Get-AzureRmStorageAccount -ResourceGroupName
  CloudMakers -Name cloudmakersvms

$vmOsDiskConfig = $vmImageConfig | Set-AzureRmVMOSDisk -Name "OS"
  -VhdUri ($cloudmakersvms.PrimaryEndpoints.Blob.ToString() +
  "vhds/webServer01-os.vhd") -CreateOption fromImage
```

Now, we can attach as many data disks as we need, empty, specifying the size of the disk. This invocation can be repeated as many times as we need, ensuring that we specify the correct .vhd filename accordingly:

```
$vmDataDiskConfig = $vmOsDiskConfig | Add-AzureRmVMDataDisk -Name
  "Data" -DiskSizeInGB 20 -VhdUri
  ($cloudmakersvms.PrimaryEndpoints.Blob.ToString() +
  "vhds/webServer01-data.vhd") -CreateOption empty
```

Finally, we can connect the VM to the virtual network by attaching the network interface that we previously created. This reveals which is the correct relationship between VNs and VMs:

```
$vmNicConfig = $vmDataDiskConfig | Add-AzureRmVMNetworkInterface -
  Id (Get-AzureNetworkInterface -ResourceGroupName CloudMakers -
  Name WebServer01).Id -Primary
```

The configuration in complete. We can now launch the VM creation process, which will be deployed in the location and the virtual network we have selected.

```
$vm = New-AzureRmVM -VM $vmNicConfig -ResourceGroupName
  CloudMakers -Location NorthEurope
```

Managing virtual networks with Operational Insight

One of the values that must be evaluated in cloud solutions is management. The application lifecycle is a long period (years) divided in phases. In a dev book, we tend to talk about development or deployment phases, which we consider to be just the first part of an application's lifecycle. However, they are just the smallest part of an application's lifecycle. The longest period is production. Every phase is subject to costs:

- Acquisition cost: It contains the following subcosts:
    - Infrastructure cost
    - Development cost
    - Deployment cost

- Production cost: It comprises the following expenditures:
    - Management cost
    - Maintenance cost
    - New development cost

- Dismiss or migration cost

One of the biggest mistakes that can be made in a solution is missing management costs evaluation. What happens is that a solution can have a cheap acquisition phase, but an expensive management phase during production. At last, what happens is that a solution can cost too much. Which are the tasks that are needed to manage a VM infrastructure? Here are some of them:

- Search and investigate to uncover valuable and actionable insights throughout your infrastructure

- Investigate your system update status and identify missing system updates across all your servers, whether they are running on your data center or on a public cloud

- Detect security breaches with security and audits by enabling an efficient, scalable, and secure way to collect and store security records

- Collect network and performance data using wire data that you can combine with other data to help you identify network activity for other processes and users
- Collect security logs, which help security analysts and system admins mine large, distributed sets of security data in order to detect suspicious activities and potential security breaches
- Detect security breaches with security and audits by enabling an efficient, scalable, and secure way to collect and store security records
- Identify differences with change tracking that will help you to know what data has been changed on your servers
- Plan for capacity to get deep visibility into your data center capacity, investigate "what-if" scenarios, identify stale and over-allocated virtual machines, and plan your future compute and storage needs

The focus of this paragraph is not "how much does it cost," and whether this is too much or not. Rather it focuses on the fact that costs exist because we need to manage resources. After focusing on why, we can discuss on how (choosing) and what (costs). This is supported by the fact that Azure and the cloud in general make management costs explicit. It is not possible to avoid them. What a cloud presents is alternatives: who needs explicit management, who prefers avoiding it. The two alternatives are:

- **Infrastructure-as-a-Service (IaaS)**
- **Platform-as-a-Service (PaaS)**

IaaS implies that you design and plan the management of the platform over which you deploy. With PaaS, you configure deployment and do not think about management. In a general sense, by controlling the platform (IaaS), you can tune your solution better than the few customizations a generic PaaS or SaaS service allows.

In this chapter, we have described the need to implement VMs and IaaS, so, as already mentioned earlier, management tasks are up to the team. We now understand what these tasks are and what can help simplify and improve management experience.

The scenario described in this chapter is just seminal about how an infrastructure can grow. Virtual networks can grow in complexity with tens, hundreds, or more VMs. All tasks previously described have something in common. Listed as follows are the features:

- Collect all the logs from different management operations in a single VM, and collect all the data for operations to run
- Collect all issues from all the VMs; operations to be repeated run in all VMs

Azure helps us solve the Operational Insights issue. Part of Microsoft Operations Management Suite is a software-as-a-service solution tailored for IT operations teams. This service collects, stores, and analyzes log data from any VM source in your deployment, applies real-time analytics tasks to process that data, and creates a dashboard that allows us to visualize, take decisions, and manage the infrastructure. It is the Azure part of Microsoft Operations Management Suite. The key features are mentioned, as follows:

- **Simplicity**: A single portal for all your management tasks and no infrastructure to maintain

- **Time to value**: Onboard, fast, no content to create, and connects to your on-premises datacenter

- **Easy to integrate**: Adds new servers, or connects to your existing management tools within minutes

- **Hybrid and open**: Manage workloads across Windows and Linux, hybrid and public clouds, Azure, and AWS

- **Optimized for System Center**: Complements your System Center investment to unleash new management scenarios

The main scenarios in OMS, as of today, include:

- **Log analytics**: Real-time operational intelligence; deliver unified management across your datacenters and public clouds; collect, store, and analyze log data from virtually any source; and turn it into real-time operational intelligence.

- **Automation**: This is simplified cloud management with process automation. It creates, monitors, manages, and deploys resources in your hybrid cloud environments while reducing errors and boosting efficiency to help lower your operational costs.

- **Availability**: This is a fully integrated availability solution, including rapid disaster recovery. Protect your data using capabilities only possible from the cloud. Enable backup and integrated recovery for all your servers and critical applications to prepare you in the event of a disaster.

- **Security**: This is a centralized control of server security. Identify missing system updates and malware status. Collect security-related events, and perform forensic, audit, and breach analysis. Glean machine data from all your servers, no matter where they are, and receive deep analytics to react quickly to issues.

The Operational Insight icon looks like this:

To create an Operational Insight account, you go on the classic portal (not yet migrated to the new portal), go to **Operational Insight | Quick Create**, and enter the respective data in the fields discussed, as follows:

- **Workspace Name**, **Public Name** that will be used in future references
- **Tier**, choosing among **Free**, **Standard**, and **Premium** that differs in quota (daily limit for free, unlimited for others) and retention period (7 days, 1 month, and 12 months respectively); **Tier** can be changed anytime
- **Location** (currently available in West Europe and East US)
- **Subscription account**

After creating the account, go to the main page of the account that guides you on the main activities for the account. The first choice is **Visit your Operational Insight account**. You go to your **Operational Management Suite** page where you can manage your resources:

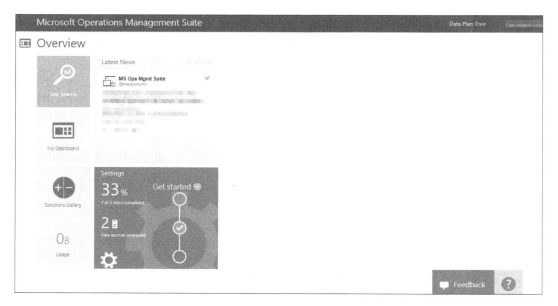

Enabling the proper set of resources for servers gives the choice between Azure Virtual Machine and On-premise server. Both bring us to the same page that lists all the virtual machines (registered or not) and all the on-premise servers already registered:

Registered means that the machine (virtual or not) has a Microsoft Monitoring Agent installed. The role of the agent is fundamental, because the software sends data logs to the OMS account (and not OMS that goes into every registered machine and gets the files). There are two options:

- For classic VMs, enable Operational Insights by just clicking on the **ENABLE OP INSIGHTS** button. It looks like the one in the following image:

- For ARM VMs and on-premise machines (virtual or not), it is necessary to install the agent manually; navigate from the OMS account to find **Settings** and then go to **Connected Sources**:

From this page, you find two important pieces of information: the workspace ID and the primary key that allows the agent to be authorized to send data to the OMS and the agent for the main server platform (Windows 32- and 64-bits, and Linux). The installation of the agent continues the installation to the selection of the Azure Operational Insights account, with the ID and key previously defined:

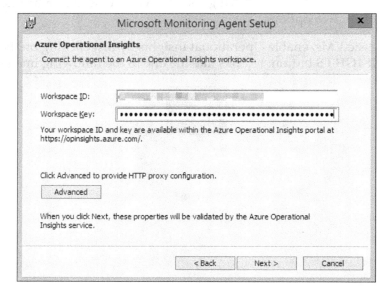

The activation of the Operational Management Suite account is immediate. The execution of the agents, which is continuous, takes some time, from minutes to hours, to collect all logs. This is because of network performance in the case of on-premise servers or size because of big or small log files.

From the empty dashboard of the Operational Management Suite, which contains just the **News** tile and the **Get Started** tile, you can manage adding a new solution pack, by selecting the **Solution Gallery** tile ⊕ . Adding it is immediate, while collecting data needs more time.

Here, it is possible to find new solutions from a continuously improving set that Microsoft adds over time. You too can include solutions. Moreover, this is compatible with the developer experience with a new set of skills that needs to be learned.

System Update Assessment

System Update Assessment helps you identify missing system updates across all your servers. The tool that can be accessed by the is tile, as follows:

It does not perform updates, downloads, and installation, but gives detailed information about:

- The servers' missing security updates
- The servers not updated recently
- Types of updates missing

The assessment operation that is performed can be identified with the dialog box that appears similar to the one in the following image:

Performing Assessment

Microsoft Operations Management Suite is connecting to your server data to perform an update assessment for the first time. This will take several hours. It is recommended you let this run overnight.

Log collection can be a long activity, so it is normal to see a message you can read on the right-hand side when you start observing update assessment. After a few minutes or hours, depending on the size and distance of machines to be analyzed, it's typical to find yourself in front of the following condition:

The sunburst charts represent some main generic queries that can give immediate information about the state of the machines. Clicking on each of them, you go deep into a detailed list of updated details that must be applied: the **TITLE**, data regarding the machine to which it is applied, the target product, main classification, knowledge base, the optionality of the patch, and whether a reboot is required.

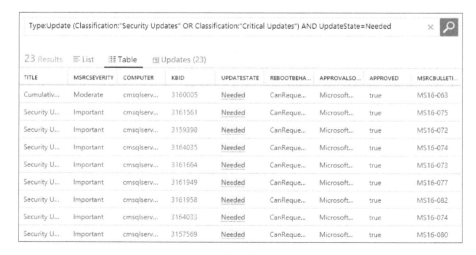

As an assessment solution, there is no automatic delivery from download to installation, out of the box, for the updates needed to update the machines. It is an awareness task. Update installation is subject to testing because of any critical impact after deployment. The reboot can mean service unavailability, an update task getting disrupted, or the machine being in an unstable state.

SQL Assessment

SQL Assessment evaluates the configuration and assesses the health of your SQL Server deployments. It considers some best practices defined by the SQL Server and Support Services teams.

As for all OMS, the number is not fixed. However, it increases as SQL teams share with OMS the newer recommendations by the services. Based on these, it provides a prioritized list of recommendations tailored to your deployments. It identifies potential issues on:

- Security and compliance
- Availability and business continuity
- Performance and security
- Upgrade, migration, and deployment
- Operations and monitoring
- Change and configuration

These areas allow you to quickly understand the health of your deployments and easily take actions to enhance your SQL Server environments.

The recommendation can be expressed in an activity that has to be implemented, some commands to be applied via SQL, or the parameters to be applied to SQL Engine configuration. One of the typical tasks to be performed is the definition of a regular backup task. Since SQL 2012, that backup can also be optimized using Azure Storage as a long-term backup storage. By connecting to the SQL Server machine and starting from SQL Server Management Studio, the Maintenance Plan Wizard can be started by going to **Management | Maintenance Plan**. This runs a guided wizard to select some of the schedulable activities in SQL Server, in particular, **Back Up Database (Full)**:

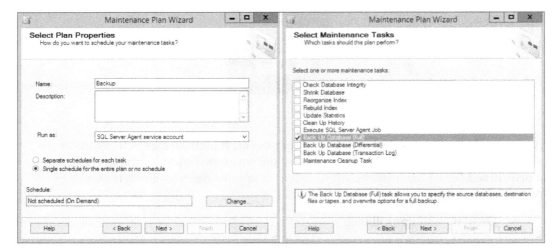

Before proceeding, a schedule must be defined because of the requirements of SQL Assessment, so the SQL agent will execute accordingly to the desired configuration.

After pressing **Next** from **Task Definition**, the following information on the backup activity can be provided:

- Databases to be backed up (**User Databases, System Databases, All Databases**)
- Destination of the backup, in this case the URL that means the endpoint of an Azure Storage

Before proceeding to configure storage, the SQL Server must be aware of the subscription that contains the storage we need. To do this, visit `https://manage.windowsazure.com/publishsettings`.

You then select the subscription of interest and submit it. The file can be downloaded with this file. It can be uploaded by selecting it from the **Browse** button from the **Destination** tab in the backup window:

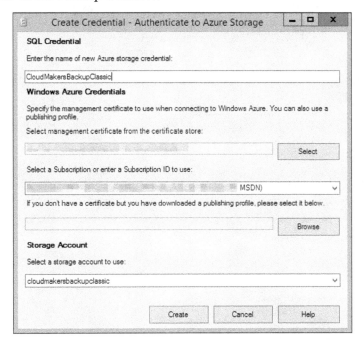

This configuration allows the SQL Server to be recognized as a valid user of the subscription and credential to authenticate to the storage. From **Define Backup Task**, Azure Storage can be configured to receive the backup files that the SQL Server will generate:

Pressing **Next** until the end will configure the SQL Server to the respective backup and thus solve one of the SQL recommendations.

Malware Assessment

Malware Assessment helps you identify servers that are infected or at a risk of infection by malware. As machines can be accessed remotely via Remote Desktop Services or through the files that can be uploaded to the filesystem via some other services, malware is always ready to cling onto some hosts or PCs.

Malware Assessment

Assessment detects whether malware software is present or not on the machine. If present, it checks if it is updated or not, if there are any running issues, and thus it recommends performing any actions useful improving security. If malware software is not present, assessment recommends providing one. In this case there are two choices:

- Bring your own license for the software that you already have the license for
- Install an extension to the virtual machine (classic VM at the time of writing this book), from the portal that comes from **Marketplace** and on a pay-as-you-go basis as that of the VM

From the portal, select the properties of a VM:

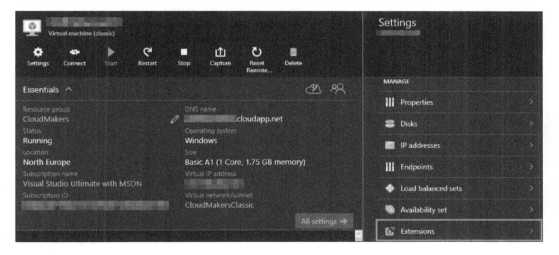

You can select the software that you want to install on the VM via the agent:

Summary

In this chapter, you learned how to connect Azure Virtual Machines in virtual networks and look for differences between the Service Manager mode and Resource Manager mode. Virtual networks are a requirement for the ARM mode VMs, so we need to understand Azure networking basics.

You also learned how to interconnect two different virtual networks in two deployment models to make use of all the current opportunities given by the two deployment models and the power of a complex, distributed, and public network.

You then understood how we can manage our IaaS assets with Azure Operational Insights and understood some of the IT pro skills that a developer needs to know when approaching Azure IaaS.

In the next chapter, we will jump into the Platform as a Service world. You will learn how to take advantage of different Azure services, and develop and deploy a frontend web application.

3
Building the Frontend

You learned how to build a comprehensive frontend composing of Azure services. This is an advanced scenario, using the Platform-as-a-Service services of Azure to reduce costs. Also, collateral services are used to improve the performance of the application.

In this chapter, we will cover the following topics:

- Catalog persisted to DocumentDB
- Advanced catalog search with Azure Search
- Blob storage and CDN for image files
- Catalog cached with Redis
- Web apps with app service

It's all about data

SQL databases have ruled the way developers store data in applications for three decades. Databases are growing in a world where applications are standalone or connected to a highly reserved and controlled Local Area Network of many machines inside a single company. Since then, the relational model has become widely used and understood. The interaction with the database is done with the SQL language, which is a standard language. This degree of standardization was enough to keep things familiar so that people did not need to learn something new to persist data when the Internet and web applications were starting their lives.

SQL databases follow the **Consistency-Availability-Partitioning** (CAP) theorem for network distributed systems: only two of the three principles can be respected. In particular, SQL databases give up to partitioning (physically organizing data of the same database in different physical containers) to guarantee consistency and availability. Consistency means that you can always read the data you have already written in database. In a relational database, consistency also means that schema validation and relational constraints are applied. Availability means that system always gives a response, even if it is an error. This result can be obtained with a relational database that is designed to run on a single machine. If you need more power because your requests increase, you need to add more computing, memory, and networking resources to that machine. Alternatively, you need to buy a new, bigger one that takes over it. A single machine means that every potential failure has an impact on the entire solution, since there is no redundant node that can take over the failed node in the case of a failure. A cluster is mandatory for high-availability system, but it is very expensive.

Consistency is all nodes of the distributed system seeing the same data at the same time. Consistency is an expensive feature. Since we perceive consistency with a `read` operation just after a `write` one, we need to understand why this costs too much. A `read` is a query over the database, and this can be done in two ways. If no ordering criteria are established, a complete table scan, that is, reading all the records in a table, is mandatory. This is because data is written in the same order as it was inserted. However, every relational database system ensures that every `write` operation is committed to the table. Ordering the content of a table is another expensive feature, if our table contains thousands, millions, or more records. Every database implements some indexing algorithm and creates a search-optimized container (an index) that is always ordered in a cheap and fast way. This relational database ensures that many indexes are updated after every write, where "many" refers to the fact that a single data from a single record can be contained in more than one index.

Redundancy is, right from the beginning, the only way to achieve performance. Data can be retrieved fast, only if we *replicate* that data and store the copy in one or more containers optimized for reads. However, what happens if we don't read or need reading after every write? The issue can be addressed by considering the following aspects:

- An ingestion system is a write-only application that does not need to read data just after it has written it, so updating indexes consistently is not so useful.

- A **Create-Read-Updated-Delete** (CRUD) application is typically a user interface-oriented application. You can use a grid of entities, insert a new data row or edit an existing one, and go back to the grid looking inside it to find that the new entity is already inserted. This is not a requirement, but generally an unrequested feature.

Redundancy is the turning point, as it is associated with the generation of copies of that data. What if we relax the index updating requirement? We transform index updating from a synchronous process to an asynchronous one that will have less priority than `write` operations. The data will be written in the indexes at last, after more critical tasks are completed. This is where a distributed system (a database is in general a distributed system, at least with one node) is violating the consistency property. Indexes can contain data that is not updated, and we say that indexes are stale. Index update time is not a "free of charge" feature, but is a feature that must be sized as a requirement so that the system can be eventually consistent in a feasible way. As the index update delay becomes important and stale data is critical, increasing the performance of the system to allow it update the index becomes a critical task.

The next step is partitioning. The explicit presence of this asynchronous synchronization task allows us to make three assumptions about it:

- The synchronization process can perform its role over a *network*, thus allowing the distribution of work over different parts of the database on different hosts

- If the process synchronizes not only an index but the write container itself in some other processes, we have distributed *replicas*, making the entire distributed system resilient over failures

- If the process moves content from a container to another over the network as a function of some parameters, it is creating a *data partition*, allowing workload distribution and high parallel data access

As we understand that an explicit process can perform synchronization, we can consider one more feature. Up to now, we implicitly needed indexing to be an automatic feature of a database management system. However, we can talk about writing data to a database, take the responsibility of writing an explicit synchronization process, and write another index in another database. In this case, we really don't talk anymore about indexing. From an application point of view, we talk about a *write model* and a *read model* where the latter one is our new index table.

Partitioning has some drawbacks, if we compare it with a **Relational Database Management System (RDBMS)**. Some of them are listed here:

- In a partitioned database, we cannot have strict integrity constraints between normalized entities. As data is distributed and data in other partitions may not be available, a partitioned DBMS cannot guarantee the constraint of the presence of an entity at the time it should enforce that constraint.

- The same constraint mechanism can guarantee the uniqueness of generic values (not to say the fields).

- If two `write` operations are required to be executed as "all or nothing" tasks, how can a partitioned DBMS guarantee the consistency of the system? In this case, we lose acid transactions and two-phase commits.

These are typically the greatest values we recognize in a relational database: indexing, normalizing data, checking constraints, transactions, and two-phase commits. As we don't apply these, we lose value on using a relational database. All these features take us far away from a partitioned database.

A partitioned DB could enforce a schema, that is, define the structure of an entity. However, the evolution of applications, the maturity of object-oriented languages, and the success of JavaScript Object Notation (JSON) to communicate entities in a network, in applications, have made this feature lose its appeal.

So, this is what we expect from a database (a generic one, not relational):

- Persisting information as fast as it can

- Partitioning data to perform a cloud-friendly, resilient system scale out

- Expressing explicit performance requirements on a read model

It is important to underline that these arguments are not against relational databases, but in favor of opportunities that the cloud gives us to propose different solutions to persist data.

The tabular model is suitable for many kinds of data, particularly when you need to pick apart data and reassemble it in different ways for different purposes.

In order to run effectively on a cluster, most NoSQL databases have limited transactional capability.

Polyglot Persistence

With all these principles in mind, we can think of two main considerations.

The first is as a database system creator, someone who can develop new database systems that can privilege some features over others (partitioning, indexing, and so on). These features, in general, differ from those that RDBMS typically supports.

The second is as a database user (the application developer). We can decide who will take over the responsibility of writing different data models we could use in our solutions. We can choose a different database engine that can differently optimize the features required by an application (storing, querying, searching, and indexing). Alternatively, we can take explicit responsibility in implementing different data stores in different database engines.

We can cite Martin Fowler:

> *Polyglot Persistence is the practice of using multiple data-storage technologies, chosen based on the way data is being used by individual applications.*

> *Why store binary images in relational database when there are better storage systems?*

Polyglot Persistence will occur all around the enterprise as different applications use different data storage technologies. It will also occur within a single application as different parts of an application's data store have different access characteristics. If we consider Azure Cloud, which already offers many different data-storage solutions, we can try mapping typical different data models to find the best database for that sort of data.

Data model	Requirements	Database service
Financial data	Needs transactional updates, tabular structure fits data, and checking constraints ensure data integrity.	SQL Azure
Product catalog	Requires a lot of reads, infrequent writes. Products make natural aggregate.	DocumentDB
Shopping cart	Needs high availability across multiple locations. Can merge inconsistent writes.	DocumentDB
User sessions	Rapid access for reads and writes. No need to be durable.	Redis
Reporting	SQL interfaces well with reporting tools.	SQL Azure
Analytics	Large-scale analytics on large clusters.	Azure Blob storage
User activity logs	High volume of writes on multiple nodes.	Azure Table storage

We must take some decisions for considering the model to be adopted:

- We have to decide what data storage technology to use rather than just going with a relational database.
- How will our development team react to this new technology?
- How will different stakeholders in the enterprise data deal with data that could be stale and how do you enforce rules to sync data across systems?

Furthermore, since we don't have much experience with the models, we don't know how to use them well, what the good patterns are, and what problems are lying in wait.

Scenario

Scenario is based on **AdventureWorks Cycles (AWC)**, a common database and fictional company used by Microsoft over the years to demonstrate the possibilities of the relational database Microsoft SQL Server.

AWC is a large, multinational manufacturing company. The company manufactures and sells metal and composite bicycles to North American, European, and Asian commercial markets.

The company needs a web application so that individual customers can navigate through the catalog, read product characteristics, view product photos, and buy a bicycle through the shopping cart.

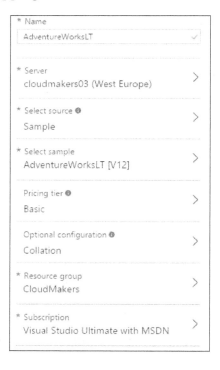

AWC has a company ERP that it uses for all daily operations and orders via legacy channels. It requires all information published on the web store to come from the ERP. This is a classic client-server application heavily based on a relational SQL Server database. Over time, the application was migrated over the cloud, moving the database to Azure SQL Database PaaS service. To recreate the ERP experience, it is possible to implement an AWC database as a sample database. From the Azure Portal (`http://portal.azure.com/`), go to **New** | **SQL databases**. The created database blade appears. You need to select:

- The **Subscription**.
- The **Server** on which the database is deployed. It preselects **Resource Group** and **Location**, the same as the server.
- The **Source Template** for the new database. You can select from **Blank database**, **Backup**, and **Sample**. When you select **Sample**, it automatically selects **AdventureWorksLT** (at the time of writing this book). In the future, there can be more samples.
- The **Pricing Tier** (for the content of this chapter, a **Basic Tier** is enough).

To create a new Azure SQL database server, we can also use a PowerShell command, as shown here:

```
$credentials = Get-Credential #prompts a UI to retrieve a username and a
password

$server = New-AzureSqlServer -ResourceGroupName CloudMakers
  -ServerName cloudmakers -SqlAdministratorCredentials $credentials
  -Location "West Europe" -ServerVersion "12.0"
```

Alternatively, you can get an existing server:

```
$server = Get-AzureSqlServer -ResourceGroupName CloudMakers
  -ServerName cloudmakers
```

To create the database by allocating a Basic edition (for our purposes), use the following command:

```
$database = New-AzureSqlDatabase -ResourceGroupName CloudMakers
  -ServerName cloudmakers -DatabaseName AdventureWorksLT
  -Edition Basic
```

To exercise database access from a development workstation, on-premise, it is necessary to open up firewall access to the database server in order to access the 1433 TCP/IP port. Do ensure that your Internet connection allows access to that port. Remember to not use this feature in production. To perform the database access action, refer to the following code lines:

```
$currentIP = (New-Object net.webclient).downloadstring
  ("http://checkip.dyndns.com") -replace "[^\d\.]"
If ((Get-AzureSqlServerFirewallRule
  -ResourceGroupName CloudMakers -ServerName cloudmakers03
  -FirewallRuleName "OnPremise") -eq $null) {
    New-AzureSqlServerFirewallRule
      -ResourceGroupName CloudMakers
      -ServerName cloudmakers03 -FirewallRuleName "OnPremise"
      -StartIpAddress $currentIP -EndIpAddress $currentIP
}
else {
  Set-AzureSqlServerFirewallRule -ResourceGroupName CloudMakers
  -ServerName cloudmakers03 -FirewallRuleName "OnPremise"
  -StartIpAddress $currentIP -EndIpAddress $currentIP
}
```

Now that the database is created, we can open up Visual Studio 2015 and start coding. The first step is to connect to the database and map all the tables to allow us to query data via C# code. So, we can create a Visual Studio 2015 C# class library named SqlDataModel and add a **ADO.NET Entity Data Model**:

Naming it AdventureWorksLTDataModel, we use the **Code First from database** convention to scaffold the database:

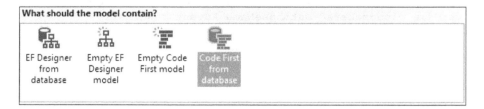

In the next step, where you define a new connection to the database, you can type details of the Azure SQL Database:

Database name	`Cloudmakers.database.windows.net` (always in the form `<databasename>.` `database.windows.net`)
Log on to the server User SQL Server authentication	Username and password used to create Azure SQL Server
Select or enter the database name	AdventureWorksLT

When the connection is established, you can store the connection string into the project.

 Remember that storing your username and password in the `connection` string is feasible only if you are the only developer in the project and if the project is not shared over the Internet.

Next in the chapter, we will see how to handle connection strings at the production stage. The wizard now scaffolds the database (the time used to make the task depends on your network connection speed), and you finally obtain an **Entity Framework DbContext** to access data programmatically.

Writing catalogs into Azure DocumentDB

One of the features of a catalog is accessing the product list and details the company sells. There is a big difference between read and write operations, favoring the first one as the most frequent. At the web stage, write operations happen only when the catalog is updated, and publishing involves just a minimal time (seconds to minutes) compared to using them (days to weeks). So, if indexing operations take a while to succeed, it is not bad. Eventual consistency is not an issue.

Product information is not flat. It is complex and structured, as information such as categorization, technical properties, and localization are not scalar properties, but complex structure themselves. Many products share the same categories or information. Again as mentioned earlier, write operations happen as catalog publishing, not product insertion. So, there are no normalization issues, as the product is already managed into the relational database-based ERP. On the other hand, the relational model is not well suited as denormalizing and loading the entire product object graph at every access can be a costly task. So, a data store that persists the entire object graph with depending information, at a product level, is a plus.

In an object-to-relational-database mapping, there can be some lazy loading issues. Loading related data can require additional calls to data sources (or the Web, in our case), so accessing products can be expensive. A product in a web application is not a set of normalized information, but a container with a clearly defined boundary. A key ID identifies and retrieves all data as one single atomic access. So, we need to define a container that atomically retrieves and delivers all relative information in a single call. Martin Fowler describes this information as **Data Transfer Object (DTO)** (http://martinfowler.com/eaaCatalog/dataTransferObject.html):

> *An object that carries data between processes in order to reduce the number of method calls.*

While our SQL data model is unique, DTOs are not. A single application can contain many scenarios (WebModel and MobileModel). The former is discussed in this chapter while the latter is covered in later chapters. Each of these are served by their specific models.

To define DTOs, we need to first create a new class library project in our Visual Studio 2015 solution. We can call it WebModel. We can define a base DTO for the library from which every DTO derives. This can give some useful information and behaviors to all objects in the library. Refer the following code for a better idea:

```
public abstract class WebModelDTO<TDTO>
    where TDTO: WebModelDTO<TDTO>
{
    public string Type { get; set; }

    public WebModelDTO()
    {
        this.Type = this.GetType().Name;
    }
}
```

In this case, WebModelDTO contains a property that is the type of string that is initialized as the Type name in the string in the parametereless constructor. As the class is abstract, it will be derived, so Type will contain the name of the derived class. The generic parameter TDTO, constrained by the same type (WebModelDTO<TDTO>) will allow us to generalize some members in the base DTO class for specific derived DTO classes, which we will see next in chapter.

In general, as defined in the pattern, the consumer needs to make a single call to obtain the DTO and to minimize communication roundtrips. What is behind that call is not defined (nor important for the pattern itself). However, it's important to us, as behind it there is a SQL database. Using the Entity Framework with the LINQ syntax, we can obtain a DTO from some entities with a two-step selection:

```
public static IEnumerable<ProductDetailDTO>
  ToDTO(this IQueryable<Product> that)
{
    var materialized = that.Select(xx => new
    {
        rowguid = xx.rowguid
        Name = xx.Name
              // ...omitted...
    }).ToList();
    var mapped = materialized.Select(xx => new ProductDetailDTO
    {
        Id = xx.rowguid,
        Name = xx.Name
        // ...omitted...
    });
    return materialized;
}
```

An extension method (`this IQueryable<Product> that`) is required in order to have an object method invocation syntax from the original entity mapped. The two stages are required, as `IQueryable` semantics works in LINQ. `IQueryable<Product>` means that we have a reference `DbSet` class (from the SQL-mapped `DbContext` class). All query invocations to this are just queries. They are not executed in front of the data source until a materialization command `ToList()` is issued. This is useful to make a minimization project in order to minimize the footprint of data that will come out from the SQL query. This is due to performances. The mapping is done in front of an anonymous-typed object, as mapped needs to be projected to the public DTO. This is necessary to correct the mismatching impedance between the SQL domain and the .NET domain. This is because in the `IQueryable` query, only a few minimal .NET commands are available. In general, in the mapping query you can:

- Change property names
- Change property types
- Invoke `Type` methods
- Change the graph's shape

DTO is a communication object that comes out from the data layer and into networks. So, it needs to be serializable to go across the connection. This can be done well in JSON notation. While a relational database is the single write-optimized container for entities, a web catalog is just one representation (among many others) of the same information. JSON is the current most widely adopted data representation over the Internet. To add serialization to the DTO, we can execute the following command via Package Manager Console:

```
PM> Install-Package Newtonsoft.Json
```

It will download the Json.NET package from the official website of NuGet (http://www.nuget.org/) and reference it. The library supports all the serialization and deserialization to JSON. We can add these two members to WebModelDTO to make all serializable:

```
public string ToJson()
{
    return JsonConvert.SerializeObject(this);
}

public static TDTO FromJson(string json)
{
    return JsonConvert.DeserializeObject<TDTO>(json);
}
```

As we are able to automate publishing data over Internet mapping data one time, we can choose to use a JSON-based document-oriented NoSQL database. There is a great variety of open source software available as NoSQL bits to be installed on a machine: this means that one of these should be deployed as IaaS. We want to choose catalog tasks using only PaaS: Azure DocumentDB is the NoSQL offer in Azure delivered as PaaS. We can start working with DocumentDB.

At the time of writing this book, there are no cmdlets in Azure SDK 2.8.1 available to manage the DocumentDB service from PowerShell. It is possible to write your own cmdlets using the DocumentDB REST API. There are some community efforts like this that you can find on GitHub at https://github.com/savjani/Azure-DocumentDB-Powershell-Cmdlets. Alternatively, it is possible to create a resource template deployment that can create just the DocumentDB account.

The first thing to understand is the DocumentDB account. It is a container for DocumentDB databases. A similar concept in the relational world is a database, but it is unfair. As a PaaS service, there is no explicit reference on the virtual hardware deployed under the service. It is not correct because at this level, there is no reference to some resources allocated (so, no pricing tier) at this stage. The only two relevant properties are:

- **Account Type**: Set to **Standard** (locked at the time of this writing).
- **Location**: Like all Azure services, this means that the account geographically locates all databases contained in it. So, to create DocumentDB databases in different locations, different accounts are needed.

Refer to the following screenshot for the **Settings** panel of your DocumentDB account:

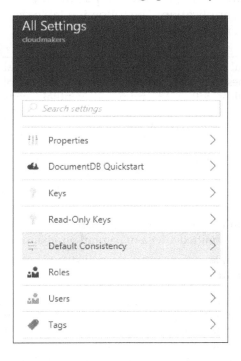

Creating a DocumentDB account is possible from `https://portal.azure.com`. Go to **New | DocumentDB account**. It's a long operation that can take minutes to deploy.

The DocumentDB account is a security boundary. As a PaaS Service, it is publicly accessible via the REST API. All requests must be authorized via **Shared Access Secret** keys. At this level, the keys are defined and managed, so all databases defined in the container are accessed with the same keys.

There is also a definition of default consistency, where *default* refers to an initial setup for new databases created that can be overridden at the database stage.

Consistency in this case refers to the property of DocumentDB to decide the level of consistency every account must guarantee, impacting the performance of the entire database and in turn the application. The following table describes the levels of consistency that are observed:

EVENTUAL	Eventual consistency allows clients to retrieve values that may be older than ones they have seen before. In the absence of any further writes, the replicas within the group will eventually converge. Eventually, consistency provides the weakest read consistency, but offers the lowest latency for both reads and writes.
BOUNDED STALENESS	Bounded staleness consistency guarantees the total order of propagation of writes with the possibility that reads lag behind in either time or number of prefixes. It provides more predictable behavior for read consistency while offering the lowest latency writes. Two parameters define it.
	Maximum lag (of operations), described as the number of writes that will be committed after a maximum number of subsequent operations
	Maximum lag (of seconds), described as the number of writes that will be committed after a maximum number of seconds
	The minimum parameter wins.
SESSION	Session consistency guarantees that clients will read their latest writes. Session consistency provides predictable read data consistency for a session, while offering the lowest latency writes. This is the default consistency setting for all DocumentDB accounts.
	This is the setting that shows consistent data for all programs that share the same work session.
STRONG	Strong consistency guarantees that a write is only visible after it is committed durably by the majority of replicas. It provides an absolute guarantee on data consistency, but offers the lowest level of read and write performance.

Now, it is possible to create a DocumentDB database, where the only information needed is just its name, for example, `AdventureWorksLT`. The operation is immediate. There are no properties at this level.

Now, it's time to understand the notion of collection. If we make a comparison with relational databases, inside a relational database, there are tables. Relational tables define the structure of entities inside them. All entities inside a table share the same structure, and relational DB guarantees it.

Remember from the initial part of the chapter that NoSQL databases use JSON to persist data, which does not define any sort of schema. So, there is no way to guarantee the structure of the document. So, at this level, what does it mean to create a container?

Consider these three simple JSON documents:

A customer	An order	A product

{
   "Type":
"Customer",
    "FirstName":
"John",
    "LastName":
"Doe"
}
	{
	   "Type": "Order",
	   "Number": 8754,
	    "Date": "2015-09-25T08:25:33"
	}
		{
		   "Type": "Product",
		   "Category": "Bycycle",
		   "Model": "Mountain Bike"
		}

We can distinguish them because we see that each one contains a different set of properties. In JavaScript, we understand, for example, that a JSON object is not an order because the `Number` property is undefined:

```
function Handle(order) {
    if (order.Number === undefined) {
        throw "This is not an order";
    }
}
```

Alternatively, we can decide that all JSON objects in our applications contain a property (type in the example) that specifies its type:

```
function Handle(order) {
    if (order.Type !== "Order") {
        throw "This is not an order";
    }
}
```

At a functional level, if our application can guarantee that all documents of the same *category* contain the same set of properties or at least that there is one classification property (always with the same name), we can create a single container in our DocumentDB database. If there no a precise way to distinguish different documents, more collections are needed, but this is not correct. If we try to create a collection, we need to decide on two properties namely, **Pricing Tier** and **Indexing Policy**. Refer the following screenshot for a better understanding:

The first one is the **Pricing Tier**. A collection (not the database) is bounded to a performance level. This means that two different collections inside the same database can have different performances levels. Collections have a size limit (10 GB, at the time of writing this book), independent of what is contained (one or many kinds of documents). No more than 10 GB can be contained. Resource Units (RU, 250/S1, 1000/S2, and 2500/S3) refer to a logical index of performances to handle work over the data collected. Every operation over DocumentDB collections consumes some RUs.

The second one is the **Indexing Policy**. Indexes are special documents that allow efficient searches by values on documents in a container, persisted in the same container. Two policies are available. The hash index policy calculates value hashes that are useful for equality. It also calculates group-by and order-by clauses. The range index policy optimizes range-inequality comparison on string values.

The policy selected at this stage is not a constraint. Indexing strategy is more complicates and deeper than just a parameter selection. Moreover, it can be changed whenever needed. Indexing needs tuning as the database is accessed, written, and queried.

Indexing impacts resource usage in the container. Indexing consumes RUs. The more the indexed data (the path parameters inside an index description), the more RUs are consumed. Default indexing policies are applied to all values in documents. This can consume a lot of space. So, in indexes, there is the notion of an exclude path that helps save space. However, this does not remove a structural limit. A collection can contain up to 10 GB of data. So, where more speed is needed, a different approach has to be applied.

A container is a partitioning tool. Different containers have to be created, and documents need to be partitioned over them. It's an explicit feature that client SDKs allow to simplify usage. There are two main strategies for partitioning:

Hash partitioning is a uniform distribution pattern over a partition key. Hash partitioning is a pattern to obtain an equal distribution of documents over a set of containers. This is obtained by identifying the container from the hash of the document.

Range partitioning is a bit more complex, as it allows us to describe more situations in date partitioning and interval partitioning.

So, let's start loading documents by migrating data from AdventureWorksDb.

Create a C# console application in Visual Studio 2015, and name it `SqlToDocumentDB`. Take references from the SqlDataModel and WebModel projects previously developed inside the solution. From the **Package Manager** console, refer to **EntityFramework** with the following command:

```
Install-Package EntityFramework
```

Create a DocumentDB client library with the following command:

```
Install-Package Microsoft.Azure.DocumentDB
```

Now, from the Azure portal, go to the DocumentDB account previously created. From **Properties**, annotate the **DocumentDB Endpoint** and **Authorization Key** into the **appSettings** part of the app.settings file, writing the relative keys `DocumentDbEndPoint` and `DocumentDbAuthKey` as:

```
<appSettings>
  <add key="DocumentDbEndPoint" value="--DocumentDbEndPoint--"
    />
  <add key="DocumentDbAuthKey" value="--DocumentDbAuthKey--" />
</appSettings>
```

Refer the values by accessing the code via `ConfigurationManager`:

```
static void Main(string[] args)
{
    MainAsync(args).Wait();
}

static async Task MainAsync(string[] args)
{
  var endpoint = ConfigurationManager.AppSettings
    ["DocumentDbEndPoint"];
   var endpointUri = new Uri(endpoint);
  var authKey = ConfigurationManager.AppSettings
    ["DocumentDbAuthKey"];
}
```

All DocumentDB services are accessible by starting from a client proxy object that maps all method calls to some REST invocations and adds the following line in the code:

```
var client = new DocumentClient(endpointUri, authKey);
```

All DTOs will be loaded into a collection. Databases and collections have a name. The full name of a collection is built as a path:

```
var collectionLink = "/dbs/AdventureWorksLT/colls/documents";
```

After configuring the SQL Database Server connection string into `app.config` and implementing a `read` loop, we can load all documents into the collection:

```
var dbContext = new AdventureWorksLTDataModel();
foreach (var productDto in dbContext.Product.ToDTO())
{
    var response = await client.CreateDocumentAsync
      (collectionLink, productDto);
    Console.Write("{0}", response.Resource.SelfLink);
    Console.WriteLine("...done");
}
```

The response object is interesting as it's full of information:

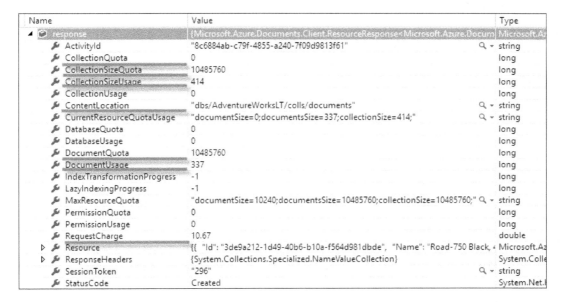

Name	Value	Type
▲ 🔵 response	{Microsoft.Azure.Documents.Client.ResourceResponse<Microsoft.Azure.Docum	Microsoft.A:
🔧 ActivityId	"8c6884ab-c79f-4855-a240-7f09d9813f61"	string
🔧 CollectionQuota	0	long
🔧 CollectionSizeQuota	10485760	long
🔧 CollectionSizeUsage	414	long
🔧 CollectionUsage	0	long
🔧 ContentLocation	"dbs/AdventureWorksLT/colls/documents"	string
🔧 CurrentResourceQuotaUsage	"documentSize=0;documentsSize=337;collectionSize=414;"	string
🔧 DatabaseQuota	0	long
🔧 DatabaseUsage	0	long
🔧 DocumentQuota	10485760	long
🔧 DocumentUsage	337	long
🔧 IndexTransformationProgress	-1	long
🔧 LazyIndexingProgress	-1	long
🔧 MaxResourceQuota	"documentSize=10240;documentsSize=10485760;collectionSize=10485760;"	string
🔧 PermissionQuota	0	long
🔧 PermissionUsage	0	long
🔧 RequestCharge	10.67	double
▷ 🔧 Resource	{{ "Id": "3de9a212-1d49-40b6-b10a-f564d981dbde", "Name": "Road-750 Black,	Microsoft.A:
▷ 🔧 ResponseHeaders	{System.Collections.Specialized.NameValueCollection}	System.Colle
🔧 SessionToken	"296"	string
🔧 StatusCode	Created	System.Net.l

The important parameters of the response object are listed as follows:

- `CollectionSizeQuota`: It is the collection quota expressed in kilobytes (currently 10 GB).

- `DocumentUsage`: It is the collection space used by documents expressed in kilobytes.

- `CollectionSizeUsage`: It is the collection space used, expressed in kilobytes. The difference with `DocumentUsage` is the space used by indexes, so it is possible to track by the overload code. It is also possible in general to insert some alert code to track whether a collection is dangerously reaching its limits.

- `RequestCharge`: It indicates the fraction of the provisioned throughput. For example, if we use a collection level S1 (500RUs/second), we can load at most an average of 50 documents per second. After that, the server will be throttled.

`ContentLocation`, `SessionCode`, and `StatusCode` are those DocumentDB calls that are REST calls which run over HTTP.

The response also contains the document persisted and augmented with specific
DocumentDB properties:

- `Id`: Each document inside DocumentDB must have a property-level
  guid-based ID. If provided with that name, then it will be used. Otherwise,
  an `Id` property will be automatically added.

- `ResourceId`: Each document inside DocuemntDB must have a service-level
  URL-based ID that is unique inside the collection. It is always provided by
  the service.

- `ETag`: This is a version marker for documents in an optimistic concurrency
  scenario.

- `SelfLink`: Every resource inside DocumentDB (database, collection,
  document, and attachment) has a `ResourceId`. `SelfLink` is the path to
  the resource built upon multiple numbers of `ResourceId` of the container
  resources. This `SelfLink` always identifies the resource.

- `AltLink`: The collection path we used to load documents with an attached ID
  is the alternative link to globally identify the document into the account. It
  is built with friendly names (aliases) for the database and collection, without
  the need to query the DocumentDB account for the single `ResourcesId` and
  `SelfLinks` of database and collection.

A simple estimate from the data read on the previous query response says a usage of
337 KB for documents and 414 KB for collection. This means that for that particular
document (not so complex or big, by the way), there is a 19 percent of "wasted" space
for indexing. Let's look inside the document:

```
{  "Id": "43dd68d6-14a4-461f-9069-55309d90ea7e",   "Name": "HL Road
Frame - Black, 58",  "ProductNumber": "FR-R92B-58",   "Color":
"Black",  "StandardCost": 1059.31,  "ListPrice": 1431.5,
"Size": "58",  "Weight": 1016.04,  "SellStartDate": "2002-
06-01T00:00:00",  "SellEndDate": null,  "DiscontinuedDate":
null,  "ThumbnailPhotoFileName": "no_image_available_small.gif",
"ModifiedDate": "2008-03-11T10:01:36.827",  "ProductCategory":
```

```
{    "Id": "5515f857-075b-4f9a-87b7-43b4997077b3",      "Name": "Road
Frames",      "Type": "ProductCategoryDTO"   },  "ProductModel":
{    "Name": "HL Road Frame",    "CatalogDescription": null,     "Id":
"4d332ecc-48b3-4e04-b7e7-227f3ac2a7ec",      "Type": "ProductModelDTO"
},   "Type": "ProductDetailDTO", }
```

All properties are indexed by default, so we can query the document without thinking what is indexed and what is not. However, if we analyze the application requirements, we will discover that, for example, while we could filter products by category, by either ID or name, we will only, for example, filter by category. The Type property, which we introduced for our purposes, will never be used to filter by category.

As we are using a bulk load console application to load the entire collection, we could also choose to relax indexing while loading so that loading will be faster.

To update indexing policies, we need to provide explicit access to the collection:

```
var documents =                   client.CreateDo
cumentCollectionQuery(databaseUri)         .Where(xx
=> xx.Id == "documents")           .ToList()
.FirstOrDefault();         documents.IndexingPolicy.IndexingMode =
IndexingMode.Lazy;         documents = await client.ReplaceDocument
CollectionAsync(documents);
```

Indexing is not disabled (IndexingMode.None). It has less priority, assigning RUs to other client tasks. RUs will be assigned to indexing tasks only if they are not assigned to other incoming requests.

Then, indexing must be reset to Consistent:

```
documents.IndexingPolicy.IndexingMode = IndexingMode.
Consistent;          documents.IndexingPolicy.IncludedPaths.
Clear();Include root path as a path required by the system:          //
"root"      var rootPath = new IncludedPath { Path =
"/" };      rootPath.Indexes.Add(new HashIndex(DataType.
String));      rootPath.Indexes.Add(new HashIndex(DataType.
Number));      documents.IndexingPolicy.IncludedPaths.
Add(rootPath);
```

Include Type so that we can filter by object type, as in the same collection, there will be mode object types:

```
// Type
var typePath = new IncludedPath { Path = "/Type/?" };
typePath.Indexes.Add(new HashIndex(DataType.String));
documents.IndexingPolicy.IncludedPaths.Add(typePath);
```

Exclude `ProductCategory` and subproperties:

```
// excluded
documents.IndexingPolicy.ExcludedPaths.Clear();         //
ProductCategory
documents.IndexingPolicy.ExcludedPaths.Add(
    new ExcludedPath { Path = "/ProductCategory/*" });
```

Include the `Id` property:

```
var productCategoryIdPath =
  new IncludedPath { Path = "/ProductCategory/Id/?" };
productCategoryIdPath.Indexes.Add(new
  HashIndex(DataType.String));
documents.IndexingPolicy.IncludedPaths.
  Add(productCategoryIdPath);
```

Exclude `ProductModel` and subproperties:

```
// ProductModel
documents.IndexingPolicy.ExcludedPaths.
  Add(                 new ExcludedPath { Path =
  "/ProductModel/*" });
```

Include the `Id` property:

```
var productModelIdPath =
  new IncludedPath  { Path = "/ProductModel/Id/?" };
productModelIdPath.Indexes.
  Add(new HashIndex(DataType.String));
documents.IndexingPolicy.IncludedPaths.
  Add(productModelIdPath);
```

Commit information back to DocumentDB:

```
       // make effective
documents = await
  client.ReplaceDocumentCollectionAsync(documents);
```

With this update, the sample document increases space usage efficiency from 81 percent to 87 percent. In general, none of the small numbers seem significant. However, on a large scale, when the document is relatively small but the occupation is reaching the collection limits, this can mean new space for thousands of millions of additional documents is allocated.

As we plan to reach the 10 GB limit, or in general, we are working on a multi-gigabyte database, partitioning is mandatory because space in collection is limited.

Partitioning is a client-side responsibility, because there is no automatic process that can work over partitions. On the writing side, there is no problem, as partition selection is just a function applied to the document that contains the parameter considered as the partition key that determines which collection should be used. It's all about querying. There are just two situations:

- If the query condition is on a partition key and is a hash partitioning, the query can be executed on the specific partition

- In all other cases, the query executes over all the partitions, and the results from each partition are merged

In any case, on the single partition, indexing plays an important role, as each single query depends on a specific collection performance level (RU number) and specific index configuration.

`PartitionResolver` is a type defined in .NET Azure SDK that allows us to configure the `PartitionKey` and the `PartitionMap`, and the rules that configure the specific partition scheme. Two basic `PartitionResolver` are available:

- `HashPartitionResolver`
- `RangePartitionResolver`

In the example, `RangePartitionResolver` is specified by:

- **Selector**: An expression that accepts a typed entity object that allows us to select the property partition key.

- **Dictionary**: Accepts a `comparable` type as a key (in this case, a `Range` object) that defines the boundaries of the partition in terms of the partition key. Associated to the key is the collection link:

```
RangePartitionResolver<string> rangeResolver =
  new RangePartitionResolver<string>
  (p => ((ProductDetailDTO)p).ProductModel.Name,
  new Dictionary<Range<string>, string>(){
  { new Range<string>("A", "M\uffff"),
  "/dbs/AdventureWorksLT/colls/productsA-M" },
  { new Range<string>("N", "Z\uffff"),
    "/dbs/AdventureWorksLT/colls/productsN-Z" },
      });
```

The partition resolver must be associated to the client object. It is no longer the responsibility of the developer selecting the specific collection, but is determined by the resolver:

```
client.PartitionResolvers["/dbs/AdventureWorksLT"] =
  rangeResolver;
```

So, when a document is inserted, there is no need for the collection link. All operations are done at the database level:

```
var response =
  await client.CreateDocumentAsync("/dbs/AdventureWorksLT",
  productDto);
```

Building up your web frontend with Microsoft ASP.NET MVC

DocumentDB is a general-purpose database based on NoSQL purposes and features. We can better understand how it works and how it can be used by recreating the classic CRUD application in ASP.NET MVC. We can add a new web project, called WebFrontEnd, of type ASP.NET Web Application to the Visual Studio 2015 solutions. We can choose the **.NET 4.6 MVC** template. Visual Studio will create the entire web project to which we need to add all the references already added to the SqlToDocumentDb project previously described in this chapter.

ASP.NET MVC is a model-based framework, where the models are C# classes. We can start using DocumentDB as the database backend for the classic CRUD approach. Before starting, in the Web.Config file, add to the project an empty controller named ProductsController. The first thing to add is the DocumentClient accessor for DocumentDB (it is the same as in the previous project):

```
private DocumentClient _client;
protected DocumentClient Client
{
  get
  {
    if (_client == null)
    {
      var endpoint =
        ConfigurationManager.AppSettings["DocumentDbEndPoint"];
      var endpointUri = new Uri(endpoint);
      var authKey =
        ConfigurationManager.AppSettings["DocumentDbAuthKey"];
      _client = new DocumentClient(endpointUri, authKey);
    }
    return _client;
  }
}
```

Since in action methods, it is common to query data via LINQ (for simplicity and demo purposes because it's better to encapsulate all the data access in some repository or DataSource pattern objects), we add a `Products()` accessor that presents an `IQueryable<ProductDetailDto>` facility:

```
protected IOrderedQueryable<ProductDetailDTO> Products()
{
  return Client.CreateDocumentQuery<ProductDetailDTO>(
    "/dbs/AdventureWorksLT/colls/documents");
}
```

So, we can add the first `Action` method, the classic `Index` action that retrieves all entities from sets of data and passes them to the `View`:

```
public ActionResult Index()
{
  var items = Products()
  .Select(xx => new {
    id = xx.id, Name = xx.Name, ProductNumber =
    xx.ProductNumber })
  .ToList()
    .Select(xx => new ProductIndexDTO { id = xx.id, Name =
      xx.Name, ProductNumber = xx.ProductNumber });
  return View(items);
}
```

The double `Select` operation is necessary because the current implementation of the DocumentDB `IQueriable` provider does not allow materializing projection over named classes, but only on anonymous one.

In the `Views\Products` folder, by convention, there should be a file named `Index.cshtml` that contains the `Razor` `C#Html` template to present items in the data as a list:

```
@model IEnumerable<WebModel.ProductIndexDTO>
<p>
  @Html.ActionLink("Create New", "Create")
</p>
<table class="table">
  <tr>
    <th>
      @Html.DisplayNameFor(model => model.Name)
    </th>
    <th>
      @Html.DisplayNameFor(model => model.ProductNumber)
    </th>
    <th></th>
```

```
    </tr>

@foreach (var item in Model) {
  <tr>
    <td>
      @Html.DisplayFor(modelItem => item.Name)
    </td>
    <td>
      @Html.DisplayFor(modelItem => item.ProductNumber)
    </td>
    <td>
      @Html.ActionLink("Details", "Details", new { id=item.id })
    </td>
  </tr>
}
</table>
```

The `Details` action queries for a single, complete DTO:

```
public ActionResult Details(Guid? id)
{
    if (id == null)
    {
        return new
          HttpStatusCodeResult(HttpStatusCode.BadRequest);
    }
    var productDetailDTO =
      Products.Where(xx => xx.id == id).ToList();
    if (productDetailDTO == null)
    {
        return HttpNotFound();
    }
    return View(productDetailDTO[0]);
}
```

The page starts showing what we expect: the list of products. The result is unlimited as the plain query has no filter condition. As a queryable result, we can use paging of ordered elements as a mechanism to limit the number of items showed at a time.

```
public ActionResult Index(int pageNumber = 0, int pageSize = 0)
{
    var items = Products()
        .Select(xx => new { id = xx.id,
          Name = xx.Name, ProductNumber = xx.ProductNumber })
        .OrderBy(xx => xx.Name)
        .Skip((pageNumber-1) * pageSize)
```

```
        .Take(pageSize)
        .ToList()
        .Select(xx => new ProductIndexDTO { id = xx.id,
          Name = xx.Name, ProductNumber = xx.ProductNumber });
    return View(items);
}
```

Applying ordering, skipping, and taking is the typical approach to perform paging with LINQ. However, there is a problem (at the time of writing this book). This code does not work. `DocumentClient` is a LINQ provider, an object that transforms the C# expressions (the lambda expressions contained in LINQ-fluent interface criteria) into provider original syntax, in this case the SQL language for the DocumentDB service. If we look at the language, we see that we do not find any ranking function that can enumerate the result set from the query, and this does not allow the provider to skip any row. It needs to be noted that `Skip` and `Take` are applicable only to an ordered result set. The `OrderBy` clause has been supported by DocumentDB since July 2015. DocumentDB is a service, like all Azure services, in a perpetually evolving state, so we can assume that `Skip` will be supported any time in the future.

We can now make some considerations:

- How can we solve paging issue with DocumentDB?
- Is this the only issue in DocumentDB?
- If I need paging, how can I solve this?

Let's start from the beginning: solving paging issues with DocumentDB. Paging is a metaphor for equally important documents that cannot be shown in a single page. Page numbering is not sorting; it is just grouping. Many web applications that need to present a big amount of data do not use paging, as the result set is single and ordered by priority indices. Sorting is not functional to searching but to prioritizing results. The first ones are more important. How "deep" we go into less prioritized results is not clearly defined. What is clear is that the user does not paginate, but "scrolls" data as the page scrolls. The retrieved number of rows is the number of rows visible on the screen. When the end of the page is reached but the user tends to continue scrolling, then this is an invocation for the system to retrieve another number of rows after the last row has been retrieved. Web applications call it *infinite scroll*. DocumentDB supports this kind of functionality with a continuation token.

DocumentDB presents a new specific type of query called `DocumentQuery`. It requires the definition of a maximum number of rows returned from execution via the `FeedOption` object. The query is executed by a specific `ExecuteNextAsync` method that retrieves the rows via classic LINQ materialization operations such as `ToList`. However, the response object returns a special string continuation parameter. Subsequent invocations to `ExecuteNextAsync`, always with the `FeedOption` parameter, supply the last continuation token. The returned result will be subsequent to the last one. The continuation action is a paging surrogate. You cannot get back, and you cannot directly access it. But you can at least scroll forward. The following code can help you get an idea about it:

```
public async Task<ActionResult> Index(Guid? categoryId)
{
  var query = Products()
  .Where(xx => !categoryId.HasValue || categoryId.HasValue
    && xx.ProductCategory.Id == categoryId)
  .Select(xx => new { id = xx.id, Name = xx.Name,
    ProductNumber = xx.ProductNumber })
  .AsDocumentQuery();

  var response = await query.ExecuteNextAsync();

  var items = response
  .ToList()
  .Select(xx => new ProductIndexDTO { id = Guid.Parse(xx.id),
    Name = xx.Name, ProductNumber = xx.ProductNumber });
  return View(items);
}
```

We started this chapter by talking about how the cloud model requires new approaches to application development, giving us the opportunity of exploring new scenarios, tools, and patterns. We started deeply exploring DocumentDB as an alternative to classic SQL-oriented databases. In fact this addresses two main topics:

- **Normalized**: The relational data model is not the only model, in favor, if applicable, of an embedded, document-oriented data model
- **Partitionable**: The embedded data model for massive scalable data storage

While analyzing the CRUD, three-tier, data-oriented infrastructure, that for years has modeled our applications, we need to consider certain factors. What does a grid mean for our applications? Is paging really a feature? What does a thousand-page grid mean? Which data should be presented into the grid? Are they the entities or something else? We can give three more answers:

- Paging is there to navigate through the pages because all rows can satisfy our needs, but there is no more ordering criteria to discriminate among them

- Paging is there to be used as little as possible

- It is necessary to minimize the result to be paged via some other criteria, such as searches

DocumentDB, like many databases, is a property-oriented (or attribute-oriented) database, so searching takes place inside properties. However, starting with the Web and search engines, the searching activity is more property agnostic. Ask tools what you are looking for, and they will provide prioritized results. It is the tool's responsibility, not the client's responsibility, to select the correct data to search.

In addition, remember one more thing that we mentioned at the beginning. As we decided that DocumentDB is a great tool to persist our data, our initial discussion gave arguments for data duplication. Store the same data in different places and in different forms, where it is found to be useful for different functionality.

DocumentDB is a great tool for data ingestion and persistence. It is a search-oriented database, based on the state-of-the-art Apache Lucene core. It is the best tool for a search-oriented data model. This is why we can introduce the Azure Search service.

Searching in catalogs via Azure Search

To create the Azure Search service, you need to enter into the Azure portal and go to **New | Data + Storage | Azure Search**. Similar to other Azure services, you need to select:

- A lowercase name for the public and global endpoint (`.search.windows.net`)

- The resource group

- The location where the service is deployed

- The pricing tier

You pay for what you use. Azure Search can be classified as a NoSQL key/value store database, as it stores JSON objects in indexes for subsequent search and access. The features include:

- The pricing is the expression of resources
- Partitions, as the data is distributed to perform searches in parallel
- Search units, as a virtual unit of computing
- 25 GB and 15 million documents per partition

 At the time of writing this book (Fall 2015), only two pricing levels are available: free tier, which is described as a non-production level service, and standard tier, which is generically expensive. It is probable that in the future, new tiers will be introduced to align to search competitor offering.

You can insert JSON documents, which can be retrieved in two ways:

- By key, to match a specific document
- By search, expressing a textual query

In general, Azure Search is not the only database to use in an application. There is always a conventional SQL or NoSQL database as a write model. Then, there are some tasks that synchronize the search read model with the original write one. Document upload can be done in three ways:

- **Explicitly using the REST API**: As Azure Search is a REST service. This is useful if there is no SDK specific for the platform or the language of choice.
- **Implicitly using the REST API**: This can be done with some existing SDKs, such as the .NET one. This is useful to synchronize database searches by an event raised in the domain of the write model.
- **Using an indexer task to be configured from the portal**: From predefined data sources, at the moment SQL databases or DocumentDB, scheduled to be executed at specific and repetitive intervals.

In a catalog search scenario, we can suppose that a product that is inserted in the write model can accept a latency of seconds or minutes to be searchable.

So, we can go on with the indexer, and from the portal blade we can choose to import data:

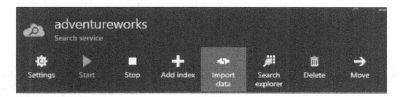

The portal asks us to define the data source to connect to by choosing the type. At the moment, only Azure SQL and DocumentDB are supported. We can proceed with DocumentDB.

We need to supply:

- Data source name
- The DocumentDB account
- The database into the account
- The document collection (in this case, a partitioned scenario is not supported, so an explicit indexer program has to be developed)
- A query that is a generic DocumentDB SQL query with a dependency to a special named parameter such as WHERE c._ts > @HighWaterMark ORDER BY c._ts"(@HighWaterMark), which marks the update timestamp

  At least, the _ts standard property in any document can be used to select the new documents to be updated.

We can use the following query as an indexing query, tested with Query Explorer in the portal:

```
SELECT c.id, c.Name, c.ProductNumber, c.Color, c.ListPrice, c.Size,
  c.ProductCategory.Name as ProductCategory,
  c.ProductModel.Name as ProductModel, c._ts FROM c

WHERE c._ts > @HighWaterMark
  ORDER BY c._ts
```

As a NoSQL database, Azure Search has a specific artifact to contain documents. This artifact is called index. Index defines the set of fields that are included in the index, and for each field. The table that follows explains the actions that can be done on it:

Key	This is a string that provides the unique ID of each document, used for document lookup. Every index must have one key. Only one field can be the key, and it must be set to `Edm.String`.
Retrievable	This specifies whether a field can be returned in a search result to be viewed in a grid.
Filterable	This allows the field to be used in the `$filter range` and equality queries.
Sortable	This allows the field to be used as a sort column in a result set.
Facetable	This allows a field containing repetitive values to be used for user self-directed filtering.
Searchable	This marks the field as full-text searchable. This means that the text can be complex, and it is internally split to be searchable by substrings.

Any selection has an impact on the index size and on the search unit consumption, so a tuning session will be necessary in the testing phase. It is important to mention that altering the structure of the index will cause a reindexing activity:

As the index is defined, an indexer can be associated to perform indexing on a scheduled time base. For example, we can schedule the indexer to be run every hour:

The indexer will be run as it is saved, and statistics about execution can be accessed from the portal blade.

To test the service, it is possible to use the Search explorer from the portal:

Now, we can implement searches in our web application. First, we need to include the Azure Search client library from the **Package Manager** console:

```
Install-Package Microsoft.Azure.Search -Pre
```

In `Web.Config` in the `WebFrontEnd` project, we need to define two settings for **Service Name** and **Query Key**. Generic applications should have a specific authorization-shared secret to query the service. This can be created in the **Search** Blade, by going to **Settings | Keys | Manage Query Keys**. You can give a name for the specific key (for example, the web role name `WebFrontEnd`):

```
<add key="SearchServiceName" value="adventureworks" />
<add key="SearchQueryKey" value="--SearchQueryKey--" />
```

A search accessor can be defined in the `ProductsController` to access a `SearchClient`:

```
private SearchIndexClient _searchClient;
protected SearchIndexClient SearchClient
{
  get
  {
    if (_searchClient == null)
    {
      var serviceName =
        ConfigurationManager.AppSettings["SearchServiceName"];
      var queryKey =
        ConfigurationManager.AppSettings["SearchQueryKey"];
      _searchClient = new SearchIndexClient(serviceName,
        "products", new SearchCredentials(queryKey));
    }
    return _search;
  }
}
```

The `Index` action has to be rewritten in front of the `SearchIndexClient` usage. A `SearchParameters` object configures search attributes, from ordering to paging information, natively supported by search:

```
public async Task<ActionResult> Index(string text,
  int pageNumber = 1, int pageSize = 20,
  string orderBy = "Name")
{
  var parameters = new SearchParameters { };
  parameters.OrderBy.Add(orderBy);
  parameters.Skip = (pageNumber - 1) * pageSize;
  parameters.Top = pageSize;
  var result =
    await SearchClient.Documents.
    SearchAsync<ProductIndexDTO>(text, parameters);
  var items = result.Select(xx => xx.Document).ToList();
  return View(items);
}
```

In the HTML code, a `search` form should be inserted to post the `text` parameter to the `Index` action:

```html
<div class="row">
  <div class="col-md-12">
    <form method="post">
      <label for="text">What are you looking for?</label>
      <input type="text" name="text" id="text" />
      <input type="submit" value="Search" />
    </form>
  </div>
</div>
```

A search can be improved if it can suggest the word you are still typing in the query field. The suggestion comes from extraction logic, such as infix matching (the only opportunity at the time of writing this book), returning all the field values that contain the text we are typing.

Suggestion is an index feature in Azure Search: one suggestion per index. If we need more suggestions, probably we need more indexes. Suggestion must be defined at index creation (at the time of writing this book, it cannot be activated where the index is already created). The most important thing is the set of fields from the index as the source for the suggestion:

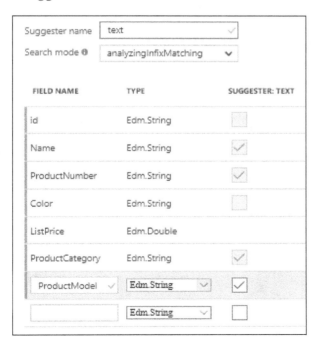

To support suggestions in the user interface, we need to use a JavaScript library. We need a functionality that shows a list of suggestions as we type a word in a textbox. From the Package Manager Console:

Install-Package Twitter.Typeahead

To enable `typeahead` on the `input` element, an invocation of the relative JavaScript method is necessary; you can enable the invocation using the following code:

```
<script src="~/Scripts/typeahead.jquery.js"></script>
<script type="text/javascript">
    $('#text').typeahead({
        hint: true,
        highlight: true,
        minLength: 3
    },
    {
        name: 'products-dataset',
        source: function (q, cb) {
            $.ajax({
                type: "GET",
                url: "/Products/Suggest?text=" + q,
                async: false,
                success: function (data) {
                    cb(data);
                }
            });
        }
    });
</script>
```

On the controller, use the following action to receive what is typed in the input and obtain the suggested list of elements:

```
public async Task<JsonResult> Suggest(string text,
int pageNumber = 1, int pageSize = 20, string orderBy = "Name")
{
    var parameters = new SuggestParameters { };
    var result = await Search.Documents.SuggestAsync
        (text, "text", parameters);
    var items = result.Select(xx => xx.Text).ToList();
    return Json(items, JsonRequestBehavior.AllowGet);
}
```

The result is that after typing a `minLength` number of characters, a dropdown appears:

What are you looking for? red|		Search
Name	Sport-100 Helmet, **Red**	**ProductNumber**
	Road-150 **Red**, 62	
HL Touring Frame - Blue, 46 Road-150 **Red**, 44		FR-T98U-46
	Road-150 **Red**, 48	
HL Touring Frame - Blue, 58 Road-150 **Red**, 52		FR-T98U-50

Storing unstructured data in Azure Storage

SQL and NoSQL databases are powerful data stores. Data persistence is one of their functionalities that gives great performance and service. However, they give their best when they can put together data with code, from data manipulation to data management, and ensuring data integrity. When the application needs to store big amounts of unstructured data, then a modern database is not the best choice, as it is the most expensive data storage service available. Moreover, it is no more convenient in terms of development, as this kind of DB has no specific primitives to handle binary large objects.

Therefore, we need a better persistence media for our Microsoft Office files, PDFs, images, videos, and so on.

While a database stores this data in some sort of binary arrays, the best artifact to store this kind of data is a file. What do we require from file storage into the cloud?

The answer is Azure Storage, one of the first services that came out in Azure in its beginning.

Azure Storage is the one of the founding pillars for Azure computing architecture, as all VHD files for virtual machines are stored in Azure Storage containers.

Azure Storage is a massive-scale storage that is able to store in a consistent way from small amounts of data for small web applications to trillions of bytes for big data needs.

Azure Storage is elastic, as any amount of space you need is always available. You just use it or release it, and you pay for what you use.

Azure Storage is a distributed data store that is accessible through four storage artifacts:

Table	This is a structured key attribute-partitioned dataset that allows us to store large amounts of data.
Queue	This provides the infrastructure for reliable messaging between cloud components.
Blob	This helps store text or binary data, associated to a media type.
File	This helps store file data and makes it accessible via the SMB 3.0 protocol.

Therefore, if we need to store media files, in particular image files, Azure Blob Storage can be a better choice.

To create a new Azure Storage account, we can use PowerShell:

```
$storageAccount = New-AzureStorageAccount -StorageAccountName
"cmadventureworks" -Location "West Europe"

New-AzureStorageContainer -Context $storageAccount.Context -Name
"webfrontendimages" -Permission Off
```

To use it from the .NET code, we need the connection string. We can generate it with PowerShell code and then save it into `web.config` (or `app.config`):

```
$accountKey = (Get-AzureStorageKey -StorageAccountName
$storageAccountName).Primary
$blobConnectionString = "DefaultEndpointsProtocol=https;Accoun
tName=" + $storageAccountName + ";AccountKey=" + $accountKey +
";BlobEndpoint=http://" + $storageAccountName + ".blob.core.windows.
net;"
$blobConnectionString
```

We now need to upload images that are originally stored into the SQL Server database. Using the mapping of the database with Entity Framework, we can access the image bits and invoke the Storage API via the .NET Storage Client SDK. To install it in a new Visual Studio 2015 console application, type the following command:

```
Install-Package WindowsAzure.Storage
```

At first, it is necessary to create a `CloudStorageAccount` object with `ConnectionString` just defined:

```
var cloudStorageAccount = CloudStorageAccount.Parse
  (ConfigurationManager.AppSettings["cloudStorageAccount"]);
```

Then, we create a blob client from this and obtain a reference to the container we created:

```
var blobClient =
  cloudStorageAccount.CreateCloudBlobClient();
var webfrontendimages =
  blobClient.GetContainerReference("webfrontendimages");
```

Now, we can upload images (saved into the database as byte arrays). Before proceeding, we need to understand that there are there are three kinds of blob object in Azure Storage:

- Block blobs allow us to create large blobs (up to 195 GB) in blocks of 4 MB each, accessing them via a block ID and writing, updating, and deleting each of them also in parallel. Up to 64 MB can be uploaded in one single upload invocation.

- Append blobs are a special case of block blobs, where blobs are optimized for performing append operations. So, you cannot access each one independently.

- Page blobs allow us to create very large blobs (up to 1 TB) to be accessed efficiently in a read/write operation of 512 byte pages.

For our needs, append blobs are alright, as no subsequent update operations are needed. Media files are updated as a single atomic element. So, to upload the files, we can use the following loop over all product elements:

```
foreach (var product in products)
{
  // …
  var blob =
    webfrontendimages.GetAppendBlobReference
    (thumbnailPhotoFileName);
  blob.UploadFromByteArray(product.ThumbNailPhoto,
    0, product.ThumbNailPhoto.Length);
}
```

Now that the images are uploaded, we can access them from the WebFrontEnd application. A `BlobClient` property accessor can be defined as follows:

```
private CloudBlobClient _blobClient;
protected CloudBlobClient BlobClient
{
  get
  {
    if (_blobClient == null)
    {
```

```
      var cloudStorageAccount =
        CloudStorageAccount.Parse(ConfigurationManager.
        AppSettings["cloudStorageAccount"]
        );
      _blobClient = cloudStorageAccount.CreateCloudBlobClient();
      }
    return _blobClient;
  }
}
```

We can expose the images via the .NET code by downloading blobs in an action:

```
public async Task<ActionResult> Images(Guid? id)
{
  // ...
  var productDetailDTO =
    Products().Where(xx => xx.id == id).ToList();
  // ...
  var container =
    BlobClient.GetContainerReference("webfrontendimages");
  var blob =
    container.GetBlobReference(
      productDetailDTO[0].ThumbnailPhotoFileName
    );
  Response.ContentType = blob.Properties.ContentType;
  await blob.DownloadToStreamAsync(Response.OutputStream);
  return new EmptyResult();
}
```

From the Detail.cshtml page, the image can be displayed with an img tag:

```
<img alt="@Model.ThumbnailPhotoFileName"
  src="@Url.Content("~/Products/Images/" + Model.id)" />
```

In this way, we expose the image in general storage content via web application. However, remember that Azure Storage is a public REST service, with a public REST endpoint. Here is an example:

```
https://adventureworks.blob.core.windows.net
```

Being REST-compliant, all blobs stored are contained resources and mapped to a URL:

```
https://cmadventureworks.blob.core.windows.net/webfrontendimages/
racer02_yellow_f_small.gif
```

By default, this URL is not accessible for security reasons. All resources are accessible only via the default storage access key. There are two possibilities to share this resource publicly:

- Shared Access Signature is a delegated access to resources in your storage account. It is possible to grant a client limited permissions to objects in a storage account for a specified period of time and with a specified set of permissions, without having to share account access keys. This is a URL-based sharing technique, as the signature is part of the URL. Here is an example (via PowerShell):

```
$storageAccount = Get-AzureStorageAccount -StorageAccountName
"cmadventureworks"

$sasToken = New-AzureStorageContainerSASToken -Context
$storageAccount.Context -Container webfrontendimages -Permission
rl
```

$sasToken will contain a URL query to append to a storage resource. Here is an example:

```
https://cmadventureworks.blob.core.windows.net/webfrontendimages/
racer02_yellow_f_small.gif?sv=2015-04-05&sr=c&sig=JpHwJktgCS3oqqI5
UwHZ4Q8sV4mhNno68T8ZfKnHoFA%3D&se=2016-01-03T05%3A05%3A49Z&sp=rl
```

This technique is great for a per-user or per-application specific lease.

- Shared Access Policy is a container- or blob-based sharing lease, as the sharing policy is applied to the container or blob for general use, not for per-user use. Via PowerShell, a blob can be shared, as shown here:

```
$container = Get-AzureStorageContainer -Context
$storageAccount.Context -Name webfrontendimages
$cbc = $container.CloudBlobContainer
# Sets up a Stored Access Policy and a Shared Access Signature for the
new container
$permissions = $cbc.GetPermissions();
$policyName = 'webfrontendimages_read'
$policy = new-object
  'Microsoft.WindowsAzure.Storage.Blob.SharedAccessBlobPolicy'
$policy.SharedAccessStartTime =
  $(Get-Date).ToUniversalTime().AddMinutes(-5)
$policy.SharedAccessExpiryTime =
  $(Get-Date).ToUniversalTime().AddYears(10)
$policy.Permissions = "Read"
$permissions.SharedAccessPolicies.Add($policyName, $policy)
$cbc.SetPermissions($permissions);
```

In this way, from our frontend application, an image is accessed as an external resource outside our main website, directly via HTTP, requiring no code in our frontend web application:

```
<img alt="@Model.ThumbnailPhotoFileName"
    src="https://cmadventureworks.blob.core.windows.net/
    webfrontendimages/@Model.ThumbnailPhotoFileName" />
```

At the time of writing this book (Fall 2015), Azure is a distributed over 28 regions around the world. The choice of the right deployment region can be based on many factors, one of which is location. However, there can be two issues:

- If we have a localized (not worldwide) application and a localized user who consumes our frontend web application is still "far" from our deployment region, there is an impact on download speed

- In a worldwide-accessed application, we don't deploy it to each of the 28 regions to speed up access

In general, for media files (images, videos, music) and in general, static content, which change so infrequently, there is an opportunity. Starting from a blob storage, such as the one we already created, we can improve our access performance with a **Content Delivery Network (CDN)** service. A CDN relies on a more pervasive presence of Azure worldwide, having Microsoft-signed national contracts, with local network providers for strategically placed locations to provide maximum bandwidth to deliver content to users.

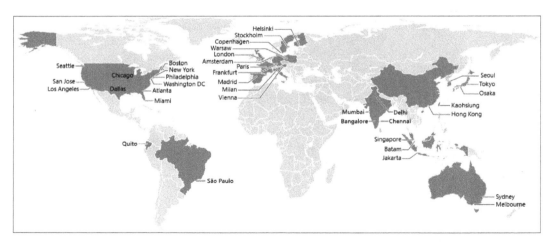

CDN offers Azure customers a global solution by caching and delivering content close to end users. As a result, instead of hitting origin every single time, user requests get intelligently routed to the best-performed CDN edge POP. This significantly increases the performance and user experience.

To create a CDN, there are no PowerShell cmdlets available. However, there is a REST API as with all Azure services, so we will see PowerShell support in future. Now, we use the Azure portal:

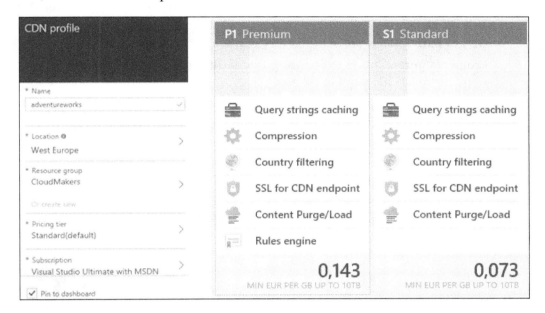

Options create an instance of an Azure Service, selecting also the **Pricing tier**, which is generally based on pricing per GB cached. The difference between the two pricing tiers is the availability of the rules engine. It allows us to customize how HTTP requests are handled, such as blocking the delivery of certain types of content, defining a caching policy, and modifying HTTP headers. For our purposes, we can use the **Standard(default)** tier:

After creating an instance (this takes quite long time), we can start creating an endpoint:

Some parameters must be entered:

- **Name**: This is the public name for the CDN endpoint to be referenced in our application.

- **Origin type**: This is the content source that will be cached. It can be selected from **Storage**, **Cloud App**, **Web App**, and **Custom Storage** (this one would be necessary in the case that our storage does not appear in the hostname list).

- **Origin hostname**: This is the public source endpoint from where are content will be cached.

- **Origin path**: This is the subdirectory relative to the origin's hostname.

- **Protocols ports**: This is to be configured if different from standard or if some protocols have not to be used.

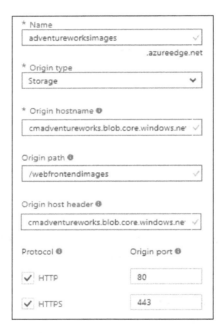

At the end of the creation process, from our application, we will reference CDN with the public endpoint:

```
<img alt="@Model.ThumbnailPhotoFileName"
  src="https://adventureworksimages.azureedge.net/
  @Model.ThumbnailPhotoFileName" />
```

The caching process is long and can take up to 90 minutes to deliver content to all the points of presence. The content will also take the same time to be updated, so take it into account when going into a production environment.

As a cache, the content loaded into CDN expires. Content expiration can be controlled:

- The default content expiration (in storage), if nothing is specified, is 7 days
- You can specify blob content duration via the `CacheControl` property in blob object by setting the TTL in seconds (the maximum is 1 year, which comes to 31,556,926 seconds):

```
blob.Properties.CacheControl = "x-ms-blob-cache-control: public,
max-age=31556926";
```

The cache can be manually cleared from the portal, thus restarting the process of loading the content from source.

Speeding up data access with caching and Azure Redis

Cloud computing brings costs that are explicit. Costs, at last, are monetary, as performance issues require services to size the requests upfront. However, the fact that we need to buy more resources does not mean that we can throw money away.

Accessing DocumentDB, for example, brings costs that are explicit. Every query result comes with a request charge that makes us aware of the real ability to answer parallel requests as demand increases. We can make a (sample) cost summary:

Service level	500RU
Sample request	12RU/request
Parallel requests (in theory)	500RU/(12RU/reqs)=41reqs

If many contemporary requests fulfill the 41 request-handling capacity of the service, subsequent requests will be throttled, and overall performance will decrease. This is true for all databases.

So, how can we handle more requests? We can make an assumption:

Many requests return the same data.

This is not unusual. How many times is a data grid refreshed and filled with the same data? How many times is a product on offer viewed in the short period after its publication?

Why do we perform the same query many times in a short period when we can assume the the result of the query is the same? Why don't we store the query result in a temporary storage that is more efficient to store the result of the query by associating it to the query itself as a key?

This is where caching patterns is helpful. It is a common technique that aims to improve the performance and scalability of a system by temporarily copying frequently accessed data to fast storage located close to the application. Caching is most effective when an application instance repeatedly reads the same data, especially if the original data store is slow relative to the speed of the cache, is subject to a high level of contention, or is far away when network latency can make the access slow.

What does "fast" mean? It can mean two things:

- We have already met the notion of DTO patterns. Make one single access to get back a complex data structure, executing all the data-access operations needed to retrieve it just once. This is true for the SQL structure of data, which means a complex task of joint data or subsequent SQL instructions.
- The persistence storage of saved data is not critical because, if lost, we can always get it back from the original data store. So, we can prefer access speed to durability, for example, storing cached items in memory.

In general, we can obtain two results:

- Lowering the pressure on the database (which is good, as the database is typically one of the most expensive services in an application)
- Speeding up the responsiveness of the system

Azure helps us with Redis cache. It's an implementation of the Redis open source platform, exposed as a PaaS service, so we can concentrate on usage rather that deployment. Different service plans offer a preconfigured Redis server infrastructure at different pricing levels. We can choose from many different nonfunctional configurations (at the developer level, all configurations are the same):

- Caching size (in MB or GB)
- Replication for business continuity scenarios
- Dedicated versus shared services

- Number of concurrent connections

We can create a Redis cache account via PowerShell:

```
New-AzureRmRedisCache -ResourceGroupName CloudMakers -Name
  AdventureWorks -Location "West Europe" -Size C0 -sku Basic
```

The creation time depends on the size of the deployment. In the sample, we use a shared deployment, which brings this time to zero. As with other Azure services, a key and an endpoint URL are necessary to programmatically access the service. We can obtain them again using PS:

```
$redisCache = Get-AzureRmRedisCache -ResourceGroupName CloudMakers -Name
AdventureWorks
```

```
$redisCache.HostName
```

```
$redisCacheKey = $redisCache | Get-AzureRmRedisCacheKey $redisCacheKey.
PrimaryKey
```

To use Redis from the .NET code at present, there is no specific API in the Azure SDK. The documentation refers to a common open source client SDK that is useful for our work. We can install the **StackExchange Redis** client in the WebFrontEnd project:

```
Install-Package StackExchange.Redis
```

We can then persist the endpoint and key into the web.config file. Now, we can implement the cache-aside pattern. In our project, we need to cache DocumentDB product details. The product ID is used to construct a cache key:

```
var key = string.Format("product_detail_{0}", id);
```

This key is used to check into Redis. If present, we send back that cached object directly; otherwise, a query to DocumentDB must be done and then directly stored into Redis for following requests. Redis cannot persist objects natively, but it can save the object state as JSON content.

```
if (!RedisDatabase.KeyExists(key))
{
  var productDetailDTO = Products().
    Where(xx => xx.id == id).ToList();
  if (productDetailDTO == null)
  {
    return HttpNotFound();
  }
  var json = JsonConvert.SerializeObject(productDetailDTO);
  RedisDatabase.StringSet(key, json);
  return View(productDetailDTO[0]);
}
else
{
  var json = RedisDatabase.StringGet(key);
  var productDetailDto =
    JsonConvert.DeserializeObject<ProductDetailDTO>(json);
  return View(productDetailDto);
}
```

As a cache, content must be invalidated as, by nature, it cannot persist for a long time. There are two possibilities:

- Specify an expiration date when adding content to Redis so that it is automatically removed from the page:

  ```
  RedisDatabase.StringSet(key, json, TimeSpan.FromHours(4));
  ```

- Explicitly remove the content from the cache. This can be done if we can evaluate some conditions in our code that invalidates cache content and then trigger content removal. This can be done by:

  ```
  RedisDatabase.KeyDelete(key);
  ```

Persisting a shopping cart with Azure Table Storage

The shopping cart is the storage where the user persists details about their intention to buy. *Intention* means it is not an order; it's different. It is just an annotation during store navigation to the effect that the user would like to buy that item.

The intention can take quite long and many trips in and out of the store. So, when it the user would like to find their shopping cart filled with elements they have not bought yet. So, user means that the shopping cart is keyed by the user and independent of the navigation session.

As items stay in the shopping cart for so long, pricing can change. So, prices need to be updated for items not ordered already in the shopping cart.

So, what is inside a shopping cart item?

- A user session identification (as the user can be anonymous at the early stages of buying) that groups all items together
- Any product in a shopping cart is, for a single user, a key in the shopping cart. No one buys the same product twice in the same shopping session
- Some product information, keyed with the product ID, for fast identification and without having to access the product catalog again to decode them
- The quantity of the element
- The unit price, as it can change
- The total price, as it can reflect calculation or discount logic
- The inserted date, as information can change over time, and it's necessary to understand how to tell the user that some information is not valid anymore

Azure Table Storage can attempt this. We already introduced Azure Storage in this chapter for blob items. In this case, a more structured storage is needed. The table storage can solve our issue as:

- It's a row-based storage, useful for data that does not require complex joins, foreign keys, or stored procedures and can be denormalized for fast access
- Quickly querying data using a clustered index, we need to access the data in a fixed way
- It's cheap

So, to start using Azure Table Storage, it is necessary to define a class that can represent a typed entity to be handled by table storage. A table entity must implement the ITableEntity interface, because an entity must fulfill some requirements:

- PartitionKey: To distribute data over multiple partitions (a requirement to scale cloud applications, as we already know this feature), we need to specify a partition key. Inside a single table, rows with different partition keys can be distributed over different partitions; rows with the same PartitionKey are stored together in the same partition.

- `RowKey`: Inside a `PartitionKey`, it identifies a row uniquely. `PartitionKey` and `RowKey` are the global unique identifiers inside the table.

- `Timestamp`: This is updated after every update of the entity.

- `ETag`: This identifies a specific version for the entity, and it is updated after every update in the table. It is useful in the concurrent scenario to test whether an object can be updated after a read.

In our solutions, we can map:

- **PartitionKey to UserSession**: All rows of the user are kept together as they are used together at the same time

- **RoweKey to ProductId**: Inside a user session, a product cannot be duplicated, because a quantity specifies the instances of the product to order

We can now implement `ITableEntity` directly on our entity, but it's more practical to derive our entity from the `TableEntity` class that implements that interface for us:

```
public class ProductCartEntity: TableEntity
{
  public string ProductDescription { get; set; }

  public int Quantity { get; set; }

  public decimal UnitPrice { get; set; }
  public decimal TotalPrice { get; set; }
  public string Currency { get; set; }
  public DateTimeOffset CreateDate { get; set; }
}
```

Table storage operations are applied through a `CloudTableClient` object, created from a Azure Storage account, in a way similar to the `CloudBlobClient`:

```
private CloudTableClient _tableClient;
protected CloudTableClient TableClient
{
  get
  {
    if (_tableClient == null)
    {
      var cloudStorageAccount = CloudStorageAccount.Parse
        (ConfigurationManager.
        AppSettings["cloudStorageAccount"]);
      _tableClient = cloudStorageAccount.
        CreateCloudTableClient();
    }
```

```
        return _tableClient;
    }
}
```

On the detail page, a shopping item form can be added to trigger the insertion of the item in the shopping cart:

```html
<form action="@Url.Action("AddToCart")">
    <input type="hidden" name="ProductId" value="@Model.id" />
    <label for="UnitPrice">Unit Price</label>
    <label>@Model.ListPrice</label>
    <input type="hidden" name="UnitPrice"
      value="@Model.ListPrice" />
    <label for="Quantity">Quantity</label>
    <input type="text" name="Quantity" value="1" />
    <input type="submit" value="Add to cart" />
</form>
```

Now, an `AddToCart` action can be defined:

```csharp
[HttpPost]
public async Task<ActionResult>
    AddToCart(string productId, decimal unitPrice, int quantity)
{
// ..
}
```

The first step is to obtain a reference to the table container:

```csharp
var shoppingCart =
    TableClient.GetTableReference("shoppingcart");
shoppingCart.CreateIfNotExists();
```

A `userSession` identifier is necessary to define the context in which the user is operating that can be used for subsequent references:

```csharp
var userSession = Membership.GetUser().UserName;
```

As we have defined `PartitionKey` and `RowKey`, we have all the information to determine the specific entity, in our case, the specific shopping cart row. All interactions with table storage are represented via some `TableOperation` objects. In our case, `retrieve` means accessing a single row via the couple `PartitionKey` / `RowKey` that uniquely identifies the row:

```csharp
var retrieve =
    TableOperation.Retrieve<ProductCartEntity>
    (userSession, productId);
var result = shoppingCart.Execute(retrieve);
var item = (ProductCartEntity)result.Result;
```

If a row is not null, then information can be updated. Otherwise, a new object must be created and initialized:

```
if (item != null)
{
  item.UnitPrice = unitPrice;
  item.Quantity = quantity;
}
else
{
  item = new ProductCartEntity
  {
    PartitionKey = userSession
    ,
    RowKey = productId
    ,
    CreateDate = DateTime.Now
    ,
    Currency = "EUR"
    ,
    UnitPrice = unitPrice
    ,
    Quantity = quantity
  };
}
item.TotalPrice = item.UnitPrice * item.Quantity;
```

This is typical for shopping carts, or in general CRUD scenarios, where objects are equally initialized with a business key and not surrogated keys to merge the two specific insert and update operations into a single one that can solve internally any specific operation to execute:

```
var upsert = TableOperation.InsertOrReplace(item);
shoppingCart.Execute(upsert);
```

Now that the item is correctly inserted, we probably need to display the shopping cart. What is important now is to retrieve all the data with a query. As a general rule, PartitionKey and RowKey are a sort of clustered index for that table, where rows are ordered naturally by the two keys. There is no generic structure for indexing, so filtering by other properties (possible) is not valuable, as they perform a partition scan. However, when one or two keys are used, performances are improved.

If we continue using the .NET SDK, we can query the table storage in LINQ as the table client is a LINQ provider. The query is an expression that must be translated into the original query language by the provider to materialize entities:

```
private IEnumerable<ProductCartDTO> ShoppingCart()
{
  var shoppingCart =
    TableClient.GetTableReference("shoppingcart");
  shoppingCart.CreateIfNotExists();

  var userSession = Membership.GetUser().UserName;
  var query = (TableQuery<ProductCartEntity>)
    shoppingCart.CreateQuery<ProductCartEntity>()
  .Where(xx => xx.PartitionKey == userSession);

  .var shoppingCartItems = shoppingCart.ExecuteQuery(query)
  .Select(xx => new ProductCartDTO {
      Currency = xx.Currency
      , ProductDescription = xx.ProductDescription
      , ProductId = xx.RowKey
      , Quantity = xx.Quantity
      , TotalPrice = xx.TotalPrice
      , UnitPrice = xx.UnitPrice
      }).ToList();
  return shoppingCartItems;

}
```

Publishing your application into Azure web apps

Now, it's time to publish WebFrontEnd to Azure, and we need to perform three steps:

1. Put the project in a source code repository.
2. Create a web application.
3. Establish a process of continuous integration.

We use Visual Studio Team Services as the source code repository. In Visual Studio 2015, right-click on the **Solution Root Tree Node** on its panel and then select **Add Solution to Source Control**. A dialog similar to the one shown as follows will open:

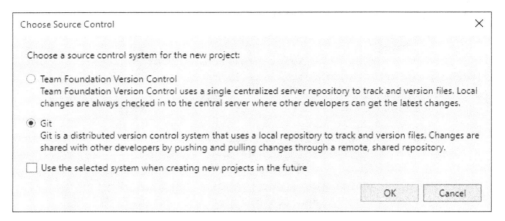

You can select the type of repository for the project code:

Team Foundation Version Control: Use this option if your team is always working connected, in the same place, and you need a strict control team working on the same files.

Git: Use it in every other case, mainly when the system is disconnected or distributed, or in general if you are confident with it. With open source, it is the de-facto standard as all public source code, including Microsoft open source code, published on GitHub is maintained in Git repositories.

So, we select Git for our projects and need to make the *first commit* to the local repository (in the same solution folder), which is a checkpoint sign to the current version of our source.

Now, by selecting **Sync**, we can merge our changes with a remote repository shared between all team members. The first time we do the synchronization, we need to create a new remote repository, or connect to an existing one if it was already created from the Visual Studio Team Services portal.

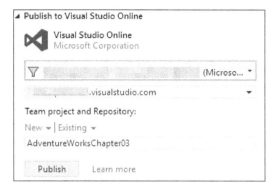

On publishing, the Git engine will calculate the changes from the local repository and the remote one to minimize the data to be exchanged (this happens at every sync; the first one is obviously longer, as the initial remote repository is empty).

In general, it is a better practice to start creating the source code repository on the first day of the development from a substantially empty solution, for three reasons. The first one is that if you work with a team, the first member creates a project and a repository and the other members "clone" the existing repository (in Git terms). The second one is the commit practice. As you can "comment" every commit, it is a best practice to commit frequently (not sync). This allows us to identify the named commits and frequent restore points in the case of lost code. The third one is branching. In the case of specific patching support, feature requests, or experimenting, it is possible to handle multiple code branches, as we can always merge them when we need it.

After the synchronization (its speed is highly dependent on your Internet connection speed), you can select a **Build** button to open the build panel.

Click on **New Build Definition**. We will be redirected by a browser window to the Team Services website.

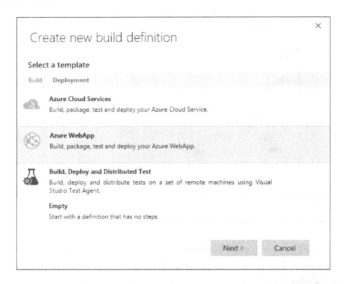

We can select a new deployment template, specifically an **Azure WebApp Deployment** template.

Every template has specific and various tasks that can be customized, added, or removed. However, in general, we find the following:

- A build task creates the *official* bits to be deployed (a local build is just for development and local testing)

- One or more test tasks verify the solution in front of functional requirements, expressed in terms of unit tests, or non-functional requirements such as load and performance testing. Failed testing, in general, stops the build process, and we need to revert to development

- Align a deployment task to a publishing environment, typically a user acceptance at the testing stage, as the testing team needs to check whether the software is compliant to the requirements that cannot be tested by automatic software (for example, the usability and user interface)

Every single step can be customized to comply to specific company requirements and conventions. Build, test, and publish tasks can be used as-is, out of the box of Team Services. We need to configure the Azure web app deployment tasks. Before that, we need to create a deployment environment on our Azure subscription.

To create an Azure web app, we need to understand three concepts. Given the current subscription, the main parameters, and the Resource Group, expressed in PowerShell as:

```
$location = "West Europe"
$projectName = "AdventureWorks"
$resourceGroupName = $projectName
$resourceGroup = Get-AzureRmResourceGroup -Name $resourceGroupName
```

The first concept we need to understand is the App Service Plan. It represents a set of features and capacity that you can share across multiple apps in Azure App Service. These plans support five pricing tiers. (At the time of writing this book, they are **Free**, **Shared**, **Basic**, **Standard**, and **Premium**). Each tier has its own capabilities, capacity, and ability to scale. Apps in the same subscription and geographic location can share a plan. All the apps sharing a plan can avail all the capabilities and features defined by the plan's tier. All apps associated with a given plan run on the resources defined by the plan.

So, we can make some considerations. You can create as many app plans as you need, but this is not strictly on a per-project decision; or, on the other hand, you can create one single app plan for company. For a solution, in general, we can have two or three deployments:

- **Testing**: This is a deployment for developers on non-functional features, such as performance, stress, and load testing
- **User Acceptance**: This is a deployment for stakeholders (in scrum terminology) to test app usability and requirement conformance
- **Production**: This is a deployment for the user's general availability

These three deployments need different resource allocations, as deployment policies and performances are different. On a per-project reasoning, we can create three different App Service Plans for these projects, with different resource allocations. On a deployment basis, we can have, for example, a single App Service Plan, where developers deploy all company apps to be tested, with no distinction of the project.

All decisions are organizational decision as they have an impact on subscription charging at the end of the month.

So, when we have decided on an organization, we can create a plan via PowerShell, where we configure the initial parameters that can be changed in the future, also controlling them via the portal. For our needs, this requires at least a Standard plan as we need slots for our operations. The following code block defines it clearly:

```
$appServicePlanName = $projectName
$appServicePlan = New-AzureRmAppServicePlan -ResourceGroupName
$resourceGroupName -Location $location -Name $appServicePlanName -Tier
Standard -NumberofWorkers 1
```

After allocating the resources, we need to create the effective application that will consume these resources. So, the second concept to understand is the app service. In our example, we are talking about the Web, but in general, the app service currently refers to four app models offered by Azure, based on the same architecture:

- **Web apps**: For HTML, a browser-based application (this is the case in our sample)
- **Mobile apps**: For JSON-based, (potentially) offline device apps
- **API apps**: For JSON-based cloud API to be consumed by other applications
- **Logic apps**: Descriptive, declarative workflow apps to automate business processes across SaaS and on-premise

Web apps provide a robust set of developer-centric capabilities such as support for multiple languages and frameworks (.NET, Java, PHP, Node.js, Python, and more), **Continuous Integration (CI)**, and cloud debugging. Web Apps can auto-scale to meet any needs and offer high-availability through deployment in several geolocations with Azure Traffic Manager.

So, to create a new web app, we need to execute this PowerShell script. It refers to the previously defined appServicePlan to select the correct resources to use:

```
$webAppName = $projectName + "App"
$webApp = New-AzureRmWebApp -ResourceGroupName
   $resourceGroupName   -Location $location -AppServicePlan
   $appServicePlanName -Name $webAppName
```

The App Service Plan can be changed in future, or it can scale without affecting the application. So, this is already enough; we have a web app up and running. But it's better to practice it with another concept during application life. The tasks are as follows:

1. Deploy a new version of the app.
2. Change the original App Service plan.
3. Do some sort of A/B testing, that is, randomly select some users of our application by testing a new version.

In the case of deployment, there is a time interval, which can be one tenth of a second long, during which the application is unavailable. To solve this, we can associate some slots (the functionality is available from the Standard level and the number depends on the level). A slot is a full-functioning app service related to the main one, with its own public endpoint URL. If nothing is explicitly created, a web application creates a default **production** slot that is our main slot. The utility of this is that we can perform anytime we need to swap two slots. Physically, this means that at any point of time, there exist two already working web apps; swap means changing the endpoint named URLs of the front automatic Azure balancer. The operation makes no service unavailable, as during a call, there is already an IP (not name) affinity. This is great during the deployment of a new version, because we can deploy to a stage slot and then make a swap.

So, the third thing we need to create is the *staging* slot where deployment will be done:

```
$developmentSlot = New-AzureRMWebAppSlot -ResourceGroupName
$resourceGroupName -AppServicePlan $appServicePlanName -name
$webAppName -Slot $slot
```

Then, there will be a **Swap** action tile that enables the swap operation to be performed directly from the Azure portal.

The swap will never be automatic. We need to verify that the application is running and then we can make the swap manually.

Configuring a web application with a Custom Domain Name

Our web application is already public when it is deployed. All instances of any Azure Services, in general, have a public URL, under a `<yourservice>.azure*.net` second-level domain, included in the service fee, running in seconds. For testing, for background or internal web services, this is great. However, frontend web applications or public and commercial web APIs need their own identity, presented by a custom second-level domain.

Having our own custom second-level domain requires three things:

- Buying a second-level domain from a domain name registrar
- Configuring a **Domain Name System (DNS)** server to hold zone and record information
- Configuring the web application, enabling it to the new DNS record name

The first thing to note is that Azure does not have a register infrastructure to buy a domain. Therefore, the yearly-based lease rules for domain names are not well suited for the pay-as-you-use services typical of cloud models. So, having a second-level domain follows this common path:

1. You have to acquire a domain name for one or more years from one of the common registrar companies.

2. Azure has integrated a register function with **GoDaddy.com** to register domain names, but you can use you own registrar of preference.

3. You have to pay a yearly based fee, with credit cards, independent of your Azure account and billing.

For example, you are buying a second-level domain name `adventureworks.xyz` from our domain name registrar of preference. It is typically configuring to some sort of automatic DNS management as some other services are already mapped over that domain name (e-mail, for example). So, you need to go to a manual configuration mode where you can add DNS zone records yourself.

 Read your register documentation carefully to understand how to make the following changes.

Given the Azure website configuration, you can retrieve records with the following PowerShell command:

```
$ws = Get-AzureRMWebApp -ResourceGroupName cloudmakers
  -name AdventureWorksWebFrontEnd
```

We need to add or change three records:

Record Name	Record Type	Record Value	Operation allowed
@ or <blank>	A	Point to the current IP address assigned by the Azure frontend balancer. You can retrieve it with a PowerShell command: `[System.Net.Dns]::GetHostAddresses($ws.HostNames[0])`	Change
awverify	CNAME	`"awverify"+ $ws.HostNames[0]`	Add
www	CNAME	`$ws.HostNames[0]`	Add or change

Now that you have committed these changes to your DNS, you could wait up to 48 hours until the changes are propagated worldwide. This is quite true if the domain was already used previously and referred to many times. In the case of a new domain, it could take anything from a few seconds to minutes.

Now, you can go to the Azure portal, go to your app service, and select **Custom Domains and SSL** from **Settings**. This brings you to a blade where you can manage DNS and certificates. In this case, we need to **Bring External Domains**:

From this blade, you can add all your custom second-level domains, which Azure already *pretends* are configured. In this way, Azure verifies resolving names, querying your domain DNS, and looking up for required DNS zone records.

After you save the changes, the web application is now configured and already accessible from the Web.

This is one of the many ways in which the configuration can be done. Listed as follows are a few of these:

- Connecting the web application (in general, the app service) to a virtual network (as we saw in an earlier chapter) to assign reserved access to backend resources or, if necessary, assigning a static IP address to the website

- Moving the primary domain name server from the registrar's domain to the Azure DNS service

- Buying the domain name and configuring DNS directly from the Azure portal

Summary

In this chapter, we have discovered that Azure offers to persist data that goes beyond the common relational database. Every data service implements different patterns that represent the best experience for different situations and that can exist together.

We have also experienced how to create a web application that uses all these data sources, manages the project inside a Source Control Manager, and uses it to enter inside a CI scenario.

In the next chapter, we will see how to create an infrastructure that can handle a shopping cart and process orders.

4
Building the Backend

Today, much of the effort for a development team of a web-based business is often dedicated to the frontend user experience. Such effort must consider, as we see in *Chapter 3, Building the Frontend*, some technology issues in order to provide quality even behind the scenes. A couple of words often used to explain some of our target indicators are:

- **Maintainability**: The extent to which it is easy (in terms of overall costs) to maintain and evolve a software artifact
- **Scalability**: The extent to which it is easy to react to growing demand without re-engineering the software artifact

In *Chapter 3, Building the Frontend* we saw how to use Polyglot Persistence to build a tailored data platform, where each logical application block has its corresponding optimal technology.

In this chapter, we will evaluate some new technologies, mentioned here, to enhance the proposed scenario in order to embrace new challenges:

- Order (and business process) management
- Identity and access management (for millions of users)

The first challenge is mainly about business. As developers, we often think that an order is just a row in the appropriate table. By thinking this, when a user clicks on the **Order** button, that's it! It's done. However, ordering is just the beginning of a series of complex business activities, and even for the technical side, it is not just about saving a record.

The second challenge may seem trivial. Almost every developer has built an authentication/authorization software block at least once. In the simplest case, the developer can write their own stack by looking for some credentials in a relation database or in a local data store. On the other hand, the developer can reuse existing technologies to build a standard **Identity Access Management (IAM)** layer for their applications.

CloudMakers.XYZ scenario evolution

One of the business missions of **CloudMakers (CM)** is to provide a scalable e-commerce software platform for its clients. This platform should be quite simple, but it has to cope with several hot points to provide at least scalability, consistency, and maintainability. Apart from the technology used to compute web pages, it is very important which data strategy is used.

We say "data strategy" and not "data tool/software," since we believe that the choice of a specific product is just a detail in the big picture of what is optimal in terms of strategy.

An example is the programming language used to compute pages. In the previous chapter, we used ASP.NET, but it is completely irrelevant whether the team knows ASP.NET, Node.js, or PHP. We can say that each language can be used to provide the same result. An exciting feature of a specific language can speed up the overall performance or the development process itself, but we can think about it as just the compute layer abstracting the backend data from the technology used to convert logic into HTML.

This same thinking exercise can be applied to data stores. No matter what data store we use to persist catalogs, order details, identities, or images, we can use the filesystem for everything.

This is why we are talking about "strategy". And these are the issues:

- Choosing the right programming language for the business drivers
- Choosing the right data store for the business drivers

The focus is on business drivers. To create some examples, try to answer these questions:

- Which programming language does the team know best?
- Is it compatible with the development area (web development) and the business goals (scalability, consistency, maintainability)?

- If not, try to identify the best language (or development ecosystem) for the business goal. Then, plan the appropriate training for the team.

- If yes, we have probably found the programming language for the project.

This simplistic and provocative approach helps us think about using what we have available, while at the same time, it leads to a choice driven by business goals. If ASP. NET does not support multithreading (requiring each web request to wait for the completion of the previous one), it would not be the best choice for the scalability requirement (in fact, it would be an epic fail for web apps). If a single developer knows PHP, even if they are the only ones who develop the whole project, the language would probably be the wrong choice for software maintainability (think about them leaving the company).

Though the preceding examples are very simple, the same thing occurs with data stores. In the previous chapter, we chose to split data among different data sources in order to achieve business goals. As mentioned earlier, we can even persist everything onto a single file in the filesystem. However, searching contents would be very hard and long, on currency would be almost impossible to achieve, and the performance would be catastrophic.

This is why we choose to use:

- **DocumentDB for the catalog**: This is well-suited to store structured data, and it has very good performance to resist web traffic.

- **Azure Search for the search engine**: This can relieve DocumentDB from an intensive workload (scalability) and, at the same time, provide developers with many out-of-the-box search features without coding a line (maintainability).

- **Blob storage and CDN for images**: This can prevent a roundtrip from the web app to the database (or to a data store), providing user sessions with resources directly.

- **Caching with Redis**: This can reduce the workload (scalability) of DocumentDB for frequently accessed data, using a technology designed just for this purpose.

Having said this, Luke, the CTO of CM, needs to find out the appropriate strategy to handle orders. A received order needs to trigger business processes in addition to just a data write. For more information, you can visit the *Handling orders* section.

Finally, since the e-commerce platform will be an enterprise, multi-tenant, and elastic platform (accessible even from the external system via APIs), a consistent Identity and Access Management system is needed. It avoids custom solutions that, despite being simpler to implement, are less maintainable while adding complexity to the surface of the entire process. You can also refer to the *Outsourcing Identity and Access Management* section.

Handling orders

As mentioned earlier, receiving an order is not just a matter of writing a row in a database. In real-world scenarios, an incoming e-commerce order triggers several business procedures. Some of them are as follows:

- Notifying the warehouse set for the delivery
- Notifying the sales agent to perform appropriate actions on the CRM
- Notifying payment information to the financial department

We can achieve these with two opposite approaches:

- **Push approach**: The application receiving an order "pushes" the notification to the involved systems
- **Pull approach**: The involved systems periodically checks for changes into a specific place in order to start business rules

Both approaches have advantages/disadvantages. They are explained in the following table:

	Push approach	Pull approach
Advantages	• Dependent systems are notified from the event source, and they have just to react to the event • Event processor can be a stupid worker	• External systems can initiate custom logic without other parties knowing of their existence • Subsequent iterations of the integration logic can fill the gaps of incomplete work by the previous ones

	Push approach	Pull approach
Disadvantages	• A failure in event/message notification results in a missing event • Separate systems, technically decoupled using appropriate technologies, are logically coupled (that is, the web app must know that someone has to be notified)	• All the integration logic must perform some sort of polling technique • Each application must keep track of processed items, and it needs to distinguish them from new items

Pull approaches are useful where we cannot (or we don't want to) touch the existing codebase. On the other hand, push approaches are generally more elegant, and they usually perform better (avoiding pulling systems for changes and reacting without delay to events).

Later in this chapter, we will see how to use a push approach to decouple the reception of an order from the underlying write to the SQL database instance.

After saving the order data into the relational data store, the company needs to analyze the huge amount of data (forecasts say a million orders per month) to provide some aggregate information:

- Order average amount
- Item most often bought
- Most-buying users

To do this, we can use the **Online Transaction Processing (OLTP)** relational database, compromising performance for the intensive usage of aggregate functions and multiple joins. Otherwise, we can transfer a custom projection of the data in a data warehouse, to perform offline analysis.

In the last two parts of this section, we will see how to use a pull approach to transfer relational data into a SQL data warehouse instance and, finally, how to predict behaviors based on data analysis.

Decoupling user actions from SQL sinking

There is a common rule while designing web applications that are going to grow (in terms of load demand): make them scalable. This requirement is not simple, since every building block of the application should be at least scalable.

The basic architecture for a B2C web application serving traffic for hundreds of thousands of users might be as follows:

- Web servers
- Database

You learned that you can add several additional blocks to perform better and to achieve resiliency and fault tolerance:

- Additional web servers (to serve more traffic)
- CDN (for faster client performance)
- Caching (for faster server thinking time)

Unfortunately, it is really hard for a relational database to scale, either because of its internal implementation or because it has to deal with **Atomicity-Consistency-Isolation-Durability (ACID)** properties. Therefore, other than web servers, more database servers cannot be just "added" to gain new computation power.

In the previous chapters, we saw that a good choice was to use Polyglot Persistence, routing the heavy load into NoSQL (which scales better) and keeping SQL outside the B2C process. When this pattern is not available, it is strongly recommended that you, at least, decouple the web traffic from the database access.

Let's imagine this simplistic scenario. The high-level requirement is to cope with a load of 200 concurrent users. Those users generate (on average) 0.5 requests/second. Each request (based on how the application is implemented) generates two to three SQL queries on the underlying database.

With these numbers in place and supposing that the rate is always constant, we have a predictable load of about 200–300 SQL queries per second.

This assumption lets us perform sizing of the SQL database in order to react to 300 queries per second. To be safer, we can think of 400 queries/second, keeping an average of 100 queries/second (25 percent of the overall power) to react to peaks.

Why is this sizing effort completely useless in real-world B2C applications? First, it is very hard to estimate in advance the specific load (in terms of SQL queries) for unknown users. Second, these users' behavior can be very different from each other. Last, but the most important, the website might experience a sudden peak of 100 percent or even 10,000 percent more than the average normal traffic.

A common scenario for an unexpected peak of traffic is represented by an unmonitored promotional campaign. If a given influencer (blogger or journalist) decides to write an article or to talk on TV about that website, millions of users might try to navigate that site immediately. This reveals that sizing systems are not useful and result very often in a waste of resources.

Going back to our scenario, we must use SQL to receive orders. We must do this efficiently and think about unpredicted peaks. One of the simplest solutions, where touching the existing code is an option, is queues. The system providing this queue needs to be something resilient and scalable. It must react well to unpredictable loads, of course. However, if such system exists, the queue can store the incoming requests (even millions in a row) to let someone else process them earlier or later.

Under those constraints, the receiving actor can read the messages from the queue and write them to the database at the same, fixed rate (that is, 300 queries/second, as imagined earlier).

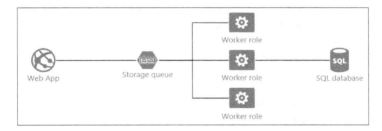

The solution proposed for this scenario is based on the first services available in Azure since its birth:

- **Worker roles**: These manage VMs running custom code
- **Storage queues**: These are REST-based **First-In-First-Out** (FIFO) queues

To edit the web application, follow these steps:

1. We need to replace the saving strategy in the generating application as follows:

```
public void ReceiveOrder(Order item)
{
  //Comment ex-Saving logic
  //WriteOrderToDB(item);
  //Introduce new Queue-based logic
  WriteOrderInQueue(item);
}
```

2. We then need to write the `WriteOrderInQueue` method as follows:

```csharp
private void WriteOrderInQueue(Order item)
{
  var connStr = "[Storage Connection String]";
  var queueClient = CloudStorageAccount
  .Parse(connStr).CreateCloudQueueClient();
  var queue = queueClient
  .GetQueueReference("orders-queue");
  queue.CreateIfNotExists();
  queue.AddMessage(new CloudQueueMessage(
  JsonConvert.SerializeObject(item)));
}
```

3. Writing the receiving application: We will setup a looping function as follows:

```csharp
public void Run(CancellationToken token)
{
  var connStr = "[Storage Connection String]";
  var queueClient = CloudStorageAccount
    .Parse(connStr).CreateCloudQueueClient();
  var queue = queueClient
    .GetQueueReference("orders-queue");
  queue.CreateIfNotExists();

  var localQueue = newQueue<CloudQueueMessage>();
  var lastSecond = DateTime.Now.Second;
  var batchSize = 250;
  while (!token.IsCancellationRequested)
  {
    var msgs = queue.GetMessages(
    messageCount: 32,
    visibilityTimeout:
    TimeSpan.FromMinutes(1)).ToList();
    msgs.ForEach(p =>localQueue.Enqueue(p));
    var currentSecond = DateTime.Now.Second;
    if (currentSecond != lastSecond)
    {
      for (inti = 0; i<batchSize&&i<localQueue.Count; i++)
      {
        var msg = localQueue.Dequeue();
        var payload = JsonConvert
        .DeserializeObject<Order>(msg.AsString);
        WriteOrderToDBAsync(payload);
```

```
            queue.DeleteMessageAsync(msg);
        }

    Thread.Sleep(1000);
        }
    }
```

4. Writing the `WorkerRole` code: We will create a new Azure Cloud Service project with a single worker role, implemented as follows:

```
public class WorkerRole : RoleEntryPoint
{
private readonly CancellationTokenSource cancellationTokenSource
  = new CancellationTokenSource();
private readonly ManualResetEvent runCompleteEvent
  = new ManualResetEvent(false);

public override void Run()
    {
        Trace.TraceInformation("DefaultWorker is running");

        try
          {
            var receiver = newOrderReceiver();
            receiver.Run(cancellationTokenSource.Token);
          }
        finally
          {
            this.runCompleteEvent.Set();
          }
    }

public override boolOnStart() […]

public override voidOnStop() […]

    }
```

Though this sample is for demonstration purposes, it shows the basic blocks needed in order to achieve decoupling between the web traffic and the database operations. Here are some comments about the preceding code:

- In step 1, we had some sort of business-logic method `ReceiveOrder` where the `Order` item can contain all the required information to persist the order to the DB. In this part, we comment the previous logic (a fictitious method writing to the DB) in order to put our method (writing to a queue).

- In step 2, we had a valid storage account represented by a connection string. We added the `WindowsAzure.StorageNuGet` package in order to use the appropriate classes to interact with queues. Through the `AddMessage` function, we write the serialized content of the `Order` item to the queue.

> The `AddMessage` function makes a REST call to the storage service under the hood.

- In step 3, we set up a class named `OrderReceiver`, with a `Run` method containing the following dispatching logic:
    - The code enters a `while` loop, checking whether someone has requested a cancellation of the task
    - Through the `GetMessages` method, we ask a maximum of 32 messages in a single batch (32 is the actual service limit) in order to minimize the REST operations

> To achieve consistency on a storage queue, the appropriate pattern to process messages is read, process, and delete. The delete operation is needed because, if the read operation itself removes the message and something goes wrong while processing, the message could be lost forever. Instead, with an explicit delete operation in conjunction with a visibility timeout (a timeout determining how long the message is hidden from new clients after the read operation), we are safe in the case of transient faults.

    - Since the high-level requirement is to perform a maximum number of 250 writes per second, we closely check whether we are in the next available time frame (by checking the current second)
    - We process the batch of messages, and for each one, we write the item and delete the message in the queue

> Note that this process does not guarantee that the write has been done neither does it say that the queue message has been deleted. Take this as just a demonstration.

    - Finally, we invoke a `Sleep` action on the current thread to avoid a continuous check against the storage service in the case of an empty queue

The storage queue service cannot block a caller in the case of an empty queue. So, to avoid incurring high and useless costs for transaction and bandwidth, a timing strategy is needed.

- In step 4, we created a new Azure Cloud Service project in Visual Studio, specifying a worker role in the project-creation wizard. The sample implementation provided by the Visual Studio template is identical to the sample proposed, except for these two lines:

```
var receiver = new OrderReceiver();
receiver.Run(cancellationTokenSource.Token);
```

An Azure Cloud Service is a PaaS providing users with an environment to execute arbitrary code and, if needed, making some customization to the underlying executing VM (Windows-based).

A worker role is a type of execution unit supported by a cloud service, and its model is summarized as follows:

- Azure checks a class implementing the `RoleEntryPoint`
- It invokes the `OnStart` method (the purpose of this method is to perform initialization tasks)
- It invokes the `Run` method that should never return, except in the case of gracefully terminating the worker role itself, where the `OnStop` method is called directly from the Azure engine.

 Using `CancellationTokenSource` is a standard method to gracefully implement the termination of continuous processes. In the preceding case, the infinite `while` loop checks its legitimacy against the `CancellationToken`. In the case of termination, the token changes its value and the process self-determines its end.

In Visual Studio, we created a cloud service that can actually wrap many roles (not just one). This reflects the following architecture:

- A single cloud service maps to a single public DNS name (the load balancer, that is, `[myApp].cloudapp.net`)
- In the cloud service dashlet (the artifact produced by Visual Studio after building the cloud service project), there are one or many roles

- For each role:

  ° A VM size is specified. Azure creates a VM to execute the code of the role.

  ° Scaling is independent. We can scale out (adding instances) a role, leaving others unaltered.

The Azure Cloud Service package can be published on Azure through the old portal, as shown in the following screenshot:

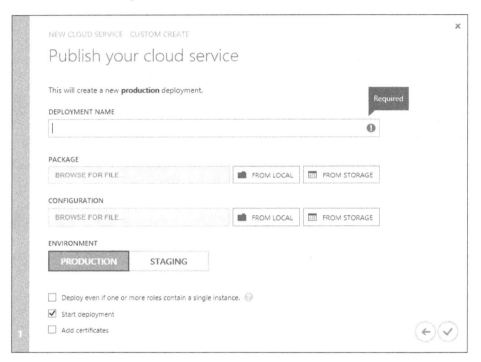

Producing denormalized data for analysis

In RDBMS development, we are used to thinking in terms of OLTP processing, where the focus of the DB interaction is on transactions and frequent reads/writes. Engineering an OLTP database involves data normalization. Data normalization is the process of organizing data to reduce data redundancy at the minimum, in order to provide users with:

- Faster search/lookup queries based on foreign keys instead of values
- Faster insertion queries

- Better maintenance, since a good normalization frees the database of data anomalies (as show in the following tables)

Let's start with the following example, showing a sample bookstore table:

BookISBN	BookName	BookPages	AuthorName	AuthorCode	AuthorCountry
ISBNX01	Very nice book	156	R. Freato	I102	Italy
ISBNX02	Awesome book	400	John Doe	U201	USA
ISBNX03	Awful book	230	R. Freato	I102	IT

As we can see in the table, the first and third books are by the same author, whose information is replaced in both the rows involved. This is probably a waste of space, and it can lead to some data inconsistencies. One insertion can differ from another one, albeit logically referring to the same information:

- In the first row, the author country is in one form, while in the third one, there is an inconsistency (the same country appears in another form)
- It is useless (and a waste of space) to repeat R. Freato over a potentially long list (of billions) of rows

This is why normalization takes place. An initial normalized version of the preceding table can be as follows:

BookISBN	BookName	BookPages	AuthorCode
ISBNX01	Very nice book	156	I102
ISBNX02	Awesome book	400	U201
ISBNX03	Awful book	230	I102

The Authors table can be represented as follows:

AuthorCode	AuthorName	AuthorCountry
I102	R. Freato	Italy
U201	John Doe	USA
I201	M. Parenzan	Italy

With this step of normalization, we just need to reference the data of the second table using a valid key (foreign key) in the first table. The foreign key of the first table must be a primary key (unique) of the second table.

We can even go further with this additional step:

AuthorCode	AuthorName	CountryCode
I102	R. Freato	IT
U201	John Doe	US
I201	M. Parenzan	IT

The `Countries` table is this one:

CountryCode	CountryName
IT	Italy
US	USA

In this second step, we applied another normalization step to the `Authors` table, and then, we minimized the redundancy of the data.

This strategy is often a valid approach for OLTP, where the quality of the data must be optimal, and the usage is characterized by a large number of short-term transactions/queries having to run with faster performance.

In OLAP processing, the tables are turned because the requirements are different. Here are some examples:

- OLAP users are few (compared to OLTP) and are focused on reads (that is, analysis of a huge amount of data)
- In OLAP, writes are usually performed in a batch periodically (that is, at night)

So, OLAP DBs are typically suited for data warehouses, and they are also implemented differently under the hood. In the following table, we have summarized the main differences:

Parameters	OLTP	OLAP
Speed	Fast, typically seconds	Slow, from seconds to hours
Purpose	Operational data	Data for decision support
Design	Very high normalization	Fewer, denormalized tables
Space used	Optimized, since data is normalized and historical data is often moved away	Larger, due to the denormalization process and the storage of historical data

Parameters	OLTP	OLAP
Availability	Critical, downtime causes losses to business	Moderate delays or downtime cause troubles to management
Queries	Typical SQL queries with filtering, joins, and projections	Complex queries involving aggregations

We talked about normalization because while dealing with data analysis, we need to denormalize our data to reduce the schema complexity in order to gain performance with queries against a huge amount of data.

In the next section, we will see how to set up a simple table for OLAP processing, using the Azure SQL data warehouse (for the database) and how to move data into it using Azure Data Factory.

Extracting, transforming, and loading data into a data warehouse

We will start this section using the `AdventureWorksLT` database, whose schema can be summarized as follows:

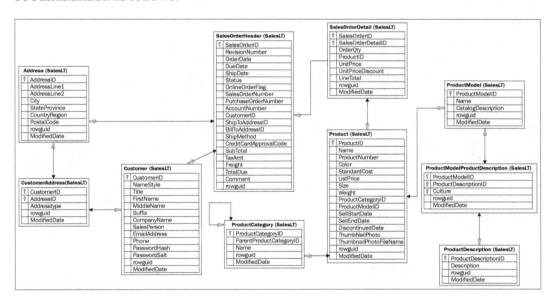

This set of tables is highly normalized, so it is well-suited for OLTP processing but is not particularly useful in OLAP scenarios. What we need to do is to think about a good transformation to denormalize part of the tables in order to obtain fewer tables with more data.

For example, starting from 10 tables with 100 records/tables, we need to design a new table set of two to three tables with thousands of records per table.

One of the most common methods to denormalize tables is to identify the tables owning details (in a master/detail model). Alternatively, to be more general, such tables are a destination for a one-to-many relationship.

 Denormalized DBs usually follow the star schema pattern. However, this pattern has a whole literature behind OLAP and data warehouses are completely beyond the scope of this book.

Looking at the preceding figure (the DB diagram), we see that three tables are a destination of only one-to-many relationships:

- `SalesOrderDetail`
- `ProductModelProductDescription`
- `CustomerAddress`

We can start summarizing data by performing a query on `SalesOrderDetail`, joining all the tables we can include in the join chain, as follows:

```
SELECT [t0].[SalesOrderDetailID], [t0].[OrderQty], [t0].[UnitPrice],
[t0].[UnitPriceDiscount], [t0].[LineTotal], [t1].[SalesOrderID], [t1].
[RevisionNumber], [t1].[OrderDate], [t1].[DueDate], [t1].[ShipDate],
[t1].[Status], [t1].[OnlineOrderFlag], [t1].[SalesOrderNumber], [t1].
[PurchaseOrderNumber], [t1].[AccountNumber], [t1].[ShipMethod], [t1].
[CreditCardApprovalCode], [t1].[SubTotal], [t1].[TaxAmt], [t1].
[Freight], [t1].[TotalDue], [t1].[Comment], [t2].[CustomerID], [t2].
[NameStyle], [t2].[Title], [t2].[FirstName], [t2].[MiddleName], [t2].
[LastName], [t2].[Suffix], [t2].[CompanyName], [t2].[SalesPerson], [t2].
[EmailAddress], [t2].[Phone], [t3].[AddressID], [t3].[AddressLine1],
[t3].[AddressLine2], [t3].[City], [t3].[StateProvince], [t3].
[CountryRegion], [t3].[PostalCode], [t4].[ProductID], [t4].[Name], [t4].
[ProductNumber], [t4].[Color], [t4].[StandardCost], [t4].[ListPrice],
[t4].[Size], [t4].[Weight], [t4].[SellStartDate], [t4].[SellEndDate],
[t4].[DiscontinuedDate], [t4].[ThumbnailPhotoFileName], [t5].
[ProductModelID], [t5].[Name] AS [ModelName], [t5].[CatalogDescription],
[t6].[ProductCategoryID], [t6].[ParentProductCategoryID], [t6].[Name] AS
[CategoryName]

FROM [SalesLT].[SalesOrderDetail] AS [t0]

INNER JOIN [SalesLT].[SalesOrderHeader] AS [t1] ON [t1].[SalesOrderID] =
[t0].[SalesOrderID]

INNER JOIN [SalesLT].[Customer] AS [t2] ON [t2].[CustomerID] = [t1].
[CustomerID]
```

```
LEFT OUTER JOIN [SalesLT].[Address] AS [t3] ON [t3].[AddressID] = [t1].
[BillToAddressID]

INNER JOIN [SalesLT].[Product] AS [t4] ON [t4].[ProductID] = [t0].
[ProductID]

LEFT OUTER JOIN [SalesLT].[ProductModel] AS [t5] ON [t5].[ProductModelID]
= [t4].[ProductModelID]

LEFT OUTER JOIN [SalesLT].[ProductCategory] AS [t6] ON [t6].
[ProductCategoryID] = [t4].[ProductCategoryID]
```

If we proceed with the other two tables using the same approach, we will build three result tables with the whole DB dataset, a starting point to build complex data analysis.

From the official Azure documentation (https://azure.microsoft.com/en-us/documentation/articles/sql-data-warehouse-overview-what-is/):

> *Azure SQL Data Warehouse is an enterprise-class, distributed database capable of processing massive volumes of relational and non-relational data. [...] SQL Data Warehouse is also deeply ingrained into Azure, it easily deploys in seconds. In addition to this, the service is fully managed and removes the hassle of spending time on software patching, maintenance, and back-ups. SQL Data Warehouse's automatic, built-in backups support fault-tolerance and self-service restore. [...] The architecture of SQL Data Warehouse introduces separated storage and compute, allowing each to scale independently. [...] Complementing this is the use of Azure Storage Blobs. [...] Using this combination of cloud-scale storage and Azure compute, SQL Data Warehouse allows you to pay for query performance storage as you need it when you need it. [...] In addition to adopting the TSQL surface area of SQL Server, SQL Data Warehouse also integrates with many of the tools that SQL Server users may be familiar with.*

The creation process of a **SQL Data Warehouse (SQLDW)** database is straightforward, and we do not cover it in this section (more information at https://azure.microsoft.com/en-us/documentation/articles/sql-data-warehouse-get-started-provision/). While SQLDW is a fully featured service, we do not investigate many of the features it provides. Instead, we just complete the previous scenario by adding a table and copying data into it.

There are some major differences between Azure SQL Database and Azure SQL Data Warehouse. In the latter, table features are limited, since SQLDW does not support primary keys, foreign keys, check/unique constraints, computed/sparse columns, and so on. Even the data types are limited to everyone except geometry, geography, hierarchy, id, image, text, ntext, (n)varchar(max) (to be used as (n)varchar(4000) instead), numeric, sql_variant, sysname, table, timestamp (to be used as datetime2), uniqueidentifier, XML, and UDTs.

The preceding SELECT query can be translated into this CREATE TABLE statement:

```
CREATETABLE [SalesLT].[MyOLAPTable] (
    [SalesOrderDetailID] [int] NOTNULL,
    [OrderQty] [smallint] NOTNULL,
    [UnitPrice] [money] NOTNULL,
    [UnitPriceDiscount] [money] NOTNULL,
    [LineTotal] [numeric] (38, 6)NOTNULL,
    [SalesOrderID] [int] NOTNULL,
    [RevisionNumber] [tinyint] NOTNULL,
    [OrderDate] [datetime] NOTNULL,
    [DueDate] [datetime] NOTNULL,
    [ShipDate] [datetime] NULL,
    [Status] [tinyint] NOTNULL,
    [OnlineOrderFlag] [dbo].[Flag] NOTNULL,
    [SalesOrderNumber] [nvarchar] (25)NOTNULL,
    [PurchaseOrderNumber] [dbo].[OrderNumber] NULL,
    [AccountNumber] [dbo].[AccountNumber] NULL,
    [ShipMethod] [nvarchar] (50)NOTNULL,
    [CreditCardApprovalCode] [varchar] (15)NULL,
    [SubTotal] [money] NOTNULL,
    [TaxAmt] [money] NOTNULL,
    [Freight] [money] NOTNULL,
    [TotalDue] [money] NOTNULL,
    [Comment] [nvarchar] (max)NULL,
    [CustomerID] [int] NOTNULL,
    [NameStyle] [dbo].[NameStyle] NOTNULL,
    [Title] [nvarchar] (8)NULL,
    [FirstName] [dbo].[Name] NOTNULL,
```

```
[MiddleName] [dbo].[Name] NULL,
[LastName] [dbo].[Name] NOTNULL,
[Suffix] [nvarchar](10)NULL,
[CompanyName] [nvarchar](128)NULL,
[SalesPerson] [nvarchar](256)NULL,
[EmailAddress] [nvarchar](50)NULL,
[Phone] [dbo].[Phone] NULL,
[AddressID] [int] NULL,
[AddressLine1] [nvarchar](60)NULL,
[AddressLine2] [nvarchar](60)NULL,
[City] [nvarchar](30)NULL,
[StateProvince] [dbo].[Name] NULL,
[CountryRegion] [dbo].[Name] NULL,
[PostalCode] [nvarchar](15)NULL,
[ProductID] [int] NOTNULL,
[Name] [dbo].[Name] NOTNULL,
[ProductNumber] [nvarchar](25)NOTNULL,
[Color] [nvarchar](15)NULL,
[StandardCost] [money] NOTNULL,
[ListPrice] [money] NOTNULL,
[Size] [nvarchar](5)NULL,
[Weight] [decimal](8, 2)NULL,
[SellStartDate] [datetime] NOTNULL,
[SellEndDate] [datetime] NULL,
[DiscontinuedDate] [datetime] NULL,
[ThumbnailPhotoFileName] [nvarchar](50)NULL,
[ProductModelID] [int] NULL,
[ModelName] [dbo].[Name] NULL,
[CatalogDescription] [xml] NULL,
[ProductCategoryID] [int] NULL,
[ParentProductCategoryID] [int] NULL,
[CategoryName] [dbo].[Name] NULL
)
```

As mentioned earlier, we need to make some changes in order to let this table be compliant with SQL Data Warehouse:

- Changed [LineTotal] from [numeric](38, 6) to [decimal](36,6)

- Changed [Comment] from [nvarchar](max) to [nvarchar(4000)]

- Removed [OnlineOrderFlag], [PurchaseOrderNumber], [AccountNumber], [NameStyle], [FirstName], [MiddleName], [LastName], [Phone], [StateProvince], [CountryRegion], [Name], [ModelName], and [CategoryName] as they are UDT

- Removed [CatalogDescription] as it is [xml]

 In the preceding sample, we removed the non compatible columns for more speed, but a valid option can be to explore the UDT in the corresponding native data types and to convert XML to plain text. Besides this, think about the real requirement to have an XML field in an OLAP table.

With such a table in the destination SQL Data Warehouse, setting up a Data Copy Activity with **Azure Data Factory** (**ADF**) remains. ADF is a cloud-based data integration service that orchestrates and automates the movement and transformation of data. The most important building blocks of ADF are:

- **Linked Service**: A linked service is an endpoint where we can fetch (or sink) the data.

- **DataSet**: A dataset is a *sliced* container or data. It can either be an *external* DataSet (where the input comes from a linked server) or a plain one (where the input comes from a copy/transformation phase).

 In ADF, we often cope with the concept of slices of data. ADF works with data at the slice level, partitioning data to scale and reacting better to failure events.

- **Pipeline**: It describes the activities between input and output datasets.

Assuming we have created the Data Factory service, we can go to the Author and deploy section and create the following items:

- Input the SQL Database linked service AW-STD: We create a linked service pointing to the SQL Database containing the source data using the following code:

```
{
    "name": "AW-STD",
    "properties": {
```

```
        "description": "",
        "type": "AzureSqlDatabase",
        "typeProperties": {
            "connectionString": "[source DB]"
        }
    }
}
```

- Output SQL Data Warehouse linked service AW-DW: We did the same for the destination data by writing the following code:

```
{
    "name": "AW-DW",
    "properties": {
        "description": "",
        "type": "AzureSqlDW",
        "typeProperties": {
            "connectionString": "[destination DB]"
        }
    }
}
```

- External DataSet fetches monthly slices from the specified table in the AW-STD source: We created a monthly sliced dataset for the SalesLT. OrderDetailsDW (which is a view created for the purpose of transformation, using the modified SELECT query built previously). The following code block is included to perform that action:

```
{
    "name": "SqlDBInputDataset",
    "properties": {
        "published": false,
        "type": "AzureSqlTable",
        "linkedServiceName": "AW-STD",
        "typeProperties": {
            "tableName": "SalesLT.OrderDetailsDW"
        },
        "availability": {
            "frequency": "Month",
            "interval": 1
        },
        "external": true,
        "policy": {}
    }
}
```

- DataSet storing results into the specified table in the AW-DW destination: We created a monthly sliced dataset for the dbo.OrdersDetails table. Refer to the following code for better clarity:

```
{
    "name": "SqlDWOutputDataset",
    "properties": {
        "published": false,
        "type": "AzureSqlDWTable",
        "linkedServiceName": "AW-DW",
        "typeProperties": {
            "tableName": "dbo.OrdersDetails"
        },
        "availability": {
            "frequency": "Month",
            "interval": 1
        }
    }
}
```

- The pipeline declaring the entire copy process: The whole process of data movement is described in this step:

    ° In the type property, we specify it is a copy activity

    ° The source is SqlSource, against the inputs specified and sliced monthly using the custom sqlReaderQuery

    ° The sink is SqlDWSink, placing copied slices into the SqlDWOuputDataset

    ° start and end have nothing to do with execution, but they represent the starting and ending points of the data, semantically speaking

This means that slices are produced based on the specified time frame with the intervals specified in the datasets. In this case, it is the time frame in one year (from 05/01/2008 to 05/01/2009) with a slice of one month. So, 12 slices will be produced by the Azure DF pipeline.

The following code block is used to perform these tasks:

```
{
    "name": "SqlDBToSqlDWOrdersCopy",
    "properties": {
        "description": "pipeline for copy activity",
        "activities": [
            {
```

```json
                    "type": "Copy",
                    "typeProperties": {
                        "source": {
                            "type": "SqlSource",
                            "sqlReaderQuery":
                              "$$Text.Format('select * from
                              SalesLT.OrderDetailsDW where
                              OrderDate>= \\'{0:yyyy-MM-dd
                              HH:mm}\\' AND OrderDate<
                              \\'{1:yyyy-MM-dd HH:mm}\\'',
                              WindowStart, WindowEnd)"
                        },
                        "sink": {
                            "type": "SqlDWSink",
                            "writeBatchSize": 0,
                            "writeBatchTimeout": "00:00:00"
                        }
                    },
                    "inputs": [
                        {
                            "name": "SqlDBInputDataset"
                        }
                    ],
                    "outputs": [
                        {
                            "name": "SqlDWOutputDataset"
                        }
                    ],
                    "policy": {
                        "timeout": "01:00:00",
                        "concurrency": 1
                    },
                    "scheduler": {
                        "frequency": "Month",
                        "interval": 1
                    },
                    "name": "SQLtoDW",
                    "description": "copy activity"
                }
            ],
            "start": "2008-05-01T00:00:00Z",
            "end": "2009-05-01T00:00:00Z",
              "isPaused": false,
            "pipelineMode": "Scheduled"
        }
    }
```

A graphic representation of the created pipeline is shown here:

Data copy executions are managed at slice level, so if something goes wrong in a slice of data, ADF notifies it and retries (if specified) or lets the user investigate the error. The following screenshot shows the status of activity runs:

In the preceding screenshot, the first execution failed (we made it fail for demonstration purposes only), while the second one was successful. After this, in the destination table of the SQL Data Warehouse database, the rows are copied from the SQL Database source.

Predicting valuable information with machine learning

Assuming we have a huge amount of historical data coming from the OLTP database, we can involve business intelligence tasks to analyze the past and the present to build predictive models for the future.

These tasks are strictly related to statistics and numerical calculus, and the whole science field is quite complex for most people. However, it is very important, for example, to predict the sell rate for a given product in a given period of time. In the last few decades, such algorithms, as long as the environments used to run those, have been the prerogative of few. Now, such algorithms have been democratized, and the underlying infrastructures often run on commodity hardware.

Machine learning is an area of computer science dealing with artificial intelligence. This means two things in most situations:

- **Supervised learning**: We *train* a machine to learn a model by giving it the input data answers from the past or the present. We expect a function as the output of the training process, which can *predict* the future results from a generic input.

- **Unsupervised learning**: We give data input to an algorithm, to find out hidden structures where there are no pre-existent classifications. We expect to find patterns, clusters, and correlations between items in the input dataset.

> It is very important to analyze real data while using machine learning techniques. Random data is useless to train models unless it is randomized efficiently.

To better understand this section, it is useful to have a reasonable knowledge of the foundations of statistics and machine learning. Two of the most famous problems that machine learning wants to address are:

- **Regression**: In regression, the goal is to find a function modeling the data domain. Regression problems are related to variables (also known as features) assuming continuous values.

- **Classification**: In classification, the goal is to classify some inputs (the features) into a given class. In the simplest scenario, we just have a single binary response (input is in X/input is not in X). When the output classes are more than one (also known as binary classification or two-class classification), we talk about multi-class classification.

For each problem, there are several algorithms to train the model appropriately. The process of selecting the appropriate algorithm is a problem per se, and it may depend on the quantity and the quality of the input data.

Problem: Finding information in a given dataset

Take a look at the dataset produced by the previous section. Try to imagine which kind of analysis we could make on it. Here is an example:

For a given customer, find the average order amount.

For a given product, find the average quantity in basket.

Generally speaking, "for a given set of features," try to "find some classification" on the dataset. Then, use the notions that follow to practice with ML.

Azure Machine Learning is a comprehensive set of technology building blocks to analyze data, produce predictive models, and integrate those models into applications. In the next few pages, we will build a predictive model with the well-known **iris** dataset.

The iris dataset is a multi-variate dataset, containing classifications of some iris flower variants (**Setosa, Virginica**, and **Versicolor**). Edgar Anderson measured 150 instances of iris flowers on four variables/features:

- Sepal length
- Sepal width
- Petal length
- Petal width

The idea behind this manual classification is as follows:

If I know four properties of 50 different instances of the same flower, I can teach them to identify new instances of this flower.

This is exactly what we want to do with machine learning.

 The Iris dataset is available at `http://archive.ics.uci.edu/ml/datasets/Iris`.

To create a predictive model based on the iris dataset, proceed as follows:

1. Download data from the link mentioned earlier.

2. Insert a new line on top of the text file to create a header:

   `sepal_l,sepal_w,petal_l,petal_w,flower`

3. Sign up for a free or standard machine learning workspace and go to `https://studio.azureml.net`.

4. Create a new DataSet (**+NEW | DataSet**) as follows:

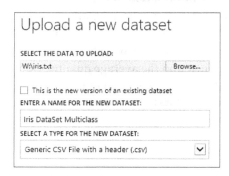

5. Create a new experiment (**+NEW | Experiment | Blank experiment**) and add an **Iris DataSet Multiclass** block and a **Split Data** block. Connect the output spot of the first in the input point of the second.

6. Configure the split data at 0.7 fraction and set up the stratified split to the column `flower`.

7. Add a **Multiclass LogisticRegression** block, a **Train Model** block, and a **Score Model** block. Connect the output spot of the first one to the left input spot of the second one. Connect the left output spot of the **Split Data** block to the right input spot of the **Train Model** block. Connect the output spot of **Train Model** to the left input spot of **Score Model**. Connect the right output spot of **Split Data** to the right input spot of **Score Model**.

8. In the **Train Model** block, launch the column selector, choose the `flower` column, and run the experiment.

9. After the process completes, right-click on the **Score Model** output spot and select **Visualize**.

Steps 1 to 5 are pretty straightforward. In step 6, we configured a block that splits the data into two separate sections. We do this to have a part of the set to feed the training and another part to verify that the output model has been set up correctly, testing/scoring it using the unused data. We divide data into 70 percent/30 percent, and through the **Stratified split** option, we instruct the splitter to perform it equally on the `flower` column.

In fact, since the splitter uses a random process, it can even take its 70 percent of rows with this pattern:

*   50 rows of Setosa
*   50 rows of Virginica
*   5 rows of Versicolor

This is clearly a bad split, since there are just five rows to train the Versicolor variant and the remaining 45 rows (to score the model) cannot score the Setosa and Verginica variants.

In step 7, we used logistic regression. We actually don't know whether it is the best choice for the given dataset. In step 8, we told the trainer to use the column in the dataset to predict the column `flower`, which is our classification result.

To evaluate the efficiency of the logistic regression, we can add an **Evaluate Model** block and connect the **Score Model** output spot to its left input spot. The following screenshot represents the accuracy of the model:

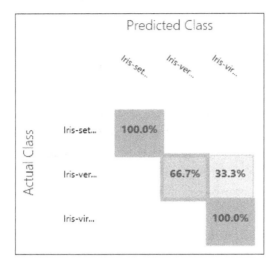

Repeating steps 7 and 8 using a different algorithm (that is, **Multiclass Neural Network**) in parallel to the previous one, we can set the right input spot of the **Evaluate Model** block with the output spot of the second-line **Score Model** block, to compare the two models and find the one that suits better.

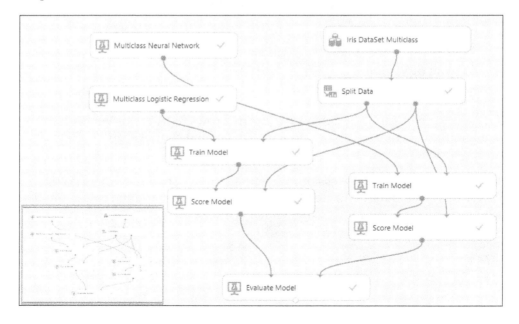

From the following result, neural networks seem to be more efficient for this dataset even with the default configuration:

We now have a good predictive model for the three iris variants (Setosa, Virginica, Versicolor). Using this result, we can build an application that uses this model to provide immediate result.

Imagine a botanical web application asking its users for the flower type. If the user does not know which variant of Iris flower theirs is, they can manually measure the properties of the actual flower by filling in a form like this one:

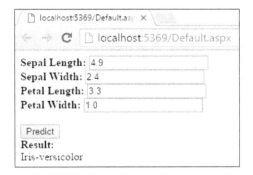

Under the hood, the web application calls the Azure ML web service to classify the input data and tells the user which variant they have.

To do this, proceed as follows:

1. Select the **Train Model** block, which best fits the problem of iris classification (the one from neural networks).

2. Publish the model as **Predictive Web Service**, as shown in the following screenshot:

3. Finally, deploy the web service to obtain the API key to call it later.

Once the web Service has been deployed, two default endpoints are available:

- **Request/Response**: This is the fastest way to retrieve a prediction, and it is the preferable way if data is needed in real time

- **Batch Execution**: This way is preferable to predict a huge group of many items

Each endpoint has its own API help page, where there is complete documentation on how to interact with the service. For reference purposes only, this is the sample code in C#:

```
public class StringTable
{
  public string[] ColumnNames { get; set; }
  public string[,] Values { get; set; }
}
static void Main(string[] args)
{
  var cl = newHttpClient();
  var url = "[service uri]";
  var token = "[api key]";

  var scoreRequest = new
  {
    Inputs = new Dictionary<string, StringTable>()
    {
      {
```

```
            "IrisProperties",
            new StringTable()
            {
              ColumnNames = new string[]
                {"sepal_l", "sepal_w", "petal_l", "petal_w","flower"},
              Values = new string[,]
                {  {"4.9", "2.4", "3.3", "1.0","0" }  }
            }
        },
      },
    GlobalParameters = new Dictionary<string, string>()
      {
      }
  };

  cl.DefaultRequestHeaders.Authorization =
    new AuthenticationHeaderValue("Bearer", token);

  var resp = cl.PostAsync(url, new StringContent(
    JsonConvert.SerializeObject(scoreRequest),
    Encoding.UTF8, "application/json"))
  .GetAwaiter().GetResult();
  var result = resp.Content
  .ReadAsStringAsync().GetAwaiter().GetResult();
}
```

> You may notice from the code that we need to pass it even a fake value for the flower property. However, this should be avoided for two reasons: first, because flower is not a feature but the class to predict and second, because it may confuse the client while calling the web method. However, omitting it causes an exception on the service side. So, why is it needed? Because we created the web service with default settings, without customization. As a tip, go to the predictive experiment and use the **Project Column** block to refine the input parameters of the web service.

To better understand what's behind machine learning, we suggest that you study the famous machine learning course of Stanford University, freely available online (at the time of writing this book) by Professor Andrew Ng. If you have already read it, you can even use the machine learning algorithm cheat sheet, available at http://download.microsoft.com/download/A/6/1/A613E11E-8F9C-424A-B99D-65344785C288/microsoft-machine-learning-algorithm-cheat-sheet-v6.pdf.

Outsourcing Identity and Access Management

I've been working for a decade with companies struggling to implement complex custom solutions for IAM. The reason is probably because standards arrived just in recent years; before, it was too easy to implement a custom solution to look ahead to the complexity and the total cost of ownership that a custom IAM may hide.

Let's recap the basic features of a (custom or out-of-the-box) IAM solution:

- Identify an individual
- Assign roles or, generally, attributes to those individuals
- Grant a valid pass to enter the application

In addition to these features, an IAM solution must provide users with a generic framework to build the company's applications by segregating the responsibilities of who develops an application and who owns the IAM process.

Tons of custom applications may handle a login in this way:

```
public static AuthUser CheckIdentity(string username, string password)
{
using (var ctx=new UserContext())
{
var user = ctx.Users.Find(username);
if (user != null && user.Password == password) return user;
else return null;
    }
}
```

The caller then puts the resulting object somewhere, using it later to check actual permissions.

Why is this approach wrong? Because the responsibility of the identity check lies with code running in the same application using it, requiring the redeployment of a potentially huge number of applications if something changes, for example, in the underlying database.

The following are changes that may occur on the preceding code:

- Developers realize that each application should pass its own identifier, to let the method apply the appropriate logic.
- Businesses require to integrate Facebook login, where the username and password are not passed to the application as the authentication workflow is completely different.

- Architects want to route those checks on a fast storage (like a cache) to increase performance and reduce the database workload. This simple feature introduces:

  ○ Code enhanced to read the `AuthUser` from the cache

  ○ Code enhanced to invalidate the cache in every single spot where the logged user changes the password for profile information

> The list of disadvantages is very long, but it is hard to understand them correctly if the running application is, for example, just one. With many applications, a single change request involving identity management may compromise hundreds of applications (requiring to traverse through them all).

- In multi-tenant applications, some users may also be routed to another store (that is, based on the tenant ID).

Under those considerations, we may look at IAM as an independent actor in the company's big picture, as shown in the following figure:

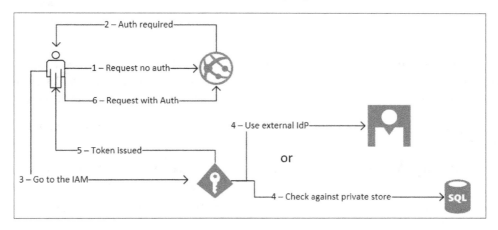

Looking at the IAM component (the one with the "key tile") as an external, independent actor, we also may consider it as an outsourced resource.

Azure AD and claims-based authentication

Let's start by describing what Azure AD is not. It is not a managed version of the Windows Server Active Directory. Though it resembles the name, Azure AD is "just" an IAM service managed and hosted by Microsoft in Azure. We should not even try to make a comparison, because they have different scopes and different features. It is true that we can link Azure AD with an on-premise active directory, but just for the purpose of extending the on-premise AD functionalities to work with Internet-based applications.

To better focus on the role of Azure AD, look at this figure:

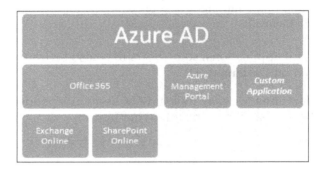

As you can see, different applications can use Azure AD as their IAM solution to provide authentication/authorization for web applications and services. As Office 365 or Azure itself uses it to authenticate users, a custom application can do that too.

You should have a sufficient knowledge of claims-based authentication to continue reading this chapter, but let's explain some basics:

- **Identity**: A set of properties that identifies a user along with its attributes, if any
- **Claim**: a piece of identity information, such as the e-mail address of a user or the role within an organization

With claims-based authentication, a simple workflow is:

1. The user asks for the resource located at a URL.
2. The application located at this URL checks whether, in the HTTP request, a valid token was issued and considered *trusted*.
    1. If not, it redirects the user to the identity provider, which can be another website, trusted by the application.
    2. The identity provider now validates the user credentials (prompting a web page, for example).

3. In the case of successful authentication, the identity provider issues a document, called a Security Token, where it puts the user information and an arbitrary number of claims, with the properties of the user.

4. Before redirecting to the application, the provider signs the token with its private key to certify the validity of information.

3. The application receives a security token. It checks whether the signature is valid (with the public key of the issuing authority).

 When can a token be considered valid? The application receiving a token must verify whether it is in the expected format, if it has not expired yet and if it has not been tampered by someone in the middle (or even generated by someone else). Steps 1 and 2 are about parsing, while step 3 is about verifying, with the proper key, whether the signature that came with the token is valid.

4. If a valid security token is found, the application reads who is the user making the request and what its properties are.

With this technique, there is no need to implement identity logic in the application, since it is completely demanded to the **Identity Provider (IdP)**, as follows:

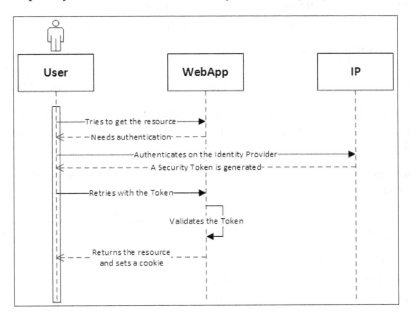

The free e-book *A Guide to Claims-Based Identity and Access Control (Second Edition)* is a good read to start using claims-based architectures. The web-based content is also available at https://msdn.microsoft.com/en-us/library/ff423674.aspx.

Think about the basic scenario where we develop a custom web application, thinking about every aspect, except identity. We would like to completely outsource the authentication process, along with the whole set of related subprocesses, such as the registration of a new user, the password recovery workflow, and the possibility of a strong-authentication mechanism (that is, multi-factor). If this is an aspect, we are supposed to plug it without touching the code. This is why claims-based security is a good choice while implementing an authentication strategy for web applications.

Azure Active Directory B2C

Azure AD is a great choice to extend the on-premise active directory with a claims-based infrastructure (to serve web-based scenarios more effectively). It is also very useful to outsource the IAM process to a reliable and managed infrastructure. However, while developing real B2C applications, some exceptions may arise:

- There is no support for self-service registration
- Output claims (the claims coming from the IdP) are limited to a few
- Some features (that is, self-service password reset) are available only with premium plans
- There is no built-in support for custom IdPs other than Azure AD itself

We can say that Azure AD was born to accomplish B2B scenarios, where the identities to manage are the ones of the owning organization or, at least, of external partners.

Imagine now you have to build the claims-based IAM infrastructure of your company. This could be the development to-do list:

- Build a custom registration process with the attributes required for registration
- Build an e-mail-validation process to confirm user opt-in
- Build a self-service process, such as *reset my password*
- Build a custom login process against the underlying provider
- Integrate external IdPs, such as Facebook, Twitter, and LinkedIn

At the end of the list (that is just a summary of the most relevant steps), someone may ask, "What if I need to customize all the properties (user attributes, external IdPs, registration/login pages, and so on) based on the caller application?" In other words, can all the processes be aware of the caller application and react consequently by showing a different IAM process (but using the same shared identity infrastructure)?

This is probably the hardest requirement to implement in the case of developing an IAM on our own, so this is another good reason to outsource the whole process.

From the Azure Documentation:

> *Azure Active Directory B2C is a comprehensive cloud identity management solution for your consumer-facing web and mobile applications. It is a highly available global service that scales to hundreds of millions of consumer identities. [...] In the past, application developers who wanted to sign up and sign in consumers into their applications would have written their own code. And they would have used on-premises databases or systems to store usernames and passwords. Azure Active Directory B2C offers developers a better way to integrate consumer identity management into their applications with the help of a secure, standards-based platform and a rich set of extensible policies. Using Azure Active Directory B2C allows your consumers to sign-up for your applications using their existing social accounts (Facebook, Google, Amazon, LinkedIn) or by creating new credentials (email address & password or username & password); we call the latter "local accounts".*

 At the time of writing this book, Azure AD B2C is in preview. Features may change considerably with the general availability.

In the next few pages, we will configure Azure AD for the company **CloudMakers. XYZ**. CM, despite working as a service provider for many clients, needs a central Azure B2C solution to centralize the identity management of the upcoming web and mobile applications.

 Since CM is a fictitious scenario, to simplify the contents, we will talk about the generic App1 as the web application to integrate with Azure AD B2C.

An Azure AD B2C directory can be created from the old portal (`https://manage.windowsazure.com`), by selecting the flag in the following screenshot:

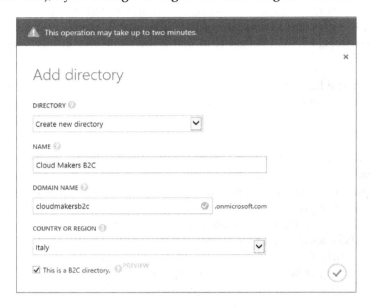

However, it can be managed using the new portal (`https://portal.azure.com`). To access it, locate this link in the directory pages:

In the following figure, the basic building blocks of Azure AD B2C are explained:

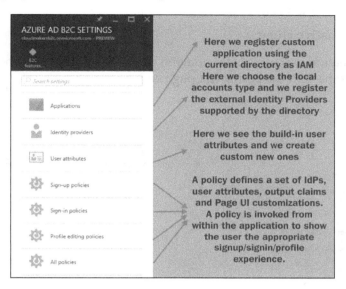

We start by creating a simple sign-up policy with local accounts as follows:

1. Add a new policy from the **Sign-up** policies blade.

2. Enter P001 as the policy name.

3. Select **Email signup** as the Identity Provider (it should be the only one available at the moment).

4. Select all the sign-up attributes (**City, Country/Region, Display Name, Email Address, Given Name, Job Title, Postal Code, State/Province, Street Address**, and **Surname**).

5. Select **Given Name, Surname**, and **Email Addresses** as the application claims.

> The difference between steps 4 and 5 is that, in step 4, we asked for some attributes to be completed by the user during the sign-up process. In step 5, we specified which attributes are passed to the requesting application as claims.

To test this policy, a new application is needed, so proceed to create a new one named **App1**, with the following options:

- **Name**: App1
- **Include web app / web API**: Yes

- **Allow implicit flow**: No
- **Redirect URIs**: http://localhost:8080
- **Include native client**: No

Confirm the creation and optionally note the client ID coming from the save process. You can now go back to the policy test page and run it:

The authorization URI has this form:

```
https://login.microsoftonline.com/[directory].onmicrosoft.com/oauth2/
v2.0/authorize?p=[policyName]&client_Id=[appId]&nonce=defaultNonce&re
direct_uri=[redirectUri]&scope=openid&response_type=code&prompt=login
```

The URL has the following aspects:

- directory is the B2C directory name (we created "cloudmakersb2c" previously)
- policyName is the name of the policy to apply (we created P001 previously)
- appId is the client ID of the application (we created App1 previously)
- redirectUri is (one of the) URI(s) of the selected application

After following the registration flow, we are redirected here:

```
http://localhost:8080/?code=[code]
```

The code is the authorization code that the app requested. The app can use this code to request an access token for a target resource.

Advanced features

In the previous section, we have set up a basic sign-up workflow, using local accounts with the built-in mechanism to store identities based on e-mail addresses (also the username and password are supported).

Let's now extend this capability by adding a couple of external Identity Providers:

- **Facebook**:
    1. Go to `https://developers.facebook.com/`.
    2. Add a new app for a website.
    3. In the **Site URL** field, enter the `https://login.microsoftonline.com/` value.
    4. Note the app ID and app secret displayed.
    5. In the **Valid OAuth redirect URI** field, enter the `https://login.microsoftonline.com/te/[directory]/oauth2/authresp` value (where the `directory` parameter is your tenant name).

- **LinkedIn**:
    1. Go to `https://developer.linkedin.com/`.
    2. Click **Create Application** and fill with the appropriate settings.
    3. Note the client ID and client secret.
    4. Select the **r_emailaddress** permission in addition to the default ones.
    5. In the **Authorized Redirect URL** field, enter the `https://login.microsoftonline.com/te/[directory]/oauth2/authresp` value (where the `directory` parameter is your tenant name).

Now, in Azure portal, perform the following steps to add Identity Providers for Facebook:

1. Add a new provider in the **Identity Providers** blade.
2. Select **Facebook** as the Identity Provider type.
3. In the **Set up this identity provider blade**, enter the client ID and client secret.

Do the same for LinkedIn too, and with these two new external identity providers registered into the B2C directory, we can now create new sign-up and sign-in policies that use them.

During the sign-up process, Azure AD checks the incoming claims from the external IdP and automatically fills the user attributes with the ones matching (that is, the LinkedIn IdP provides Azure AD with the `Job Title` attribute, as long as Facebook provides first and last names). However, the remaining fields have to be completed by the user explicitly, during the two-step registration flow.

Finally, we would like to customize the UI of the sign-in page, using the specific feature of Azure AD B2C. Since the governance of the authentication process should stay on the Azure side, it is conceptually wrong to create a custom page with server-to-server backend calls to manage authentication. It is also wrong to put hard-coded sign-in URIs into custom web pages, since they can be subject to change.

Hence, the idea behind UI customization is as follows (based on **Cross-origin resource sharing (CORS)**):

- We create a custom UI page with no logic (nor JS) but placeholders
- We specify that page URI into Azure AD
- The Azure AD sign-in page will run in the client browser and, via JavaScript, it will load the page contents and style from the previously specified location

 CORS is a mechanism that allows cross-origin requests from the browser code. To test it, go to `http://client.cors-api.appspot.com/client`.

To test this scenario, we can download the sample HTML UI customization available at `https://azure.microsoft.com/en-us/documentation/articles/active-directory-b2c-reference-ui-customization-helper-tool/`.

We edit the `Index.html` file like this one:

```
<!DOCTYPE html>
<html>
  <head>
  <title>Home</title>
  <meta http-equiv="X-UA-Compatible" content="IE=edge"/>
  <meta http-equiv="content-type" content="text/html;
    charset=utf-8"/>
  <meta name="apple-mobile-web-app-capable" content="yes"/>
  <link href="[absoluteURI]/auth/CSS/styles.css"
    type="text/css" rel="stylesheet"/>
  </head>
  <body>
```

```
<div id="logo">
  <p id = "logoTitle">
  <imgsrc="[absoluteURI]/auth/Images/logo.png"/>
   CloudMakers</p>
</div>

<div id="api" data-name="IdpSelections">
  <div>
    <ul id="menu">
      <li>
        <button class="accountButton"
          id="LinkedInExchange">LinkedIn</button>
      </li>
      <li>
        <button class="accountButton"
          id="FacebookExchange">Facebook</button>
      </li>
      <li>
        <button class="accountButton"
          id="SignUpWithLogonEmailExchange">Email</button>
      </li>
    </ul>
  </div>
</div>
</body>
</html>
```

We add those two CSS directives in the `styles.css` file:

```
#LinkedInExchange{
  background-image: url("../Images/ms.png");
}

#LinkedInExchange:hover{
  background-image: url("../Images/ms_mouseOver.png");
}
```

Then, we upload the contents to a public blob container and enable CORS on it. Once we do this, `Index.html` is published at a URL like this:

```
https://cloudmakers.blob.core.windows.net/auth/Index.html
```

We put it into the **Page UI customization** blade of the selected sign-in policy:

This customization process is available for sign-in (IdP selection, error), sign-up (IdP selection, local account sign-up, social account sign-up, error), and profile editing (IdP selection, profile update, error) policies.

Summary

In this chapter, we talked about two important areas where the development effort often goes: input management and identity management. We looked at how to build a resilient and scalable order-ingestion system and how to integrate data into a different data store. Through machine learning, you learned how to predict data (and how to apply it to real-business data). With Azure AD B2C, you finally learned how to outsource the identity management to **Identity-as-a-Service (IDaaS)**.

In the next chapter, we will look at how to enhance mobile application development with Microsoft Azure, Visual Studio, and open source technologies.

5
Building the Mobile Experience

In previous chapters, you have discovered how we can develop cloud services and web applications that can be consumed with browsers installed on a desktop or mobile computer. The revolution started with the introduction of smartphones has introduced two new ways of consuming the Web: mobile browsers and mobile apps. In this chapter, we will discover the world of mobile app development from the hybrid app point of view. We'll also discover how Azure helps mobile developers with vertical scenario services to simplify and accelerate app release and management.

In this chapter, you will learn:

- How to develop hybrid mobile apps with HTML5, JavaScript, and Visual Studio Tools for Apache Cordova
- How to create fast and easy vertical cloud services for mobile applications if you are a focused mobile developer
- How to code Azure services in Node.js

The technical community case study

SQL Saturday is a technical event, where IT developers and professionals, typically in hourly-based sessions, present technical content about SQL Server and other data-oriented content. It is a community event organized in a city, by some tech people once a year. It's a spare time activity for those tech people, based on sponsorship and volunteer contribution.

There are many organizational issues: one of these is giving all information to attendees, such as general information, day scheduling, session information and session feedback. In general, all of this information can be given on paper: print off the scheduling and post it on the wall or print sheets so every attendee can take it. When the session is done, everyone picks up an evaluation sheet, completing it by using a pen and then putting it in a closed box. In this case, organizers need to rearrange all the sheets, read and compile a temporary Excel workbook, and have event and session statistics.

During the last event, attendees were asked if they could publish photos and messages on social networks to make some noise and help in making the event more visible: this is even more possible now that everyone has a smartphone connected to the Internet.

The idea is to allow every attendee carrying out all these tasks from their smartphone to use an app, but there is no app available about this. This brings up some "business" considerations:

- There is relatively little money from sponsor contributions, so money in general cannot be spent on software development. An app is a plus.
- It's a spare-time activity, so there is not much time to develop it.
- It's a one-off activity, so the app would only need to be used for just one day.

We can make some technical considerations:

- We need to develop a multiplatform app that runs on major smartphones
- An app produces data that needs to be collected
- Data collection is not regular during the day: there are some peaks once a session ends
- Data collection can be huge: this kind of event can bring one or two hundred people that give up-to-date feedback in a few moments of the day

As a general rule, these objectives can be reached with all technologies that we have already described in previous chapters. We have described generic, "horizontal" services that are valuable in every situation. But many times, there are resource constraints (time or money, in general) that need to be accomplished with vertical, more specialized services. They can be limited in functionality but are deployed more rapidly and in general, are more cost-effective.

Writing mobile applications

Developing a mobile application is a challenging activity, as we need to target some specific objectives.

The first one is **User eXperience (UX)**, which is how a user interacts and uses the application.

Smartphones have in general, a small visible surface, compared to regular PCs or at least notebooks. So specific attention is paid to which information is presented on a specific view of the application. Smartphones, paired with tablet-related devices, and the possibility to rotate the screen, impose a specific focus on the "responsiveness" of the application, that is, the ability to adapt content layout, as visibility or rearranging, to different and mutable resolution specification. This specifically means that orientation can change during the same running application, as the device can be rotated during usage. And generally, we cannot develop different versions for any specific resolution, as today we already have many different current resolution specifications available.

It is now common in this field to speak about:

- **Capability**: It is the current capability of the device, in terms of functions available, function specification, and limitations.
- **Touch and gestures**: It is the interaction with a device is not limited by a keyboard and mouse, as smartphones and tablets do not have a keyboard and mouse. Fingers, or our hand, are our input device, or at least a stylus, or, with modern hybrid devices, all of these at the same time.
- **Visibility**: It is what we need to show or hide because of space constraints.
- **Views**: Data needs to be represented, and different capabilities, visibilities, or inputs need different representations of the same information.

This information is about resource constraints. We speak about UX because all decisions that are needed to be taken because of resource constraints depend on how a user generally accepts the application.

In general, there is a common acceptance and sharing about the rules that regulate responsiveness of an application; but there is also generally little experience of the ability to create responsive user interfaces.

This text is not about User eXperience, so some decisions will be taken on experience, opportunity, and speed. We invite readers to extend their knowledge on the topic with specific content that can be easily found on the Internet

The second mobile application challenge is portability, which is how a software project can be reused for the different mobile platforms available. As a general rule, different platforms mean different software projects, as there are different mobile operating systems and platform services, development languages and software development kits are not compatible. This is the situation when developing native applications for mobile devices: this is how a device developer writes their apps and how professionals develop the most performant application possible. Performance can be measured as:

- Computing resource usage such as CPU, memory, and storage space for maximum performance
- Screen resource usage as specific UI gadgets can be used to represent some information
- Feature resource usage, such as camera, GPS, compass, and so on

Writing mobile applications is a modern career with many skills required, which in general, current traditional desktop applications developers (the legacy career that can be considered similar to mobile developer) do not have. Web Developers, on their own, already have a matured experience on issues typical of mobile development. Browser is a resource constrained environment that influences applications responsiveness. HTML pages can be consumed on screen of different sizes so that content should be rearranged consistently. Application functionalities should use specific browser features, or simulate them if features are missing.

Web developers have also solved the portability problem, as the application is defined in terms of web standards, such as HTML5, CSS3, and JavaScript.

Today, HTML5 represents modern content organization. Data is placed into the HTML5 markup language, feeding text, images, and references as raw as possible to be represented dynamically to the specific needs of screens and features that are available during usage. Data in markup is adorned by four markup metadata:

- **Tags**: Data organizational elements that are useful to navigate data.
- **The ID attribute**: A specific instance of the data, which can be referenced just once into a HTML5 document.

- **The name attribute**: The name of the data contained, which can be instantiated multiple times into a HTML5 document. It is not mandatory to specify a different ID for elements that refer to the same name.

- **The class attribute**: It is the semantic attribute that specifies the roles associated to the data.

CSS3 is the modern content presentation method. All data contained in HTML5 can be represented crossing current device capabilities (known as media queries) with metadata. The most theoretical description of the CSS3 rule is:

 Data contained in a specific composition of markup, inside a current media query, is represented specifying some style attributes....

JavaScript is considered by some as the "assembly language" of the web. Many development tools are becoming JavaScript code generators. The biggest moment for the language was the modern development of highly performing JavaScript virtual machines inside browsers, executing this interpreted language without suppressing other languages.

This portable nature of the Web has been used by different software producers to apply a new mobile application development approach with the notion of hybrid apps. Hybrid references the web technologies just described and is applied inside a smartphone with an app experience. The app experience refers to some specific features:

- The application is not consumed inside a generic Internet browser, but inside a dedicated app. Users do not need to type any web address to consume the application, they just need to select the app from their device console.

- In general, JavaScript code executed into a web browser is run in a sandbox, as resources outside that sandbox (outside the browser) are not accessible. All possible features available are mapped as JavaScript APIs. Web browsers expose a fixed set of features, such as local storage, audio, and high-performance graphics. New mobile devices have introduced a new set of features that also can be optional and the application has to handle this variability. These include camera, GPS, contact, calendar, and so on. The app needs to be authorized using these capabilities.

In general, native app developers are opposed to this approach, speaking about performance and the ability to implement all required functionality inside the app. But there is also a fraction of potential developers that are asked to develop a mobile application, reaching all target mobile platforms, without having all the different skills required.

On this wave of developers, Apache Foundation have funded the project that is today known as the Cordova Project. It is a framework that offers the application infrastructure a model to develop a mobile application and a model for plug-ins, the pluggable features that are required on the application basis. The code is written in JavaScript, the UI in HTML5 and CSS3. The app is mainly a customized browser view running as a store-based application with its features and constraints.

Microsoft has embraced this mobile application development (besides other models, such as the native model for Windows Phone 8.1 and Windows 10 mobile devices, or the Xamarin development model) including the Apache project into a specific Visual Studio 2015 extension and template.

Building a mobile app with Visual Studio Tools for Apache Cordova

Visual Studio 2015 (starting from the Community Edition) already contains Visual Studio Tools for Apache Cordova (TACO), and it is continuously updated as features are optimized and incremented. As with all projects in Visual Studio, we can create a new project from the menu item: **File | New | Project**:

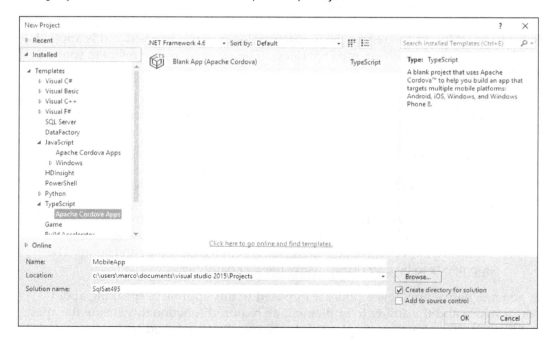

We can choose between two kinds of template groups, as in the JavaScript world the TypeScript superset language is also available. It is recommended to move on to TypeScript as we can obtain compiler and IDE support on strong typing.

The template is quite complex as it contains many different folders:

www is the main folder as it contains the core application structure as on ordinary HTML5 + CSS3 + JavaScript web sites. Typically, index.html is the main page from which the application starts.

Dependencies is a folder containing external packages of JavaScript software components downloaded from Bower (http://bower.io/). It is a central repository where all software component developers publish their code. Developers do not need to navigate elsewhere on the Internet, but just to this central repository. This is a general tool for JavaScript components, besides the usage inside a mobile application. There are some major advantages of using this way of management.

The first one is that Visual Studio integrates a **Bower Package Manager** (**BPM** – right-click from the project root in **Solution Explorer**) that contains a **Package search** tool.

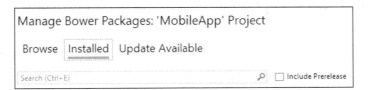

You can search by name, find it, and click on **Download**. The packages are copied in a local `bower_components` folder and registered by key and version in a `bower.json` file.

```
{
  "name": "MobileApp",
  "dependencies": {
    "bootstrap": "3.3.5",
    "font-awesome": "4.4.0"
  }
}
```

When the projects build, each bower package is copied under a `www/lib` folder to be referenced in the running application. The folder structure will be similar to the one shown in the following screenshot:

The `bower.json` file has two roles. The first one is managing the project under Visual Studio Team Service and configuring cloud-based builds or Continuous Integration; packages can be automatically downloaded by the services without the need to check inside the single project. The second one is that at any time we can go back to the BPM and check if referenced packages have some updates that can be automatically downloaded and referenced.

The file `config.xml` in the root folder contains the Cordova project-specific settings, about the interaction with the underline mobile OS and the specific features of each of the mobile platforms supported and plug-ins. These are specific packages that contain HTML5 and JavaScript resources to interact with local hardware services.

They provide a platform-agnostic API that decouples mobile developers from the specific platform details that make the custom code portable among the different OS versions.

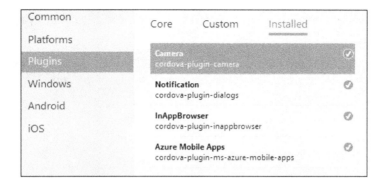

The `scripts` folder under the project is the custom code for the application. If the project code is written in the TypeScript language, it contains all the `.ts` code files. At each build, the compiler generates all the `.js` files, based on the `tsconfig.json` configuration file:

```
{
    "compilerOptions": {
        "noImplicitAny": false,
        "noEmitOnError": true,
        "removeComments": false,
        "sourceMap": true,
        "inlineSources": true,
        "outDir": "../www/scripts",
        "target": "es5"
    }
}
```

As many other dynamic languages, JavaScript does not have any static type information that is necessary to control code syntax in the editor and at the compiling stages. TypeScript has static type information for TypeScript code: but if you refers to Bower packages or plugins, written in JavaScript, you are still missing out on static information and IntelliSense support. For this work, TypeScript uses files with the extension `d.ts` as files containing typically TypeScript interfaces that completely describe packages in a typed manner, and that are contained under the `scripts/typings` folder.

A public open source effort contained in a GitHub repository (`https://github.com/DefinitelyTyped/DefinitelyTyped`) contains public contributions to more than 1,600 packages that are already typed and maintained. These typings are also contained in NuGet, so they can be downloaded directly in Visual Studio from NuGet Package Manager (`packages.json`) searching for `DefinitelyTyped` along with the package of interest.

In the `scripts` folder, there is an `Application.ts` file that contains the application module (in TypeScript terms). The file has the following code in it:

```
module MobileApp {
    "use strict";

    export module Application {
        export function initialize() {
            document.addEventListener("deviceready",
                onDeviceReady, false);
        }

        function onDeviceReady() {
            // handle the Cordova pause and resume events
            document.addEventListener("pause", onPause, false);
            document.addEventListener("resume", onResume, false);
            // todo: Cordova has been loaded. Perform any
                initialization that requires Cordova here.
        }

        function onPause() {
            // todo: This application has been suspended.
                Save application state here.
        }

        function onResume() {
            // todo: This application has been reactivated.
                Restore application state here.
        }
    }
}
```

It is necessary to handle the main global mobile app events exposed as JavaScript events:

- `deviceready`: Cordova is completely loaded, so plugins are already available and we can interact with device-specific features, such as the camera, accelerator, and so on.

- `pause and resume`: The two events that happen during app navigation when you get out of or reenter the app. We need to remember that the smartphone is considered a resource-constrained device, so resources must be saved. Every time you close an app (for example, clicking on an anchor and getting redirected to the browser, or receiving a phone call) the app is paused and the state must be serialized on a storage device. Doing this is a dev experience, as an automatic task cannot know what to store when pausing and what to restore on resume.

The entry point for the events is exposed as an `initialize` function that can be invoked on the `windows.onload` event as we are inside a browser:

```
window.onload = function () {
    Application.initialize();
};
```

Now that we have a substantial overview on how the Cordova project is organized, we can proceed with application development. As this is an HTM5 + CSS3 application we need content organization and presentation. Cordova does not force any decision and you freely start from scratch implementing HTML5 code. To improve productivity and access to a multitude of open contributions on the Internet, a good starting point is using Bootstrap (http://getbootstrap.com) and you can download it from Bower. We have already used it in previous chapters. You can find many app themes implemented over it. What is important is that Bootstrap contains semantics in terms of predefined classes that manage the responsiveness of the app, allowing the framework to rearrange contents due to running screen resolution and orientation changes.

We can define a generic HTML page inside a mobile app as a bunch sequence of section tags that contains the content groups of a page. Inside it, the HTML is adorned with bootstrap classes:

```
<section id="about">
    <div class="container">
        <div class="row">
```

```
            <div class="col-lg-12 text-center">
                <h4>Welcome to #SqlSat495, Pordenone 2016</h4>
            </div>
        </div>
        <div class="row">
            <div class="col-lg-4 col-lg-offset-2">
                For the third time the PASS SQL Saturday went
from Pordenone. Like last year the event will be held in February
(Saturday 27) and will be, as is customary, completely FREE. Needless
to say, the contents are very diverse. However we tried to keep a
pretty simple form of separation of the three available tracks. The
location is still the University Consortium of Pordenone (see below
for details) and we will have three classrooms fully dedicated to the
event. But let's digress…

            </div>
        </div>
    </div>
</section>
```

What is specific for apps is the col-xx-xx classes in class attributes in div
tags. These are the classes that are controlled by the CSS3 media queries that make
an app responsive.

> It is not an objective of this text to teach how to make an app
> responsive. There is a lot of content on the Internet to learn from or
> refer to text books such as: https://www.packtpub.com/web-
> development/bootstrap-essentials.

Typically, a responsive application that needs to respond to a small screen contains a
navigation bar that can collapse to the typical "hamburger" button:

```
<nav class="navbar navbar-default navbar-fixed-top">
    <div class="container">
        <!-- Brand and toggle get grouped for better mobile
          display -->
        <div class="navbar-header page-scroll">
            <button type="button" class="navbar-toggle"
              data-toggle="collapse" data-target=
              "#bs-example-navbar-collapse-1">
                <span class="sr-only">Toggle navigation</span>
                <span class="icon-bar"></span>
```

```
                <span class="icon-bar"></span>
                <span class="icon-bar"></span>
            </button>
            <a class="navbar-brand" href="#page-
                top">#SQLSAT495</a>
        </div>

        <!-- Collect the nav links, forms, and other content
            for toggling -->
        <div class="collapse navbar-collapse" id="bs-example-
            navbar-collapse-1">
            <ul class="nav navbar-nav navbar-right">
                <li class="hidden">
                    <a href="#page-top"></a>
                </li>
                <li class="page-scroll">
                    <a href="#about">About</a>
                </li>
                <li class="page-scroll">
                    <a href="#what-is-new">What's new</a>
                </li>
                <li class="page-scroll">
                    <a href="#sessions">Sessions</a>
                </li>
                <!--<li class="page-scroll">
                    <a href="#goodies">Goodies</a>
                </li>-->
                <li class="page-scroll">
                    <a href="#contact">Contact</a>
                </li>
            </ul>
        </div>
        <!-- /.navbar-collapse -->
    </div>
    <!-- /.container-fluid -->
</nav>
```

This is a configured navigation container of HTML local anchors that refers to the defined sections adorned with the id attribute. Every click on the Navigation bar, typically locked on the top of the screen, takes you directly to the specific section of the page.

A typical app can be defined in two ways:

- **As a single page application**: This means that the application has a single HTML page (such as index.html) and all content is managed via code contained in Application.ts.

- **As a web site application**: This means that content is mainly statically contained in many different HTML files. In this case, code must be organized into more .ts files.

Here, we will adopt the second approach. Every page (for example index.html) has a related index.ts code module that compiles to index.js. It can be defined as:

```
module MobileApp {
    "use strict";

    export module Index {
        export function initialize() {
            // invoke some custom code
            do_something();
        }

        function do_something(): void {
            //
        }
    }

    window.onload = function () {
        Application.initialize(); // reattach application events
          for the page
        Index.initialize(); // initialize specific page code
    };
}
```

As HTML content, JavaScript code must be referenced (only the main code block is presented, the others are omitted for simplicity):

```
<!-- bower dependent lib code for HTML and JavaScript lifetime
  content -->
<script src="lib/jquery/dist/jquery.js"></script>
<script src="lib/bootstrap/dist/js/bootstrap.js"></script>
```

```
<!-- Cordova reference, this is added to your app when it's
  built. -->
<script src="cordova.js"></script>
<script src="scripts/platformOverrides.js"></script>
<!-- application page specific code -->
<script src="scripts/application.js"></script>
<script src="scripts/index.js"></script>
```

Now that the initial content is defined, it's time to test the app for the first time. As we need to target the three major mobile platforms, we need to use all the different devices to test it. As it is expensive testing code during development, with all the different devices connected to dev machines and it's quite heavy and longer deploying an app to the remote device, it's common in a mobile dev experience using emulators. These are complex pieces of software that emulate the hardware platform, giving developers the experience of the real device. Emulation is a complex software creation art and it's never completely correct. But we can consider that all the major developments, up to an arbitrary 90% or 95% of the development activity, can be done with emulators, right up to the end of the development period, testing over the real platform. There are many emulation opportunities: one of these is Ripple, a mobile emulator that is hosted inside Google Chrome and emulates either iOS or Android devices. Testing in an emulator is equivalent, in Visual Studio, to running the app. So pressing the *F5* key is enough to run it. The first time, or in the late dev activity stage, we can configure which device to emulate:

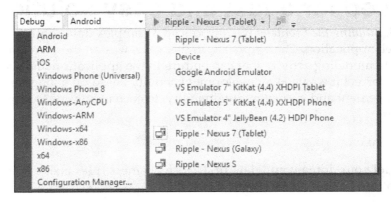

The result is like this:

The need for a fast and easy solution

In *Chapter 3, Building the Frontend* we introduced a complex data solution for a frontend web application. The emphasis, in that case, was on the correctness of the frontend data modeling activity that can endure in the application lifetime. This approach is correct if we need a development activity based on a long-term vision of cost management and correct maintainability, to correct bugs or to implement new features.

As a general rule:

- Model your domain and data first, close business rules inside a domain, and then think about applications, if possible
- Develop your application and model data according, to application usage if really needed

There are some scenarios where this activity is not cost-effective:

- **Prototyping**: This is necessary to prove the idea so the emphasis is on composing the application and verifying the idea, not fine-tuning the entire solution.

- **Short-term application**: This is when time is constrained and we need to have a functional application as fast as we can.

- **Mobile development**: In a modern, complex software world, mobile development is a vertical development scenario that requires specific development skills. It is mainly a frontend development that concentrates on UX, rather than backend plumbing. But a mobile experience is not useful if not connected. If a mobile developer cannot participate in a team with complete skills or does not possess specific web services skills, he needs some prefab vertical services to access basic cloud functionalities.

In this scenario, the focus is not on maintenance or a long-term data model. It is more on the application, and data is just a problem about object serialization and deserialization. The **Create-Read-Update-Delete** (CRUD) acronym gives a general, intuitive, rapid approach to operating on data with the four basic operations, moving data management responsibility out of the domain and typically moving in other tiers, for example presentation. We have two possibilities:

- Data is just a very simple data model, in the same way we can consider text files or Excel workbooks as a database

- Data is a view model, strongly dependent on presentation metadata and information, so a storage table is a sort of staging storage where data will be temporarily stored while waiting to be processed and imported into a corporate database

Introduction to mobile apps

Technically speaking, a mobile app is not different from a web App: it is part of App Services and it is a REST API service, over HTTP or HTTPS. Besides other common settings coming from App Services, mobile apps are characterized by a vertical set of features, implemented in App Services, that are typically required by a mobile application.

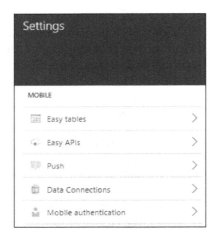

Easy tables (ET) is a bundle of a CRUD API service backed by the SQL Azure database or Azure Storage, with a client API capable of handling offline state, storing pending changes locally in the device with local storage, while there is a connection.

 At the time of writing, not all features are available to all platforms. For example, Cordova does not support offline data management, in our case.

You start defining a data row and Azure builds up an entity, the service handler, and the Web App to support it. The required initial configuration is just to create instances of the two functionalities a mobile app is built upon.

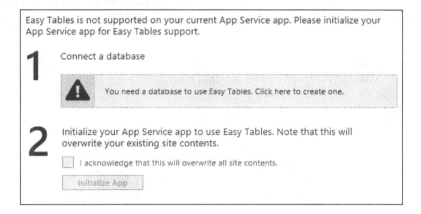

Choosing the database is specifically the selection of a data connection; the choice is between a SQL Azure database or Azure Storage. Because of this level of abstraction, we cannot pretend to configure a SQL database with all DBA criteria of strict strong typing or normalization. As a REST service, the database is just a mere JSON object persistence media that can enforce typing loosely.

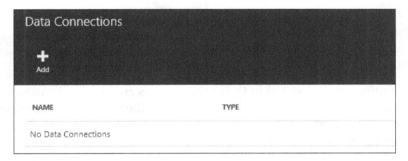

As pervasive in all Azure services, that depends upon a data connection, that can be selected from the existing one in the same subscription or created at the time of the app definition. There is no practical difference between choosing a SQL Azure Server or Azure Storage to persist service data, from an application experience. This is more dependent on how you process data after data acquisition.

 Azure Storage emphasizes the role of mobile services towards the data, as Azure Blob storage data takes forms as a log file.

So you can select an existing one if applicable.

All specific settings are persisted in the mobile app as custom application settings that can be changed after service creation. In case of the SQL Azure Connection String, the name is wired up as MS_TableConnectionString as recognized by the application template written in the mobile app.

When a data connection is established, we can proceed with the app creation. The mobile service is deployed, applying a predefined application template that supports the sequential addition of code, for each single table defined. It is based on code generating tasks (which we will see in the next chapter).

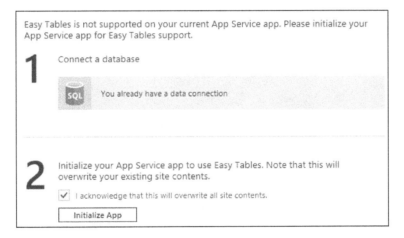

It will take some time to deploy the entire service; in the notification area, you can check deployment execution with a progress bar:

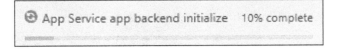

Now we can start adding easy tables:

The first thing we need to define is the table name and the access rights to it. As we can see, access rights are modeled on specific HTTP verbs, as any single operation is backed by a specific REST service method:

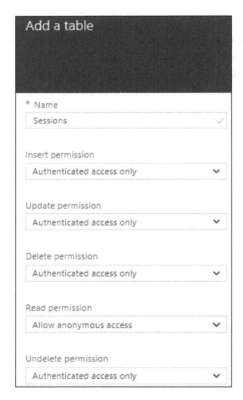

For every operation, there are three selectable options:

- **Allow anonymous access**: The access is public without any authentication.
- **Authenticated access only**: The access requires authentication (we will discuss authentication in the next chapter).

- **Disabled**: The HTTP verb is not applicable. For example, the delete operation can be disabled as we need to avoid it or implement some sort of "soft delete" with a `Boolean Deleted` field that we can use for filtering data.

Each operation can be selected independently according to an application scenario:

- Read only data (this means the table is filled up with data by the application developer)
- Append only (this means the service for data ingestion, when data will be processed by another application or service, distinct from the collecting application)
- Generic CRUD form editing

With the **Manage schema** functionality, we can define the structure of the entity container. Every entity we create already contains a set of fixed properties that mobile apps use for entity lifetime management:

- `Id, createdAt`: This is the identity index composition
- `Version, updatedAt`: This is an optimistic entity concurrency update management implementation
- `deleted`: This is a soft delete entity implementation

You can add properties to the entity that maps the column to the table. The property type is limited by JSON semantics, so the types are the typical TypeScript (or JavaScript) type system:

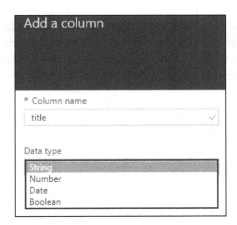

We can compose a session table that contains all information we need to compose a visible table. That's the main difference between this approach and what is described in *Chapter 3, Building the Frontend*. Entities (either SQL or Storage) are strictly created to support client user interaction, with data ready for presentation. In fact, for example, time can be expressed as a string already presented in textual form without formatting; it can be expensive fine-tuning that function in a client app.

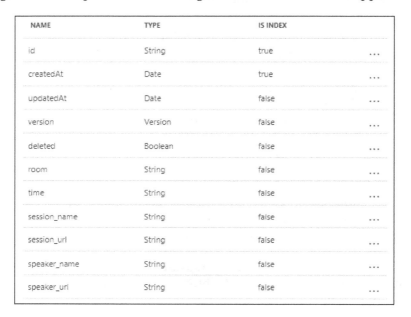

NAME	TYPE	IS INDEX	
id	String	true	...
createdAt	Date	true	...
updatedAt	Date	false	...
version	Version	false	...
deleted	Boolean	false	...
room	String	false	...
time	String	false	...
session_name	String	false	...
session_url	String	false	...
speaker_name	String	false	...
speaker_url	String	false	...

To populate the data, we remember that the table is backed by SQL Azure. Session information is public read-only data and it needs to be initially loaded once, not necessarily with a custom application, directly into the database. We can connect to SQL Azure from Visual Studio 2015, selecting the defined server and database:

Data can be prepared and copied, for example, from an Excel file and pasted directly into the table data editor:

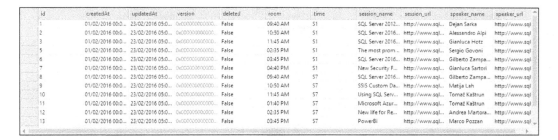

Getting data from the service

Now we are ready to connect our Cordova mobile app to the simple table just created and populated. Every mobile platform has its own connection SDK. In our case, we have chosen Cordova. So right-clicking from the project folder in Visual Studio 2015, we can open the command prompt and type the following command:

```
>cordova plugin add cordova-plugin-ms-azure-mobile-apps
Fetching plugin "cordova-plugin-ms-azure-mobile-apps" via npm
Installing "cordova-plugin-ms-azure-mobile-apps" for android
Fetching plugin "cordova-plugin-inappbrowser" via npm
Installing "cordova-plugin-inappbrowser" for android
>
```

This downloads the Cordova plug-in for mobile apps and references it from the project. Before proceeding with the code, we have to remember that we need to write Cordova code in Typescript, not just JavaScript. The plug-in code is just JavaScript: if we proceed in this way, when we type code working with the Azure mobile package we will not have any IntelliSense help from editors as type information is missing. TypeScript supports the reuse of JavaScript packages that miss out TypeScript type information, implementing the notion of TypeScript definitions. These are files that are referenced in code (such as C/C++ language header files), defining classes and interfaces that completes the original package code.

So, we need to add mobile app TypeScript definitions. There are so many JavaScript packages available and widely used on the Internet that Visual Studio and Microsoft cannot support all of them alone. Definitely Typed is an open source initiative that collects contributions from many developers worldwide. If a developer needs a TypeScript definition for a package but it is missing, he can undertake the hard work of creating a new definition file and then share it on DefititelyTyped, helping other developers by making things less tedious. The entire contributions are shared in a GitHub repository (`https://github.com/DefinitelyTyped/DefinitelyTyped`).

Type definitions are available as NuGet packages, so we can download and reference them inside Visual Studio and search for, `azure-mobile-apps.TypeScript.DefinitelyTyped` package:

The mobile service is exposed from a REST HTTP endpoint, typically `http://<servicename>.azurewebsites.net/` (if not, a second-level custom domain name is assigned).

This URL is useful to initialize the client proxy object that encapsulates the inner HTTP(S) logic to invoke and serialize/deserialize data.

```
var mobileAppsClient = new WindowsAzure.
    MobileServiceClient(   "http://sqlsat495.azurewebsites.net");
```

The client gives access to all vertical services exposed by mobile services: in our case, the table service. In this case, table service is exposed by another proxy that hides the internal complexity to communicate:

```
            var sessionsTable =
                mobileAppsClient.getTable("Sessions");
                Table object expose in Typescript an
                API that is quite similar LINQ for C#,
                as the already known function where,
                orderby, take, skip. read() are the
                materialization function, that converts
                the query exposed by the tool to some
                serialized/reserialized object.
module MobileApp {
    "use strict";
```

```
export module Index {
    export function initialize() {
        reload_sessions("http://sqlsat495.azurewebsites.net");
    }

    function reload_sessions(url:string): void {
        var mobileAppsClient = new
          WindowsAzure.MobileServiceClient(url);
        var sessionsTable =
          mobileAppsClient.getTable("Sessions");
        sessionsTable.read().then((result: any) => {
            var table = $("#sessions-table > tbody");
            $(result).each(function (index: number, element:
              any): any {
                var session_url: string = element.session_url;
                var sid: string =
                  /\d+/.exec(/sid=\d+/.
                  exec(session_url)[0])[0];
                var id = element.id;
                table.append("<tr><td><a href='" +
                  element.session_url + "'>" +
                  element.session_name +
                  "</a></td><td><a href='" +
                  element.speaker_url + "'>" +
                  element.speaker_name + "</a></td><td>" +
                  element.time + "</td><td>" + element.room +
                  "</td><td><a href='score.html?id=" + id +
                  "'>Score</a></td></tr>");
            });
        }, (error: any) => {
            alert(error);
        });
    }
}
```

Initialization functions are attached as callbacks for `window.onload` events, for a one-off initialization.

```
window.onload = function () {
    Application.initialize();
    Index.initialize();
};
}
```

Accessing the Internet from code is always considered harmful because we need to beware of malicious code that can put the device and other features at risk. Mobile apps run inside a sandbox that require the declaration of the endpoints need to be reached, stopping invocations that are not predefined. Cordova allows this, adding at page level a meta tag that declares which unsafe code can be executed, a list of patterns in JavaScript code that are allowed:

```
<meta http-equiv="Content-Security-Policy" content="default-
    src 'self' data: gap: https://ssl.gstatic.com 'unsafe-eval';
    style-src 'self' 'unsafe-inline'; media-src *; script-src
    'self' 'unsafe-inline' 'unsafe-eval'
    http://sqlsat495.azurewebsites.net">
```

The result is an HTML5 table filled dynamically, where the mobile page is loaded with data rows as expected:

SESSIONS

Title	Speaker	Time	Room	
SQL Server 2012-2016 Columnar Storage		S1	09:40 AM	Score
SQL Server 2016 JSON support		S1	10:50 AM	Score
The most prominent wait types of your SQL Server 2016 (IT)		S1	02:35 PM	Score
SQL Server 2016 Temporal Database Support (IT)		S1	11:45 AM	Score
SQL Server 2016: Maturazione dell'In-Memory OLTP		S1	03:45 PM	Score
New Security Features in SQL Server 2016		S1	04:40 PM	Score

If you click on any of the **Score** buttons, the application will switch to a **Detail** page needed to vote the session. The session data is reloaded for the specific speaker: the **Score** button contains the ID of the session that is useful to perform the query over data and get more details. The ID can be recovered directly from the URL:

```
var id: string = /\d+/.exec(/id=\d+/.exec(document.URL)[0])[0];
```

In this case, the dataset is the same, but could be different in general. Data needs to be reloaded. The `where` method can be used to compose a query and perform a specific filtering on an `id` attribute:

```
var mobileAppsClient = new WindowsAzure.MobileServiceClient(url);
var sessionsTable = mobileAppsClient.getTable("Sessions");
sessionsTable.where({
    "id": id
}).read().then((result: any) => {
    var element: any = result[0];

    $("#session_name").html(element.session_name);
    $("#session_url").attr("href", element.session_url);
    $("#speaker_name").html(element.speaker_name);
    $("#speaker_url").attr("href", element.speaker_url);
}, (error: any) => {
    alert(error);
});
```

Sending data to the service

The page is loaded and buttons are available to vote for the session. Pressing a **Vote** button is an invocation to the service to add a new row in the table, passed as a JSON object:

```
function vote_session(url: string, session_id: string, vote:
  string): void {
  var mobileAppsClient = new
    WindowsAzure.MobileServiceClient(url);
  var sessionsVotesTable =
    mobileAppsClient.getTable("SessionsVotes");
  sessionsVotesTable.insert({
    session_id: session_id
    ,
    vote: vote
  });
}
```

The function is referenced once per button; specifically, the **Vote** button refers to:

```
$(document).find("#vote_more").click(function () {
    var id: string =
    /\d+/.exec(/id=\d+/.exec(document.URL)[0])[0];
    vote_session("http://sqlsat495.azurewebsites.net", id,
        "more");
});
```

During a community event it is important to create a lot of "noise:" posting on the Internet, messages, photos, tagging people, and sharing contacts and emotions. Publishing content from participants reveals whether it's successful and can be useful to collect historical multimedia information. From the "pure web" application, only text can be collected immediately. Collecting photos is a little more "tricky." You already have photos in your storage; if not, you need to switch to the camera, take a photo, get back to the app, add metadata, and send it. Many people don't do this. It would be interesting if the app had this as a native feature.

The camera is one of the native capabilities a mobile app can access and make it customizable by the application. Camera usage is possible because there is a specific plugin supporting it. From the Cordova command line, we can add a camera support plugin:

```
D:\            >cordova plugin add cordova-plugin-camera
Fetching plugin "cordova-plugin-camera@2.1.0" via npm
Plugin "cordova-plugin-camera" already installed on android.
Plugin "cordova-plugin-camera" already installed on ios.
Plugin "cordova-plugin-camera" already installed on windows.
Plugin "cordova-plugin-camera" already installed on wp8.
D:\            >
```

Camera shoot is configurable via a JavaScript object using some parameters:

```
{
    quality: 100,
    destinationType: Camera.DestinationType.DATA_URL,
    sourceType: Camera.PictureSourceType.PHOTOLIBRARY,
    mediaType: Camera.MediaType.PICTURE,
    encodingType: Camera.EncodingType.PNG,
    saveToPhotoAlbum: true
}
```

There are some interesting parameters:

- `destinationType`: This lets us specify how to reference the captured photo that will be stored locally in the device. For app usage, `Camera.DestinationType.DATA_URL` is useful because photo bits are stored in a string formatted as a Base64-encoded URL. In our case, this is the best solution because we can reuse bits and send them to our service.

- `sourceType`: The same API can be reused to capture a photo with the camera or just selecting an existing photo from storage.

- `mediaType`: This allows us to select the camera mode, to shoot photos or videos.

- `encodingType`: This sets the image format, currently JPEG or PNG.

As a TypeScript or JavaScript API, the called function handles results asynchronously, giving the result image as a parameter of a callback function. We can wrap the camera invocation inside a custom function, only leaving open the possibility to handle the callback result:

```
function get_picture(handler: (data: string) => any): void {
    navigator.camera.getPicture(
        handler
        , function (error: string): void {
            navigator.notification.alert(error, (): void => {
            });
        },
        {
            quality: 100,
            destinationType: Camera.DestinationType.DATA_URL,
            sourceType: Camera.PictureSourceType.CAMERA,
            mediaType: Camera.MediaType.PICTURE,
            encodingType: Camera.EncodingType.JPEG,
            saveToPhotoAlbum: true
        }
    );
}
```

A new object can be composed and sent to the mobile service:

```
var picture_post: {
    hashtags: ['sqlsat495']
    , twitter_handles: [speaker_twitter]
    , photo: data
};
```

In the case of this object, we need to consider the biggest difference from the previous `session_vote` object: the size. A photo property that contains the Base64-encoded photo can be big. In general, we don't want to store this image inside a row in SQL Azure, as there is cheaper and more efficient storage to handle this kind of data: Azure Storage blobs. But we have already defined the use of simple tables backed by relational tables.

There is another opportunity inside mobile apps: the definition of a custom API, instead of using the fixed CRUD ET API. From the **Service** blade, we can add a new instance of a Photo API:

It's always an API, as we have the same verbs available with the same selectable permissions. The difference is with what is backing this particular API, as there are no other parameters that can be specified. The answer is under the **API details** blade, after the API is created where, besides representing the same parameters, we can find an **Edit script** button.

This button opens up an entire new environment named after the project name **Monaco**; it runs under the **App Services Kudu** environment:

This web IDE allows modifying already published service code directly on the service. It's an HTML5 + CSS3 + TypeScript developed environment that shows the entire folder-based structure. We can find our new API expressed in terms of two files (`Photos.js` and `Photos.json`). But it's also interesting seeing that the previously defined ET services are substantial API services on their own.

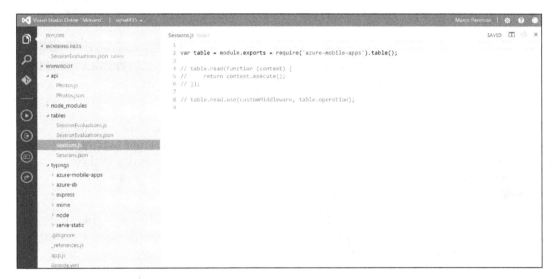

The language definition, as we can see, is TypeScript, and the entire environment runs under Node.js.

Azure and Node.js

The Node.js website (`https://nodejs.org/`) describes it as a JavaScript runtime built on Chrome's V8 JavaScript engine. `Node.js` uses an event-driven, non-blocking I/O model that makes it lightweight and efficient. It can be used inside a desktop application (for example, it runs Microsoft Visual Studio code, built on the Electron open source project) and inside Internet Information Server or Azure, handling requests and responses, from an HTTP connection, inside an HTTP Server service, for web applications or API applications.

With `Express.js` framework, Node.js can be considered as a competitor for Microsoft ASP.NET stack-based applications. They overlap in many ways but many considerations have to be made:

- Then resemblance that these languages share is a great reason to choose the language, so those confident with C# compared to JavaScript (or the TypeScript superset) can favor one language over another

- Besides the current Microsoft involvement with open source initiatives, JavaScript and Node.js are a great investment in an alternative language and environment, as Visual Studio 2015 currently deploys Node.js and JavaScript

- Microsoft is rebuilding all its tools (for example, ASP.NET Core 1.0 and NuGet) to the Node.js world, or embracing them, such as Grunt or Bower

- Technically speaking, Node.js, with a non-blocking I/O model, is a great performer for a front HTTP JSON service that dispatches calls to backend services; the ASP.NET model is more oriented to blocking I/O and CPU-intensive tasks, that need thread scheduling, and that Node.js does not support

Since the beginning of Azure websites and the underlying **Kudu** environment, JavaScript and Node.js have become Azure first-class citizens. The **Monaco** IDE is written entirely in JavaScript and Node.js and most commands depend on the *npm Node packages* system. Mobile services that generate code from the service configuration natively generate JavaScript code.

If we look inside what is generated behind the scenes, we will discover that mobile app extensions are built entirely over the Node.js structure of the project. Easy tables and custom APIs correspond to the folder structure of the service:

The `tables` folder corresponds to the easy tables, while the `api` folder corresponds to the custom API. This seems like a convention, but actually it is a configuration issue. If we look inside `app.js`, we will discover the nature of a Node.js application, enhanced by the Azure mobile app. The following code is similar to what you will find in the file:

```
var express = require('express');
var azureMobileApps = require('azure-mobile-apps');
var bodyParser = require('body-parser');

var app = express();
var mobile = azureMobileApps();
```

The `express` function is the main function object that builds up the main express framework web server object that handles all the HTTP requests. `require` is one of the main functions of the `Require.js` framework that handles all the module and dependency injection components in the JavaScript project. `azureMobileApps` is the function object that is an extension for `express` to handle the vertical specifications of the mobile apps service. `mobile` becomes the instance of the mobile services:

```
mobile.tables.import('./tables');
mobile.api.import('./api');
```

`mobile` is then configured from the `tables` folder, where the folder name is configured and updatable, like the `api` folder, with import function from relative `tables` and `api` objects. Inside the two folders, we can discover two kind of files: `<tablename>.json` and `<tablename>.js`.

The first one is the configuration file that describes the table service configuration, the same parameters we have already found in the blade portal configuration:

```
{
    "softDelete" : true,
    "autoIncrement": false,
    "insert": {
        "access": "anonymous"
    },
    "update": {
        "access": "disabled"
    },
    "delete": {
        "access": "disabled"
    },
    "read": {
        "access": "disabled"
    },
```

```
    "undelete": {
        "access": "disabled"
    }
}
```

These are parameters that are read and assigned to the instantiated objects as they can also be configured by code. These parameters can be changed directly from these files, as portals directly read from them, so there are no problems with service configuration consistency.

In the .js file, there is the main handling code. As Azure mobile service implements a complete mapping of CRUD operations over table storage in SQL Server and maps it to HTTP verbs, the code is just one line:

```
var table = module.exports = require('azure-mobile-apps').table();
```

But we can see that a `table` object is explicated as we can customize and handle the four CRUD operations. For example, in the case of a `read`, the basic handling is something like this:

```
table.read(function (context) {
    return context.execute();
});
```

Custom APIs are exactly the same. The configuration file removes the unnecessary table extensions, such as soft delete and auto increment, while sharing the same HTTP verb accessibility attributes. The .js file for an API is just an exposure of HTTP verbs in a JSON object:

```
module.exports = {
    get: function (req, res) {
        res.status(200).type('application/json').send({ currentTime:
Date.now() });
    }
}
```

To finally initialize the Node.js application, we initialize mobile tables and then pass the entire `mobile` object to an express app object. The app finally listens to HTTP requests:

```
mobile.tables.initialize()
    .then(function () {
    app.use(mobile);
    app.listen(process.env.PORT || 3000);
});
```

Now we are ready to implement our photo handler. We need to handle a POST request, as our Cordova mobile app will post a photo in the body. In detail, the photo will be a Base64-encoded binary image inside a JSON object, so data can travel with its metadata.

To handle a POST request with JSON-formatted information, we need to add another extension inside the `app.js` file. Node.js uses JavaScript and JSON to configure itself. To handle the JSON body, it is necessary to add a module that is written to do this. So it is necessary to add the following code to ensure that you have a correctly parsed `body` object inside a `request.body` object:

```
var bodyParser = require('body-parser');
app.use(bodyParser.json());
```

Now we can work on the POST request for storing a photo. It is posted to the service as a JSON body, with some metadata such as its filename. This handler is necessary as we are not required to persist the image in a SQL Azure table field, but it is more efficient for costs and performance for big binary files in Azure Storage. To reference the Azure Storage Node.js client SDK, we need to download the package with the `npm` command from the Monaco console:

```
\> npm install azure-storage
npm WARN package.json azure-mobile-apps-quickstarts.backend.node.EmptySite@0.0.1 No
README data
npm WARN package.json dateformat@1.0.2-1.2.3 No repository field.
npm WARN package.json eyes@0.1.8 No repository field.
npm WARN package.json string_decoder@0.10.31 string_decoder is also the name of a node
core module.
```

From the `Photos.js` file we need to reference the package with its required function. As Azure Storage is secured by Shared Access Signature, we need to read the `ConnectionString` from the Azure portal blade:

```
var azure = require('azure-storage');
var connectionString = "<azurestorageconnectionstring>";
```

Now we can implement the body of the post function. We need to instantiate the Blob service with `ConnectionString`, ensuring a reference to the Blob storage container. As the image is a string inside the body, we can use the `createBlockBlobFromText` function to store the data into the storage.

The method finally sends back an acknowledgement message to the client, completing it with an HTTP status that confirms the correctness of the operation:

```
module.exports = {
    post: function (req, res) {
        var photoName = req.body.photoName;
        var photoData = req.body.photoData;

        var blobService =
          azure.createBlobService(connectionString);
        var containerName = "sessionphotos";
        blobService.createContainerIfNotExists(containerName);
        blobService.createBlockBlobFromText(containerName,
          photoName, photoData);

        res.status(200).type('application/json').send( {
            "success": true,
            "photoName": photoName
        });
    }
};
```

Now back to the Cordova client; we can now complete the photo experience. As we need to invoke a custom API, we must fill in the photo information and the InvokeApiOptions object, which add specific custom API options, such as the method used to invoke the service. From the MobileServiceClient object, we can invoke the Photos API, with a specified options object.

```
$(document).find("#takePhotoAndShare").click((): void => {
    get_picture((photo: string) => {
        var options: Microsoft.WindowsAzure.InvokeApiOptions = {
            body: {
                photoData: photo
                , photoName: Date.now() + ".jpg"
            },
            method: "POST"
        };
        var url = "http://sqlsat495.azurewebsites.net";
        var mobileAppsClient = new
          WindowsAzure.MobileServiceClient(url);
        mobileAppsClient.invokeApi("Photos", options).done(
            (result: any): void => {
                alert("Picture posted");
            }
```

```
          , (error: any): void => {
              alert("ERROR:" + error);
          }
      );
   });
});
```

Summary

In this chapter, we explored the complete experience of a mobile solution development with the device app and the app service. We have approached a complete JavaScript and TypeScript language experience. On the client side, Cordova is a portable, multiplatform framework to develop a hybrid application; on the Azure side, a mobile app from app services can be developed as a Node.js application.

Our app and our service work with entities: what happens if data sent by clients is not in the form of stateful objects, but rather events that log something that has happened?

In the next chapter, we will explore the API experience in greater depth, writing more general, powerful, complex but maintainable, and long-term API projects.

Building the API Layer

6

It can be said that, these days, we have definitely been immersed into the API era. This period has been defined as the *API Economy*, the term corresponding to the SOA period. However, as many have experienced, this is not an "era" but a growing ecosystem of independent actors running complex software, exposing their interfaces through the REST API over HTTP.

Start-ups are building entire business models on top of API publishing, building communities of developers to raise attention for their API and boost their adoption.

APIs are ubiquitous due to the standardization process of protocols and formats for the underlying communication, which is now happening majorly via JSON over HTTP. This simple requirement enables almost every third-party technology to integrate with APIs, from legacy software written in an ancient language and framework to the latest mobile operating system. The only requirement is, in fact, to support HTTP, which is the most mainstream concept of IT today.

Though API development commonly tells us that it's easy to develop even complex integrations, this is only partially true. Today's technology enables us to develop APIs in almost any language and platform with minimal effort, while frameworks provide foundation services. However, building a good API involves some design skills and even strategic ones since the API (when public) represents a contract between you (the publisher) and others (the consumers). This is why many API-development activities, after going live, are actually related to maintaining specific endpoints with previous versions.

In this chapter, we'll cover the following topics:

- How to build a realistic scenario of API development
- Deployment and long-term management, with specific attention to this last aspect, which is often an underestimated part of the overall process

CloudMakers.XYZ scenario evolution

In the past few years, CM developed a proprietary GIS database with a huge amount of data. This has led to further discussion about building a software layer to monetize this data and, at the same time, build new business models around this evolving project.

After establishing that CM has the data in a format accessible through a business logic library written in .NET, it is now the goal of the company to expose this dataset through a REST API, adding features as they become available.

API business is important, and it deserves the respect of any other software engineering application field; so, do not start with coding!

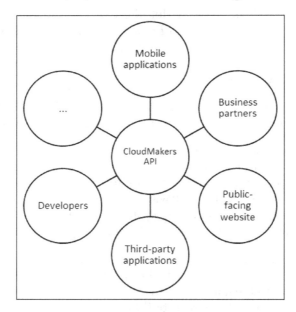

These are the main stakeholders of the CloudMakers API infrastructure. It is imperative to keep them in mind before designing the API representing a good strategy.

This is not rocket science, but some questions should be addressed before going forward:

- Who are the consumers of the API?
- Is the API a read-only API (for data consumption) or a read/write API (for data ingestion)?
    - ° In the latter case, authentication or authorization isn't an option
- Are we considering a private API or a public/open API?

 Private APIs are generally developed for business partners or internal usage only, while public/open APIs are developed to be used from a previously-unknown group of consumers (for example, the OpenWeatherMap API: `http://openweathermap.org/api`).

- Who are the consumers of the API?
- Are some of the end users paying users?
    - ° Are we planning to give support to the APIs?
- Can we introduce new features (or major changes) on existing APIs?

These seem like simple questions, but the corresponding answers can tell us:

- **How to write an API**: This can be done by embracing a pure REST approach, preferably with open APIs or a pragmatic REST approach. This problem is related to design and data formats and, eventually, to API documentation.
- **How to manage versions**: This can be done by declaring support and building a contract with consumers; an API cannot simply stop responding. This problem (and many others) is related to versioning.
- **How to manage user access**: This changes everything between a private/public API in terms of identity management. In the latter case, things are quite complex, and they are even more challenging in the presence of data ingestion. This point also has legal/compliance implications.
- **How to survive traffic**: With public APIs, new challenges arise in terms of performance and traffic management. In private APIs, or when the business case is predictable, this is a negligible aspect.
- **How to perform monitoring and billing**: If the usage of the API is related to billing, another interesting challenge must be addressed.

Despite this introduction, in the rest of the chapter we approach API development sequentially, starting with development, documentation, and deployment. Then, we introduce the importance of the API gateway using Azure API Management; finally, we look at some advanced concepts related to debugging complex API workflows using App Service and Azure Service Bus.

Building the API

A pure REST approach may use all of the HTTP methods detailed in the following table:

HTTP Verb	Sample URI	Task performed
GET	/cities/10	Retrieves the city with ID 10
DELETE	/cities/10	Deletes the city with ID 10
POST	/cities	Creates a new city
PUT	/cities/10	Updates the city with ID 10
PATCH	/cities/10	Performs a partial update to the city with ID 10
OPTIONS	/cities/10	Returns all the available operations on the city with ID 10
HEAD	/cities/10	Returns only the HTTP headers

However, in order to enforce compatibility with old clients of the platform with a restricted set of available HTTP options, we can also choose to be pragmatic and perform every operation with a single verb using HTTP headers to specify the operation, as follows:

```
POST http://api.cloudmakers.xyz/geo HTTP/1.1
Accept: application/json
x-cm-operation: PUT
```

This method requires an adapter at the API endpoint in order to provide routing to the appropriate operation type.

This approach applies to responses as well:

- With a pure REST approach, the API can return one status code from the dozens available in HTTP (that is, 405 Method not allowed, 413 Request Entity Too Large)

- With a pragmatic approach, the API can return just a subset of some main status codes (except the 200 OK), such as the following:

  ° 4xx Bad Request, Not found, Forbidden, and so on

  ° 5xx Internal Server Error, Service Unavailable, and so on

 An API developer can also decide to always return 200 OK, even in case of errors. In these cases, the error code and message can be wrapped into the response as a normal payload.

Using the ASP.NET Web API

The ASP.NET Web API is an API framework that provides users with a foundation stack of services and classes to easily build the REST API. Each API implementation stands around the ApiController class:

```
...public HttpActionContext ActionContext { get; set; }
...public HttpConfiguration Configuration { get; set; }
...public HttpControllerContext ControllerContext { get; set; }
...public ModelStateDictionary ModelState { get; }
...public HttpRequestMessage Request { get; set; }
...public HttpRequestContext RequestContext { get; set; }
...public UrlHelper Url { get; set; }
...public IPrincipal User { get; set; }
```

The ASP.NET Web API indicates this pattern for the development of APIs:

1. Create a controller class inheriting from ApiController class.

2. Implement the REST methods.

Those two simple steps may or may not use conventions; for example, take a look at the following scenarios:

- If the controller name ends with the Controller phrase (that is, GeoController), it will be resolved automatically by runtime

- If the REST methods are named like HTTP verbs (that is, GET), they will be automatically mapped to the corresponding HTTP verb

In the following code sample, we use conventions:

```
public class GeoController : ApiController
{
    public GeoAddress Get(string address)
    {
        return new GeoSolver().ResolveAddress(address);
    }
}
```

The ASP.NET Web API automatically binds the inputs to the method parameters as long as it marshals the output with the most convenient output data format:

- The address parameter comes from either the query string or, if the method allows it, the body of the request
- The GeoAddress object that is returned is formatted as XML or JSON depending on the request itself

For this sample /api/geo?address=dome,milan query string called from Chrome, the result is as follows:

```
<GeoAddress xmlns:i="http://www.w3.org/2001/XMLSchema-
    instance" xmlns="http://schemas.datacontract.org/
    2004/07/CM.Geo.BL">
    <Address>
        Milan Cathedral, Cathedral Square, 201213 Milan Milan, Italy
    </Address>
    <Latitude>45.464160919189453</Latitude>
    <Longitude>9.1916046142578125</Longitude>
</GeoAddress>
```

Now, let's analyze the request-processing pipeline.

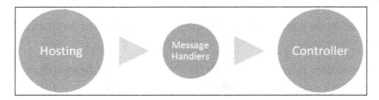

The blocks discussed in the preceding diagram are discussed as follows:

- The HTTP request arrives at the hosting layer
- One or more message handlers can be processed in the cascade to refine the input

The binding and serialization process takes place between handlers and the controller, which is hidden from the developer by default. However, it can be customized too, of course.

- The actual controller is invoked

After the controller has been invoked, the response passes into the same chain (but reversed) of message handlers, and finally the output is produced.

The message handler model is actually an onion architecture, where in the request the output of the outer layer is the input of the inner layer; in the response, the same happens in reverse.

Through message handlers, we can build our logic; for example, take a look at the following two steps and implement the three different handler examples as they come:

1. Inject user information in the controller.
2. Log each call of the services.

Let's see this in an example with three handlers:

- **Handler 1**: This first handler resolves the user calling the service by reading a custom header:

```
public class InjectUserHandler : DelegatingHandler
{
    protected override Task<HttpResponseMessage>
            SendAsync(HttpRequestMessage request,
CancellationToken cancellationToken)
    {
        if (request.Headers.Contains("x-cm-identity"))
        {
            GeoUser user = UserManagement.FromIdentity(
                request.Headers.GetValues("x-cm-
                    identity").FirstOrDefault());
            request.Properties["USER"] = user;
        }
        return base.SendAsync(request, cancellationToken);
    }
}
```

- **Handler 2**: This second handler logs each request:

```
public class LoggingHandler:DelegatingHandler
{
    protected override Task<HttpResponseMessage>
        SendAsync(HttpRequestMessage request,
          CancellationToken cancellationToken)
    {
        var logEntry = string.Format("Call to: {0} from
          {1}",
            request.RequestUri.ToString(),
            request.Properties.ContainsKey("USER") ?
            request.Properties["USER"] : "Unknown");
        GeoLogger.Log(logEntry);
        return base.SendAsync(request, cancellationToken);
    }
}
```

- **Handler 3**: The third handler appends a session custom header to the response:

```
public class SessionHandler:DelegatingHandler
{
    protected override async Task<HttpResponseMessage>
        SendAsync(HttpRequestMessage request,
          CancellationToken cancellationToken)
    {
        var response=await base.SendAsync(request,
          cancellationToken);
        response.Headers.Add("x-cm-session",
          Guid.NewGuid().ToString());
        return response;
    }
}
```

This code enables the handlers and defines the precedence:

```
config.MessageHandlers.Add(new InjectUserHandler());
config.MessageHandlers.Add(new LoggingHandler());
config.MessageHandlers.Add(new SessionHandler());
```

The ASP.NET Web API has tons of features and extensibility points in addition to the few mentioned here. However, this book is about Azure, and these tips are the minimal concepts required to build an API that makes sense.

ServiceStack

ServiceStack is an open source project (developed and maintained by the community) that represents a great alternative to the ASP.NET Web API in the field of API development. It has been designed to:

- Be fast
- Reduce the complexity of the infrastructure code
- Expose services in multiple forms (REST/JSON, SOAP/XML, and CSV)

Further more, since it is a mature technology, it is now widely used by the community and enterprises.

After adding the ServiceStack reference to our project, a few configuration touch points must be implemented:

- A custom handler in the `web.config`
- A basic AppHostBase implementation to initialize from the `Global.asax` `Application_Start` method

 The AppHostBase implementation is very useful in order to define dependencies that are eventually injected into the actual services.

The concept behind ServiceStack is as follows:

- RequestDTO contains information about the route and the input parameters (it is generally one per method)
- ResponseDTO contains the properties of the response (these can be reused)
- A service implementation defines the operation as long as HTTP methods are involved

CM GeoService can be ported as follows:

1. **Implement RequestDTO:**
   ```
   [Route("/api/geo/{Address}")]
   public class Geo
   {
       public string Address { get; set; }
   }
   ```

```
Implement (or reuse) the ResponseDTO:
public class GeoAddress
{
    public string Address { get; set; }
    public double Latitude { get; set; }
    public double Longitude { get; set; }
}
```

2. **Implement the Service**:

```
public class GeoService : Service
{
    public GeoAddress Any(RequestDTO.Geo request)
    {
        return new GeoSolver()
                .ResolveAddress(request.Address);
    }
}
```

It is nice to note that, by default, a `/metadata` endpoint shows every Web Service along with the various supported protocols/formats. The following screenshot explains this:

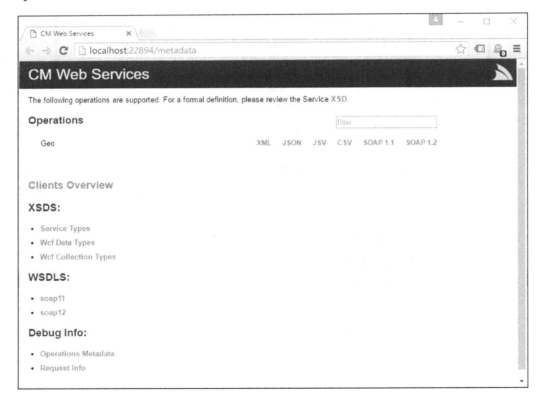

Documenting the API with the Swagger/ OpenAPI

In the SOAP era, interoperability through web services has been possible thanks to standards and well-known protocols and formats. **Service Providers** (SP) published web services with **Simple Object Access Protocol (SOAP)**, describing their endpoints with **Web Services Description Language (WSDL)**. WSDL has been designed to completely describe the operations provided by the SP as their input/ output arguments in order to enable interoperability scenarios.

One of the most important and adopted applications of WSDL has been enabling the creation of proxies between the client and the server (or the consumer and the provider) to hide communication complexity in order to let consumers work. This is because they are invoking operations on a local library instead of having to deal with serialization and message protocols.

With the evolution of the API ecosystem — despite the REST approach being born to free everyone from the unnecessary complexity of protocols/formats — the need to document APIs had been growing until someone invented an efficient format (based on JSON) to document APIs. An excerpt of the swagger document for the popular Pet Store API is as follows:

```
1   {
2       "swagger" : "2.0",
3       "info" : {
16      "host" : "petstore.swagger.io",
17      "basePath" : "/v2",
18      "tags" : [{
37      "schemes" : ["http"],
38      "paths" : {
39          "/pet" : {
40              "post" : {
41                  "tags" : ["pet"],
42                  "summary" : "Add a new pet to the store",
43                  "description" : "",
44                  "operationId" : "addPet",
45                  "consumes" : ["application/json", "application/xml"],
46                  "produces" : ["application/xml", "application/json"],
47                  "parameters" : [{
48                      "in" : "body",
49                      "name" : "body",
50                      "description" : "Pet object that needs to be added to the store",
51                      "required" : true,
52                      "schema" : {
53                          "$ref" : "#/definitions/Pet"
54                      }
55                  }
56              ],
```

Despite Swagger being born as a community initiative, it has been used a million times as it represents a good way to document APIs, enabling code generators and derivative projects. This is why recently SmartBear (the USA-based company behind the Swagger project) donated the specification to the Open API initiative (under the Linux Foundation Project) to reach an even wider audience.

Swagger comes with some useful tools, such as the following:

- **Swagger UI**: This is a collection of HTML/JS/CSS that generates documentation from a valid JSON Swagger-compliant document (an example of the Swagger UI is available at `http://petstore.swagger.io/`)

- **Swagger Editor**: This is a web application with an online editor for Swagger files like the code generators used to build sample server/client projects based on the API specifications

 Many frameworks and languages are supported by the Swagger format, including Android, C#, Java, JavaScript, Objective-C, PHP, Python, Ruby, Scala, Swift, and so on.

How the Swagger Editor UI looks shown in the following screenshot:

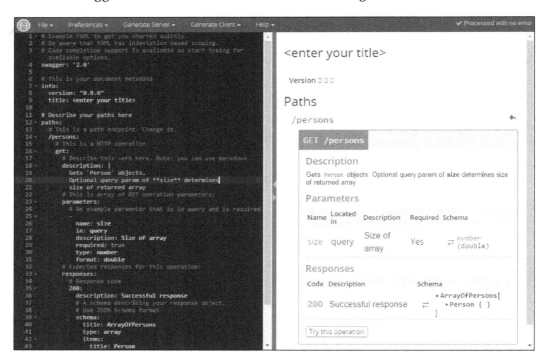

Another option is to provide Swagger documentation by reverse-engineering the actual API code, as done by the Swashbuckle project and the ASP.NET Web API. Simply by adding the NuGet reference to an existing project, Swashbuckle generates a Swagger endpoint, and includes the Swagger UI into the web application.

Deploying the API

Cloud conversation is pretty much about deployment. Existing infrastructures relying on traditional VPS are being moving to IaaS, while new software are moving to PaaS. So, from one perspective, cloud isn't really a new initiative but a new approach to existing problems.

Deploying a web application (and, consequently, a web API) should be a straightforward process either to reduce friction between the development process (dev/test cycles), or to be "agile", letting teams deploy and continuously minimizing the administrative effort.

This figure highlights that the deployment phase in every process can occur multiple times and must be easy to achieve:

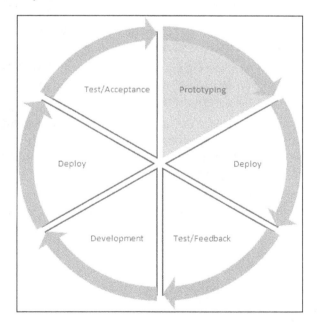

So, our focus is on two main things:

- Providing developers (and us) with frameworks and tools (even cloud tools) to reduce the friction between subsequent deployments during the pre-roll phases
- Providing the entire company with a consistent solution to cope with this continuous process in a production environment

From the developer's perspective, it is important to push up the code frequently with no barriers when deploying the update. From the company's perspective, the main goal is to provide business continuity to clients' applications, adopting appropriate the processes and technologies.

We can now see how Azure App Service helps teams enhance the development process, with an API gateway being an advantage in exposing critical API assets to the public.

Advanced App Service features

We have already discussed App Service a bit in previous chapters; here is a brief recap:

- App Service is a technology that provides an isolated runtime environment to web applications written in various languages
- The unit of scale in App Service is the App Service Plan. A plan is the representation of a hardware topology when the applications (even multiple ones) are deployed:
  - For example, an App Service Plan can be of the *standard* type (which defines features), medium size (which defines the machine type), and with four nodes (which defines how many machines are allocated to that plan)
  - One or more applications can be associated with this plan, which means that all of them are deployed to all the nodes of the ASP

- The underlying software that provides isolation and features to the runtime environment is called Kudu, and it is an open source project hosted on GitHub

- App Service abstracts from the physical topology of the web farm, and it is one of the most advanced PaaS in Azure and in the entire cloud computing panorama

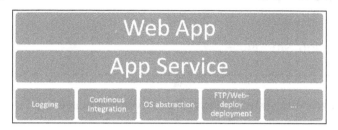

App Settings management

Under some circumstances, due to pressure related to certain development activities—or simply because of a distraction on the part of the deployment manager—the test configuration arrives and runs on the production environment. Has this ever happened to you or your team?

App Service lets you put your sensitive data on the Cloud side, directly bypassing the data arriving from the configuration file or the dev/test environment. Take a look at the following screenshot for clarity:

This is a great method to separate who writes the code and, sometimes, deploys it in production from who owns the deployment process. To check what App Service is "seeing", we can use the **Site Control Manager** website of Kudu, which is available at `https://[mySite].scm-azurewebsites.net`.

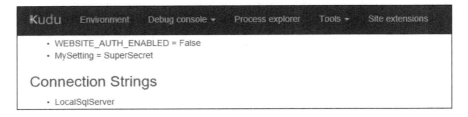

This is the Kudu website showing several environmental settings, including the ones defined by us.

Slots and traffic routing

In previous chapters, we learned how to create a parallel deployment slot to hot-swap them in production in order to avoid runtime. This is made possible because of the balancer actually involved in the process, which listens on `http(s)://[mySite].azurewebsites.net`. Working on it, the Azure Engine can redirect traffic to one of the available deployment slots depending on the configuration.

This means that the *swap* process is, in fact, a mere change to the balancer configuration (nothing is physically moving anywhere).

Using this technique, App Service provides us with the capability of using the secondary slots of a given website in order to split the production traffic and realize some interesting scenarios (that is, A/B Testing). Let's assume we have these slots:

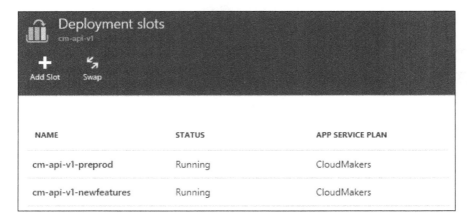

We can easily tell App Service to serve a mix of actual deployments based on a split rule defined as follows:

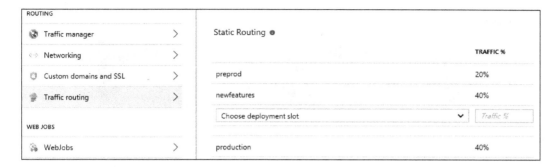

Here, we reserve 40% of the total traffic for the `newfeatures` slot (having a new version of the website/API), 20% to the `preproduction` slot, and the remaining 40% to the actual `production` slot.

Continuous deployment

Behind App Service, there is Kudu, which—among other features—offers the capability of handling deployments from the source control system, including VSTS, GitHub, Bitbucket, and external (or even App Service-hosted) repositories.

 It is also possible to configure source control integration between App Service and Dropbox or OneDrive. This is a fancy but interesting method of deploying the code.

While integrating with VSTS is incredibly powerful, the simplest scenario to explain is the one with a local Git repository setup inside App Service. Once configured, a Git URI like this is available: `https://$[mySite]@[mySite].scm.azurewebsites.net:443/[mySite].git`.

We can push our code here and, in the Azure portal, a new deployment will be triggered. A subsequent push will be deployed and will automatically have the latest code always published on the website. Of course, it is always possible to revert a deployment to a previous one, choosing from the following list:

Hybrid connections

Sometimes (actually very often), it so happens that a company is not completely ready to move to the cloud or, precisely, to PaaS. This is because there are major constraints with the existing software, making it hard to adapt it to Platform-as-a-Service.

One of the most common scenarios is to use an on-premise SQL Server despite the actual website being able to be deployed to App Service.

In the following figure, the on-premise SQL Server uses a Hybrid connector (a client software to be run on the on-premise machine), which initiates an active TCP outbound connection to the public BizTalk service endpoint.

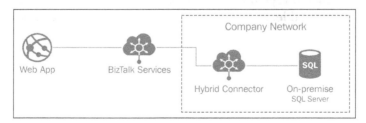

This, passing through the firewall, avoids complex IT configuration on the company side and, at the same time, enables the **BizTalk Services** endpoint in order to reuse the TCP connection in a bidirectional way to route traffic coming from the public-faced web app.

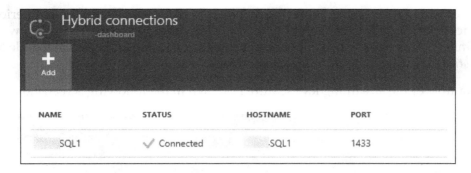

This shows a website hosted on App Service, communicating with an on-premise SQL Server database through a Hybrid connector.

Application logs

App Service captures the default output of many execution engines to route it to a data store. In the **Diagnostics logs** section of the portal, it is possible to define log shipping to the local filesystem (not to be intended as a persistent data store) or to the blob/table storage, which is to be intended as the right option for production workloads. The configuration pane of the logging features of App Service looks like the one shown in the following screenshot:

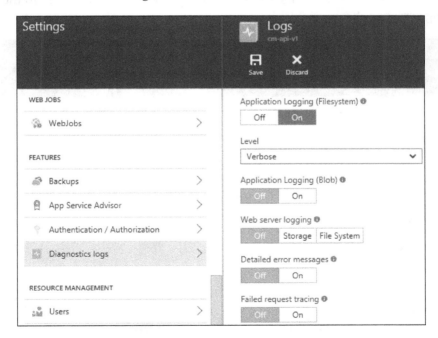

After activating the logging on the filesystem, it remains active for a limited period (this does not apply to other shipping methods) in order to avoid letting it grow indefinitely. This feature also allows you to attach a console to the actual log file to get a *streaming experience* of the application logs.

An example of the streaming logs feature is shown in the following screenshot:

Backup and restore

As the title suggests, App Service offers a native backup experience at the site level. This means that you can configure a backup schedule to run periodically, saving the entire website content, its configuration (the App Service one), and, optionally, its connected databases. The backup feature of App Service is displayed in the following screenshot:

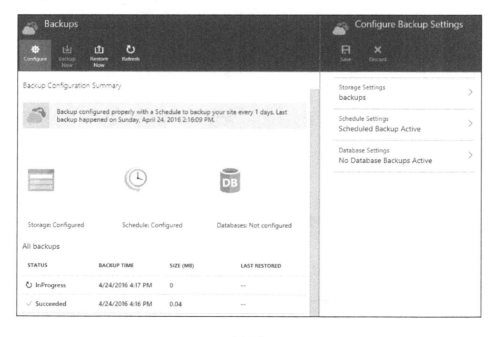

The restore feature can restore the website using one of the backup sets of the same site (the **App Backup** option), or it can browse other backup sets in a given storage account (the **Storage** option). In either case, the restore overwrites the existing website or moves to another website:

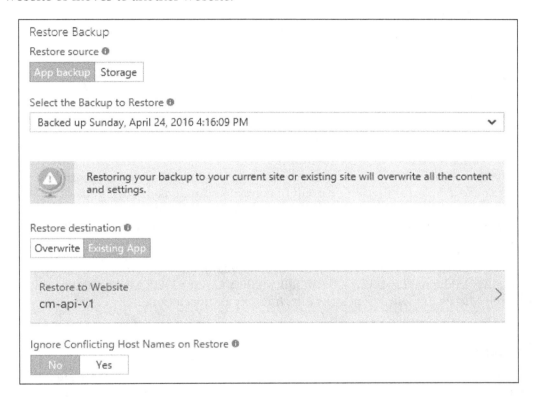

API Gateway

API development does not finish with the deployment of a working environment; in fact, it begins with it. Once an API endpoint is published on the Internet, it becomes public, and the underlying API starts to become a public API.

At the start of this chapter, we discussed the importance of the creation of a public API, a fortiori if used by the general public. Some of the most important aspects to be addressed are as follows:

- URLs and HTTP verb definitions
- Versioning the underlying API

- Exceptions and HTTP error codes
- Content negotiation and formats
- API documentation
- Security and authentication
- Pagination and caching
- Traffic management and throttling
- Logging
- The developer portal

All of these aspects can, of course, be addressed on the web app side by implementing them accordingly. However, existing APIs can miss some of these features and, if they are put on the Internet, issues can arise. On the other hand, an architect can decide that, since there are several APIs to be developed, centralizing some of these features in a single point of control and management can be done. Based on these assumptions, an API management layer can help consistently speed up the process and give more control to the company serving the APIs.

The strategic role of an API management solution (or the API Gateway) has been gaining the attention it deserved in the last few years, with the growth of the API economy. In the next section, we will talk about the Azure API Management service and the Microsoft cloud offer for this technology requirement.

Using Azure API Management

Azure **API Management** (**APIM**) is a SaaS product to administer, orchestrate, and manage even complex API workflows. It comes on `*.azure-api.net` and, by default, a new endpoint creates the following:

- `[myEndpoint].azure-api.net`: An endpoint hosting the API Gateway logic
- `[myEndpoint].portal.azure-api.net`: An endpoint hosting the developer portal

APIM can be configured to use personal domain names as personal SSL certificates, as shown here:

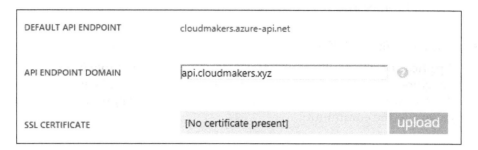

Once the APIM endpoint is configured, we can navigate the developer portal to see it in action. The screenshot that follows shows the developer portal displaying the sample **Echo API**

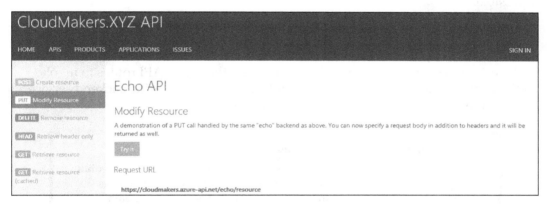

Each developer can subscribe autonomously with a simple e-mail opt-in mechanism. Every aspect of the developer portal, including the frontend site graphics and e-mail templates, can be customized in the administration website. At the time of writing this, these touch points are supported:

- **Site culture/language**: 10+ languages are supported along with every time zone.

- **Google Analytics support**: The public Developer Portal website can track usage on GA by including the tracking ID.

- **Custom robots.txt**: This customizes what is visible/hidden to spiders.

- **Navigation**: The developer portal menu can be customized as well.

- **Widgets**: Some widgets are available in the frontend engine (based on Orchard).

- **Media Library and Blogs**: These contain content and offer an integrated blog engine.

- **Contents**: Basic CMS features are supported to create custom content.

- **Applications**: Since the developer portal should be the touch point for developers building their apps based on the exposed APIs, it is possible for them to submit apps to the portal. If approved, these apps are visible in the gallery to the community.

Creating an API

In a new APIM instance, there is a sample API called the **Echo API**. This API is useful when it come to checking endpoint status in production, so do not delete it, if possible.

Creating a new API is the process of creating a root-level URL suffix, such as `https://[myEndpoint].azure-api.net/[newApi]`.

Each API can have multiple operations, which are the actual API routes to invoke methods on the backend services. By default, an API has a specific backend service, and it is replaceable in policies according to the rules engine.

Importing an API with Swagger

The importance of Swagger has been covered earlier. If a public API has a Swagger endpoint, an API can be created (and its operations can be inferred) through its Swagger metadata document using the import API action.

Each API can stay in one or more *products*. A product, in APIM, is a collection of APIs that share some common logic, such as the following:

- The title and the description
- Legal terms
- Subscription requirements (who can subscribe to the product)
- Usage quota (traffic limiting can occur at the product level)

The backend service behind the public endpoint of APIM can be either an Internet-faced endpoint or a private endpoint in a VPN (VPN connectivity is a premium feature, requiring a more expensive tier).

Despite VPNs having been used for years, they just add a layer of security, tunneling the public Internet, but they cannot do anything more. This is why it is strongly recommended that you protect API endpoints at each stage; merely designing a good VPN-based network infrastructure is not enough.

For example, a secure API can be also exposed safely on the public Internet, by following these rules:

- The API endpoint must reply only on HTTPS/TLS
- The API must ask for authentication (even basic authentication)
- The API must be presented with a valid client certificate for mutual certification

Under these assumptions, an API can be considered secure even if publicly accessible.

This is the configuration page for client certificates used by APIM to communicate securely with backend APIs:

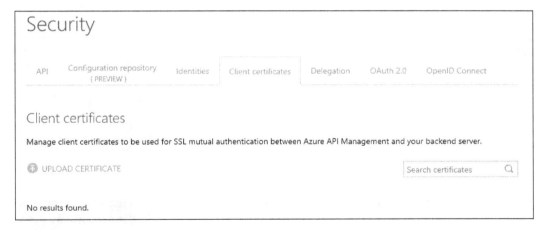

After an API is created, we need to add operations. For each operation, we can set up the following:

- The HTTP verb (GET, POST, and others)
- The URL template that triggers the APIM engine
- The rewrite URL template to forward the request to a backend service
- The display name and description

As part of the API operation, we can set up the request parameters as the response codes and types. This is not required to make the API Gateway working; instead, it is useful in building the automatically updated documentation on the developer portal.

 If we use Swagger to import the API, we automatically have the operations imported as long as the Request/Response documentation is filled.

After filling in the basic details in the **Signature** tab, we can enable caching as follows:

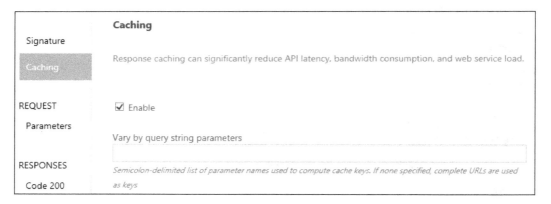

APIM comes with built-in support for caching included in the service fee (the size of the cache depends on the service tier). Since we deal with HTTP, the caching system automatically caches the content of the response using the input URI as the cache key. To customize this behavior, we can set up the **Vary by query string parameters** or **Vary by headers setting** rules for advanced caching.

Using policies

The majority of the features of APIM is created by policies. The policy engine is the engine triggered by an HTTP route that's incoming to the APIM endpoint. A policy is XML that contains the logic to be plugged in the request pipeline in order to inject custom behaviors and even complex workflows:

```
<policies>
  <inbound />
  <backend>
    <forward-request />
  </backend>
  <outbound />
</policies>
```

The basic building blocks are as follows:

- The `inbound` section: This includes rules to be applied in the request phase before any backend service is called
- The `backend` section: Here, the backend API is called
- The `outbound` section: This includes rules to be applied in the response phase after the response from the backend API service

A policy can be applied at the following levels:

- **The product level**: Every API in the product will inherit the policy
- **The API level**: Every operation in the API will inherit the policy
- **The operation level**: Only the specific operation is affected by the policy

 By default, in order to inherit the base rules from the upper levels, an XML tag `<base />` is placed in the appropriate section.

A complete set of examples of the usage of the policies is beyond the scope of this book, but here is a list of the currently supported policies with a brief description:

- **Access restriction policies**:
  - ○ **Check the HTTP header**: Check the existence of a header in a set of values specified in the policy. It can block the pipeline if there's something missing.

- ○ **Limit the call rate**: Check the call rate of the current API by subscription (the user coupled with a product) or by key (a custom value):

```
<policies>
    <inbound>
        <base />
        <rate-limit-by-key  calls="5"
                renewal-period="30"
                counter-key="@(context.Request.IpAddress)"/>
    </inbound>
    <outbound>
        <base />
    </outbound>
</policies>
```

- ○ **Restrict caller IPs**: Set up a list of allowed or denied IP addresses for callers.

- ○ **Set the usage quota**: Set the usage quota of the current API by subscription or by a custom key:

```
<policies>
    <inbound>
        <base />
        <quota-by-key calls="1000" bandwidth="20000"
          renewal-period="7200" counter-key=
          "@(context.Request.IpAddress)" />
    </inbound>
    <outbound>
        <base />
    </outbound>
</policies>
```

- ○ **Validate JWT**: Validate the content of a JWT extracted from a specific header value. This is an advanced policy that performs a complex outbound activity.

- • **Advanced policies**:

  - ○ **Control flow**: This is the corresponding version of the `switch` C# statement:

```
<choose>
    <when condition="Boolean expression | Boolean
      constant">
```

```
        <!— one or more policy statements to be applied if
           the above condition is true  -->
     </when>
     <when condition="Boolean expression | Boolean
        constant">
        <!— one or more policy statements to be applied if
           the above condition is true  -->
     </when>
     <otherwise>
        <!— one or more policy statements to be applied if
           none of the above conditions are true  -->
</otherwise>
</choose>
```

- **Forward the request**: This simply forwards the request to the backend service.

- **Log to EventHub**: Writes a payload into EventHub; it can be a log entry or anything else as well.

- **Return the response**: Aborts the pipeline execution and returns the specified response to the caller:

```
<return-response response-variable-name="myVariable">
   <set-status code="404" reason="Not Found" />
</return-response>
```

- **Send a one-way request**: Sends a fire-and-forget request; this is useful in notifying an unreliable actor or sending a noncritical notification:

```
<send-one-way-request mode="new">
<set-url>
https://hooks.slack.com/services/...</set-url>
      <set-method>POST</set-method>
   <set-body>@{
         return new JObject(
new JProperty("username","myUser"),
new JProperty("text", "Notification")
      ).ToString();
      }</set-body>
</send-one-way-request>
```

- ◦ **Send a request**: This is a complex policy that makes an HTTP request and stores the response in a local variable. With other policies, it is then possible to reuse this variable and compose a response (or other subsequent requests):

```
<send-request mode="new|copy" response-variable
  -name="" timeout="60 sec" ignore-error
  ="false|true">
    <set-url>...</set-url>
    <set-method>...</set-method>
    <set-header name="" exists-
      action="override|skip|append|delete">...</set-header>
    <set-body>...</set-body>
</send-request>
```

- **Authentication policies (from APIM to the backend service)**:
    - ◦ **Basic authorization**: Sets the username and password authentication
    - ◦ **Certificate authentication**: Sets a certificate (from those uploaded into the appropriate APIM section) in the request to the backend service:

```
<authentication-certificate thumbprint="....." />
```

- **Transformation policies**:

    - ◦ **Convert JSON to XML and XML to JSON**
    - ◦ **Find and replace a string in the body**:

```
<find-and-replace from="a" to="b" />
```

    - ◦ **Mask URLs in the content**: This changes the URLs in the response body returned by the backend service, making them point to the APIM gateway URI
    - ◦ **Set the backend service**: This changes the default backend service based on rules applied earlier:

```
<policies>
    <inbound>
        <choose>
            <when condition="@(context.Request.Url.Query.
              GetValueOrDefault("version") == "v1")">
                <set-backend-service base-
                  url="http://cloudmakers.xyz/api/v1/" />
            </when>
```

```
<when condition="@(context.Request.Url.Query.
    GetValueOrDefault("version") == "v2")">
        <set-backend-service base-url="
            http://cloudmakers.xyz/api/v2/" />
    </when>
</choose>
<base />
</inbound>
<outbound>
    <base />
</outbound>
</policies>
```

° **Rewrite the URL**: This changes the incoming URL to another one before forwarding the request to the backend service

There are four advanced caching policies and three policies to work with cross-domain calls (CORS, JSONP).

> In the previous XML sample (*Set backend service*), we learned how to perform API versioning with policies. In the sample, we used the *version* query string parameter to switch the backend service to the right version. The client can use the same web API URL with a different parameter value to query the specified API version.

Identity and Access Management

APIM has built-in support to register/log in developer profiles. However, in order to integrate the existing systems, delegation can be configured. With delegation, the workflow can be as follows:

* The developer goes to the developer portal and clicks on **Sign Up** or **Sign In**
* APIM redirects the user to the delegated endpoint, which owns the user process until a login/registration has been performed

The delegated endpoint redirects back to the developer portal.

From a security perspective, the SSO experience is through the exchange of a **Preshared key (PSK)**, which must be used to sign the URIs between parties. Each party (the APIM portal and the company website) must verify the signature and proceed accordingly. The delegation feature of APIM can be seen in the following screenshot:

Delegation

Delegation allows you to use your existing web site for handling certain user operations like sign-in and sign-up as opposed to using the built-in functionality in the developer portal.

A special delegation endpoint on your web site must act as the entry point for any request initiated from the developer portal.

☑ Delegate sign-in & sign-up

Delegation endpoint URL:

https://www.cloudmakers.xyz/signup

Delegation Validation Key:

I8eNTdz5ZwTHmiziGBKNpZ0j05TKQrBdizXJCGLg+4WcMY3Kn0bo7huDOhU2m5J9VWcbkpaguqCZUWł   Hide   Generate

Advanced APIM Management

In the past few years, as users of APIM, we lacked some governance features; these have finally arrived in the product. Integration with Git is a powerful touch point to work on APIM from outside the browser and, at the same time, to track changes in APIM configuration.

Since almost everything in APIM is about policies, it is recommended that you use Git integration to keep track of the several policies we set up for each product, API, and operation. Integration with Git is performed behind the scenes by Kudu.

The process is as follows:

1. Initialize the Git repository on the APIM side.
2. Create a first commit in the master branch from the portal.
3. Clone the Git repository on the client side.
4. Commit/push new versions from the local environment.

Git integration always shows the latest commit in use by the platform and it is shown in the following screenshot:

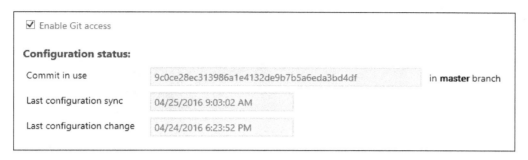

Another great management option is to back up/restore the entire APIM configuration in order to enable several scenarios:

- Be ready (in minutes) with a new environment if something goes wrong with the APIM instance
- Clone an existing instance for test/staging purposes
- Perform versioning of the entire configuration, including the CMS contents (at the time of writing this, backup retention is limited to 7 days)

Backup/restore is available only through the REST Management APIs calling this method:

```
POST https://management.azure.com/subscriptions/{subscriptionId}/
    resourceGroups/{resourceGroupName}/providers/
    Microsoft.ApiManagement/service/{serviceName}/
    backup?api-version={api-version}
```

This can be done only using a valid Azure AD identity that has the **Access Azure Service Management** delegated permission enabled.

Debugging complex API workflows

The more we complicate the topology of the API workflow, the more complex the debugging activity around it will be. Now imagine this scenario:

1. The user calls `https://api.cloudmakers.xyz/api/v1/users`.
2. `v1` in the URI determines that the backend URI, `https://cm-api-v1.azurewebsites.net`, has to be called.

3. APIM performs some activities (due to the policies) and calls the backend service.

4. After that, it calls another service to compose the response and returns it to the client.

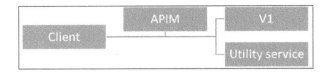

Now, suppose that the client has an error code and we need to determine where it occurred:

- Has it happened on the **V1** side?
- Has it happened in the **Utility service**?
- Has it happened on the **APIM** side (due to policy execution errors)?

The first instrument we can use to diagnose what happened is the API inspector of APIM, a feature that traces calls in order to troubleshoot the pipeline.

If we can replicate the error conditions (hopefully), then we can call the APIM endpoint, specifiying an additional header:

```
ocp-apim-trace: true
```

This tells APIM to return, in the response, the location to which the trace file of this request in the header should be downloaded:

```
ocp-apim-trace-location :
  https://[storage].blob.core.windows.net/
  apiinspectorcontainer/[blob]
```

Analyzing this file can drastically reduce the troubleshooting effort by pointing out which actor involved in the pipeline has failed. If the backend API is failing, then we need to troubleshoot/debug it directly.

Debugging App Service with remote debugging

In the Advanced App Service features, we learn how to enable application logs to ship logs to various data stores, including a filesystem provider that is then used by App Service itself to offer the streaming logs feature.

This is a great help when debugging in order to understand the process, but sometimes it is not enough to identify where an exception is occurring.

This is why App Service can enable remote debugging on the target website.

Keep the following points in mind:

- This feature lets us attach a Visual Studio debugger to the w3wp process of the remote website. This means that, if we breakpoint on a method that is being executed for each request, we are potentially blocking every user on the website.

- Use this feature only outside production workloads. If there is a specific need to debug a production workload, replicate the production in another website slot (with cloned settings) and debug it. The rule is "do not remotely debug a website that is being accessed by the public".

- Turn off the **Remote Debugging** feature when finishing: despite it turning off automatically after a period of time, it is recommended that you close it manually.

Apart from this, remote debugging can sometimes save hours of troubleshooting; a common case is when the runtime has library issues, a scenario that is hard to replicate locally.

The following screenshot tells us how to attach the Debugger on Visual Studio using the **Cloud Explorer** pane:

Using a Service Bus relay to debug REST services

In this last section of this chapter, we learn how to use one of the most interesting services/features of Azure Service Bus to perform debugging. Since its launch, Service Bus relay was explained as a public HTTP relay, where on-premise services can connect—in order to be discoverable from the outside Internet—without complex network configurations on the company side.

This is true, and for production workloads it can save an incredible amount of time/resources.

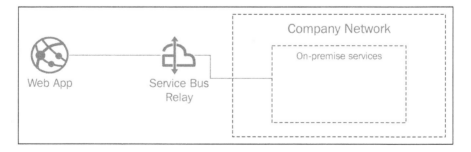

However, why not use it elsewhere? Let's come back to this scenario, where Azure APIM is involved in a complex workflow, calling multiple APIs:

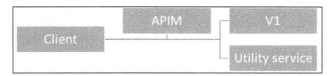

If we understand the issue on the **V1** side, is there a more efficient method to debug it without involving the App Service Remote Debugging feature?

Or, again, if we are developing the API infrastructure and we need to test policies continuously, is there a more efficient method to develop, instead of deploying, attaching, or debugging in the cloud? The answer is yes, and it is connected to the usage of the Service Bus relay.

First, we need to create a Service Bus namespace (a standard tier) on the Azure subscription (Service Bus features are available only in the old portal at the time of writing this):

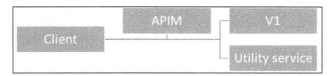

As with the image, relays are created dynamically from the client, so there is no need to do anything on the portal side.

Second, we need to create a WCF-ready service with this service contract:

```
[ServiceContract(Namespace = "urn:CloudMakers.XYZ.APIs")]
public interface IHandlerAdapter
{
    [OperationContract, WebGet(UriTemplate = "/{*route}")]
    Stream Get(string route);

    [OperationContract, WebInvoke(Method = "POST",
            UriTemplate = "/{*route}")]
    Stream Post(Stream data, string route);
}
```

We need to create the service with an empty implementation like this one:

```
public class ServiceBusRelayHandlerAdapter : IHandlerAdapter
{
    public Stream Get(string route)
    {
        return new MemoryStream();
    }

    public Stream Post(Stream data, string route)
    {
        return new MemoryStream();
    }
}
```

This WCF enables raw HTTP calls via GET and POST methods, passing the following:

- For the GET method, the `route` string after the root prefix
- For the POST method, the `route` string along with the POST body through a `Stream`

Now, in order to attach this service to the Service Bus relay, we can use this code:

```
var sh = new WebServiceHost(typeof(ServiceBusRelayHandlerAdapter));
sh.AddServiceEndpoint(typeof(IHandlerAdapter),
    new WebHttpRelayBinding(EndToEndWebHttpSecurityMode.Transport,
    RelayClientAuthenticationType.None),
    ServiceBusEnvironment
    .CreateServiceUri("https","[namespace]","apis"))
    .Behaviors.Add(new TransportClientEndpointBehavior
    {
        TokenProvider = TokenProvider
        .CreateSharedAccessSignatureTokenProvider(
            "[keyName]", "[keyValue]")
    });
sh.Open();
```

What is the purpose of this sample? Hosting this service means that we expose our local running process through a public URL such as `https://[namespace].servicebus.windows.net/apis/{route}`.

Inside the GET/POST methods discussed earlier, we can implement our test API, and we can use the public Service Bus URI in APIM in order to make it call our Visual Studio instance directly, speeding up the development process amazingly.

Summary

In this chapter, we discussed APIs. We learned how to use the ASP.NET Web API as ServiceStack and how to document it with Swagger. We saw how Azure App Service helps manage the entire life cycle of API/web development, and we underlined the fundamental role of a API Gateway when building complex API infrastructures.

With APIM, we learned how to implement a rational process of API Management, and finally we looked at some tricks to perform efficient debugging with distributed environments.

In the next chapter, we'll learn how to deal with messaging systems in order to create distributed applications that should be scalable, resilient, and robust.

Working with Messages

7

In *Chapter 3, Building the Frontend* we availed ourselves of some of the many opportunities that Microsoft Azure data service offers to developers when dealing with data. A data service should not be a constraint: it should be an opportunity to choose the best data service from many after reviewing the requirements of the solution.

We classified data services on a usage base, evaluating principles, typing, speed, and accessibility. But all data has one thing in common: it all represents the current state of an entity. We always spend a lot of time speaking about the current state.

We also introduced the concept of stale data. A distributed application contains copies or parts of the same state at different times because it is not possible to update all the instances at the same time. How do we sync all the state copies around the system? We need to introduce a couple of new kinds of data.

In this chapter, we will learn how to:

- Use messaging in solutions for asynchronous communication between applications
- Understand the notion of message, command, and event
- Send messages to a Service Bus Queue and Topics and process them with Azure WebJobs

Dealing the future with commands

Consider a scenario where we have a CRUD application over the Internet backed by a relational database. One of the big issues in this scenario is concurrency.

There is no connection open to the database, so we cannot lock record(s) to avoid concurrency problems. If we had the connection, we can limit concurrency with exclusive access to that record.

So, we need to deal with optimistic concurrency. Create a snapshot of the records (marked as original records); change data with the client application; then send it back to the Web. What could happen? If another user performs the same operations at the same time, starting from the same copy of the data, the application can do two things:

- If only the ID is used to query the original records to update (and this practice is used more times than we could imagine), the second user updating wins and overwrites the changes of the first user because the app has no way of knowing that there is concurrency. The first user has no notion that his changes have been lost. Data is corrupted.

- If the original records are retrieved with a query matching of all original field values, the second user will cause the update process to fail, as the original records, with that original values, would be gone. There is no data corruption, but a second user would have lost time performing an operation that is not useful.

The greatest mistake in this scenario is giving the client application the responsibility for the entity update. The presentation tier knows how an entity is composed and prepares it for the data layer. This is a mistake because data can become stale. But there is another problem, known as coupling. We intend to couple the knowledge of a part of the application, for example, the presentation tier, with the data access tier. If the database changes, the presentation needs to change consistently. The presentation tier is responsible of tasks that should not be its responsibility. So, any structural change to the database is a costly change as other tiers of the application need to reflect this change, through having them updated and retested.

We can express a question in two ways:

- Why does an application change an entity?
- Why does a user need to change an entity with an application?

The difference is substantial. An application has "no brain" of its own, so to be precise, the first question is a mistake. An application doesn't change an entity: an application is requested by a user to change an entity. So, the real question is "why" a user needs to change an entity.

Suppose again that two users starting from an empty order or basket need to add an item into it. The classic entity-based way is: get the entity, add the item, then save the entity; then you have concurrency problems. If instead the two users don't update the entity but ask, "Add the item to the entity," they would send the request to an independent party (or tier) that can act correctly because it is the only subject enabled to access the original entity and update it consistently.

The expression of the intention, the data that describes the need to perform an operation, is known as a *command*.

Messages and queues

Commands are messages. This is a way to distinguish the kind of information that describes the actions on an entity, instead of describing the state of an entity. Messages describe the cause and effect of an action over an entity.

Command messages are time-bound, that is, the time in a command is described when a command is issued but not yet executed.

Commands bring arguments necessary to execute the action on the entity.

As data, messages need to be persisted. The point is that a traditional store (such as a database, as we normally refer to them) normally handles entity states, but this is not useful because it would not be optimized to the specific features of the messages:

- Messages are useful only if correctly ordered in time; messaging systems handle unordered messages as an issue
- Messages should be handled once
- Message execution should be idempotent, that is, executing a message twice should not affect the system the second time
- Messages should be marked as *consumed*

These requirements match with a sort of empowered queue. As a pattern, it can be implemented, probably over some other data structures (our recurrent database), but it is better experienced when a specific service is built from the ground up and optimized for this usage: a Service Bus.

Azure Service Bus is a generic, cloud-based messaging system to connect just about anything—applications, services, and devices. Service Bus is a Platform-as-a-Service.

Azure Service Bus implements some specific messaging patterns:

- **Relay messaging**: As described in *Chapter 6, Building the API Layer,* it enables the building of hybrid applications that run in both an Azure data center and in its own on-premise enterprise environment

- **Notification hub**: It provides an easy-to-use, multiplatform, scaled-out push infrastructure that enables you to send mobile push notifications from any backend (in the cloud or on-premise) to any mobile platform (not covered in this book)

- **Brokered messaging**: This enables the scenario of a decoupled system, where either the message producer or consumer handles messages at different times

Brokered messaging offers many advantages:

- The consumer does not process the message at the time the producer sends it, but only when it is available. This is an effective infrastructure to manage workload and planning resource allocation.

- It is the correct pattern to handle parallel consumers that can distribute processing over many workers.

- Producers do not wait for the message to be consumed, so in this way a real async process is implemented.

- Every message can be serialized, so it can also be used to log the message arrival and process a debug in case of problems.

- Every message can be temporarily ordered and can recognize the correct message arrival, implementing a read **First In First Out** (**FIFO**) process.

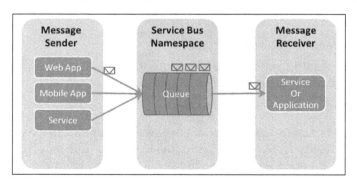

Commands are well suited to be handled with queues, as we require one-time processing of the message.

The scenario

An online shop shows a catalog of products that can be added to a basket. It is an ASP.NET MVC application with a page that receives and sends data through Ajax. It is authenticated, as a basket is associated with the username, and referred to as `UserId`.

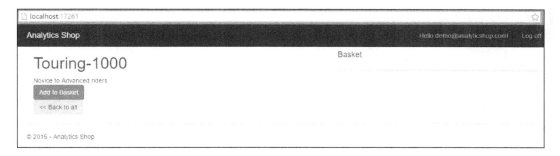

Add to Basket is associated with a JavaScript function that composes the request to the API controller:

```javascript
function AddToBasket(productId) {
    $.ajax({
        type: "POST",
        url: "/api/commands/addtobasket",
        contentType: "application/json; charset=utf-8",
        dataType: "json",
        data: JSON.stringify({
            productId: productId,
            quantity: 1
        })
    }).done(function (msg) {
        ViewItems();
    });
}
```

Sending messages with queues

At the time of writing this, managing a **Service Bus** is possible only from the classic portal:

The common concept at the heart of a service bus is the namespace. Every service needs a public endpoint reachable from the outside. So, the first thing to do with a service bus is assign a name that will be used under the `.servicebus.windows.net` DNS name. There is no standalone way to create a namespace without creating a specific service, such as a queue, relay, topics, notification hub, and EventHub, but it is possible to then create every other service.

So, we need a queue to send commands to act on a basket. We select **MESSAGING** from the dialog box, type the namespace name in the field, and select the Messaging Tier, between the **BASIC** and **STANDARD** ones. The difference between these refers to the capacity to handle a given number of messages. It is always possible to change this during the lifetime of the messaging tier as performances require.

 At the time of writing this, a new messaging tier, Premium, is available for structural high-performance and high-availability capabilities, but the is beyond the scope of this book.

It is also necessary to specify the region in which the service is hosted. This is unchangeable after creation, so it is necessary to always correctly select where the queue is located.

 Getting deeper into the service bus is beyond the scope of this book. For now, we move ahead considering that it is necessary to create just one queue. So, in a distributed scenario where a web application is distributed in more that one region and balanced in the frontend with **Traffic Manager**, we can consider creating a queue for each web application, in the same region where the web app is.

We now need to create the basket queue to send commands to the basket worker from the selector inside the service.

You can create a queue by just typing its name, which will be used as a reference.

Without entering in more specific details, authentication for each service bus (SB) service is enabled by the **Shared Access Secret** (**SAS**) policy. We can decide among three rights (listen, send, and manage), and we assign a name (typically the role or the app that will use it) to the policy. The common rule is to create more policies, one for each actor, granting the minimum rights required for each one.

From the **Configure** tab, we can define the policy that goes into action by clicking on the **Save** button.

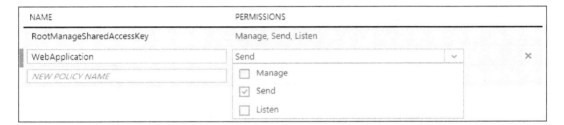

To authenticate, the queue client requires the generated access key (accessible at the bottom of the **Configure** page) or via **ConnectionStrings** from the root SB page. The second proposal is the choice of preference, as all the information is contained in one string.

 It's a good practice to configure connection strings and application settings in a **WebApp**, in a production environment, after the deployment of the web app. From Azure portal, open WebApp blade, select Settings, and search for **Application Settings**. Then write on any value at this stage overrides any value previously written in web.config before deployment.

Now, it's time to code. In a .NET project, the service bus is accessed via the SDK library downloadable from NuGet, referencing in the project with **Package Manager**:

```
Install-Package WindowsAzure.ServiceBus
```

The **Commands ApiController** receives the Ajax request to add a product in the basket:

```
public async Task PostAsync(string id)
{
    var command = JsonConvert.DeserializeObject<JObject>
      (await Request.Content.ReadAsStringAsync());
    switch (id) // id is the command to be sent
    {
        case "addtobasket":
            await SendQueueAsync("basket", new
            {
                CommandType = "AddToBasket",
                ProductId = command["productId"].Value<string>(),
                Quantity = command["quantity"].Value<int>(),
                UserId = User.Identity.Name
            });
            break;
        default:
            throw new NotSupportedException("Command not
              supported");
    }
}
```

The request is contained in the body and is sent in the JSON format. It can be parsed with `DeserializeObject` from the `Json.Net` library. The `id` gives an identity to the command that should be executed and is useful for the following reasons:

- **Tracing**: We can save the command with the ID and then debug (if necessary) the command trip, from the client to the server, and to the queue

- **Idempotency**: We can discover whether a command with a specific ID was already submitted, check the command execution result, and decide whether any command with the same ID needs to be re-executed (if never run) or discarded (if already executed)

An invocation is an immediate selection of the way we execute, and this is described by the body of the method. The code inside the method is immediately executed. We need to couple the "pure" execution with the way we handle nonfunctional aspects such as logging, rejecting, and delaying.

A message declares in one single atomic element (the message) the requirements of an execution and the arguments needed to parameterize the execution. The invocation is just the nonfunctional part of the execution:

- Check whether we can execute and reject the message if needed

- Log the invocation to possible future needs

- Delay execution, pushing the request message inside a queue, and giving the opportunity to check whether execution is possible or not

This is also a declarative approach. We requested an execution and we are not interested, at this stage, how execution is implemented: we trust it will be executed in the correct way. This is great for coupling and project maintenance: as the execution implementation can be updated, we do not need to change how the execution is invoked.

From the API controller that receives the Ajax request, we can send a new message inside a queue with code similar to the following:

```
protected async Task SendQueueAsync<T>(string name, T target)
{
    var queue = QueueClient.CreateFromConnectionString(
        ConfigurationManager.ConnectionStrings["ServiceBus"].
            ConnectionString, name);
    var json = JsonConvert.SerializeObject(target);
    var message = new BrokeredMessage(json);
    await queue.SendAsync(message);
}
```

The `queueclient` is directly created parsing the connection string as the first argument, and the name of the queue as the second parameter.

`BrokeredMessage` is the object that contains all the information necessary to be enqueued. It stores the parameters that can be customized at this level; these are beyond the scope of this book. What is most important is that `BrokeredMessage` is a container for specific application information, which can accept a .NET serializable object as an argument. Here are some possible uses:

- Passing a generic .NET object that needs to be XmlSerializable
- Passing a generic .NET object specifying a custom XmlCustomSerializer
- Passing a stream that contains the serialized object
- Passing a string or a byte array that contains the serialized object

In general, the choice is a matter of coupling and deciding how much the two parties in communication know each other. For example, the two parties can share knowledge in the form of a library of classes containing a common set of model type DTOs. Using a custom XmlCustomSerializer introduces too much coupling and must be used only in very limited and specific scenarios, for example, a very high-performance infrastructure that needs to minimize latency. If another serialization is necessary or preferred, a string or binary array can be used as *automatically* serializable. We use this in the example, as it introduces no coupling in parties and everyone is free to handle the object as needed.

After the message is sent into the queue, the client application does not receive any results. The successful invocation without any exception confirms to the client the correctness of the request. The request has finished, but the execution is not yet started. The request will be executed somewhere in another process, sometime in the future, asynchronously.

Processing messages with workers

When a command is inside a queue, the producing application has completed its work, but the command processing has not yet started. An independent process or role, besides the frontend web role, has to receive the commands and process them.

A worker role is a noninteractive process that works in the background and perhaps also far from the user, continuously receiving messages and processing them. Technically speaking, from an operating system and Azure point of view, it is just a process, and for .NET it is just a console application. What distinguishes a worker from normal processes is the nonfunctional aspects that need to be considered:

- Deployment
- Scaling
- Resiliency

Deployment means the description of the environment around the worker that handles its lifetime, from creation to completion, through execution. The worker needs resources and configuration, and the deployment needs to give all the information necessary to the process. This models our "console application" with some specific environment configurations, objects, and parameters, besides the plain program class of a command line application.

Scaling refers to how a worker can guarantee workload completion as it increases. It's normal to consider that a worker must "scale out", meaning a worker is instantiated more than once when processing its workload in parallel. There are some requirements that need to be satisfied in order to scale out. One of these is decoupling workload requests from execution, and this is one of the main usages of the service bus.

Adapting the dictionary definition, resiliency refers to the ability to recover from failures. This means:

- How does a worker handle failures?
- How does a worker retry previously interrupted works?
- How does a worker guarantee continuity of the work?

The most important general rule is: the higher the quality of the service and **Service Level Agreement (SLA)**, the more complex the implementation. Because of this, as often in Azure, we can find abstractions implemented by some services that help in our work.

To host our worker code in Azure, we have the following:

- **Virtual machine**: As Infrastructure-as-a-Service, we have control over the entire operating system and virtual devices, and we have the opportunity to choose the operating system: Windows or Linux. This is the most powerful but also the most complex one to understand.

- **Cloud Services V1**: The Platform-as-a-Service original service that can host any Win32/64 executable. This is very flexible: it solves only the deployment experience, but doesn't offer any particular vertical scenario.

- **Service Fabric (Cloud Services V2)**: This is the new offering in Azure hosting stateless and stateful services: and guarantees highly resilient services that offer high scalability. At the time of writing this, it is a high-end solution, which is not well suited for solutions that need to start small.

- **Azure WebJob**: This builds on top of app services and the Kudu platform. It shares the same service plan with web app, mobile app, logic app, and API app. In fact, it is the backend worker role of any of these and it is deployed.

Azure WebJobs is suitable to use with this kind of solution: great code with good usage of coding patterns and Azure Service will minimize the impact of moving code to more powerful hosting solutions.

From Visual Studio, we can create an Azure WebJob from the relative project template. If we already have a console project, it's just a matter of adding a reference from NuGet through the Package Manager console:

```
Install-Package Microsoft.Azure.WebJobs
```

This package configures natively only the usage of Azure Storage (and relative queues), and does so in the WebJob project template. So because we need a service bus, we need to add ServiceBus WebJob extensions in the same way from NuGet:

```
Install-Package Microsoft.Azure.WebJobs.ServiceBus
```

The main function of a console app, as the entry point in a worker, should be an endless loop that polls for a condition and then executes the specific handler. In WebJobs, there is a prefab class, JobHost, which implements the loop for us:

```
public static void Main()
{
    JobHostConfiguration config = new JobHostConfiguration();
```

```
ServiceBusConfiguration serviceBusConfig = new
  ServiceBusConfiguration
{
    ConnectionString =
        AmbientConnectionStringProvider
        .Instance.GetConnectionString
          (ConnectionStringNames.ServiceBus)
};
config.UseServiceBus(serviceBusConfig);

JobHost host = new JobHost(config);
host.RunAndBlock();
}
```

The default implementation of a WebJob supports just one Azure Storage account and one Service Bus account at a time. If we need access to more than one Azure Storage or Service Bus accounts, we need to make a custom implementation of the WebJob code or customize the WebJob SDK source code. The following link has an example of this operation:

`https://github.com/Azure/azure-webjobs-sdk`

A specific Azure Storage account is needed for non-functional requirements, not for potential work but to store log files as WebJobs performs its tasks. It creates two containers for this:

- `azure-webjobs-host`: Where the worker logs its lifetime nonfunctional events, such as heartbeats and ID generation
- `azure-job-host-output`: Where the worker logs its functional event handling triggers

What are triggers? A trigger is the pattern implemented by WebJobs to give the developer an abstraction on a fully-fledged message handling implementation. A trigger can be signaled by:

- A new row in an Azure Table
- A new message in an Azure Storage Queue
- A new or updated blob in an Azure Blob container
- A new message in an Azure Service Bus Queue
- A subscription triggered by an Azure Service Bus Topic

In our case study, we use the Azure Service Bus queue, but the pattern is implemented in the same way. A trigger is associated to a parameter in a static function accessible by the `WebJob` object: it polls the source of the triggers until it happens and retrieves the object triggered in the associated parameter, consistently with the specific message. The function runs in a sort of saga: the source object is peaked. If the handler completes correctly, the message is automatically completed and removed from queue. Otherwise, in the case of an exception, the WebJob retries (as a message is not removed from queue) for a configurable number of times to complete the handling, or the message is finally moved to the poison messages queue:

```
public async static void HandleBasket(
    [ServiceBusTrigger("basket")] BrokeredMessage message
    , [ServiceBus("events")] ICollector<BrokeredMessage> events)
{
    var command =
      JsonConvert.DeserializeObject<BasketCommand>(
      message.GetBody<string>());
}
```

The parameter is automatically deserialized consistently to its type, or we can deserialize as `BrokeredMessage` in order to manually perform operations on it. Again, the plumbing is hidden, so we can concentrate on our functional tasks. This is probably not sufficient for all scenarios, but it's a great simplification if we need to start with it.

So, now we can execute the command. The rule in our scenario is that a user has a single basket per session, so `UserId` can be a key for the basket. For this code, we store baskets in Azure Storage. We can look to see if this is the correct way to implement baskets (as we discussed in *Chapter 4, Building the Backend*). In this case, it is now appropriate to demonstrate another feature of the solution.

So, the command is typed by the `BasketCommand` class:

```
public class BasketCommand
{
    public CommandType Type { get; set; }
    public string UserId { get; set; }
    public int Quantity { get; set; }
    public int ProductId { get; set; }
}
```

The `UserId` can be used to retrieve a blob from an Azure Storage Blob container containing:

```
var storageConnectionString =
  AmbientConnectionStringProvider.Instance
```

```
    .GetConnectionString(ConnectionStringNames.Storage);
var storageAccount =
    CloudStorageAccount.Parse(storageConnectionString);
var blobClient = storageAccount.CreateCloudBlobClient();
var basketContainer = blobClient.GetContainerReference("baskets");
var basketBlob =
    basketContainer.GetBlockBlobReference(command.UserId);
```

If the basket exists, then it is deserialized from JSON, or an empty object is created if a blob does not exist:

```
if (basketBlob.Exists())
{
    json = await basketBlob.DownloadTextAsync();
    basket = JsonConvert.DeserializeObject<Basket>(json);
}
else
{
    basket = Activator.CreateInstance<Basket>();
    basket.UserId = command.UserId;
}
```

The basket is an object, better described as an **Aggregate Root (AR)** if we describe it in terms of **Domain-driven Design (DDD)**. A command expresses the intention of the user on the result, not how to do it, so the worker has to map the command arguments to the relative member of the AR. There should be a method for each command. This is the most correct way of handling this scenario as the AR is the only testable object we can create in a scenario where it can be difficult testing it by sending all possible commands in the bus.

It's beyond the scope of this book to explore basket implementation in depth (you can read the sample code that comes with this book). A class contains private entity classes that it has the responsibility to manage. The command handler has to dispatch the correct command to the correct method:

```
switch (command.Type)
{
    case CommandType.AddToBasket:
        var unitPrice = 1m; // lookup ProductId on a PriceList
            service
        basket.AddProduct(command.ProductId, command.Quantity,
            unitPrice);
        break;
    default:
        throw new NotSupportedException("Command not supported");
}
```

The basket is then serialized back to JSON and stored back into a blob:

```
json = JsonConvert.SerializeObject(basket);
await basketBlob.UploadTextAsync(json);
```

> To be fully consistent to the DDD methodology, the Azure Storage code, up to serialization and deserialization, should be encapsulated into a repository pattern – do it as an exercise.

Dealing the past with events

When we implement code handling the command message, we may contextually make some mistakes, such as:

- Executing some other operation on another entity, for example, because it needs to change consistently with the first operation
- Tracing the fact that the operation has been executed in a log file

Forget testing how command execution is performing in terms of speed and resource usage. Each of these mistakes has some effect on how we handle the entire project.

The first mistake is a matter of responsibility. For example, when we add an item to the basket we need to change the product availability into the store (that is, another entity). Is it correct that the same code that updates the basket updates the store? No: basket and store are two entities (or better, aggregates in DDD terms) that have two different lifetimes and responsibilities, so they need to be well separated into different places. The store should be informed that a basket has changed and it must change accordingly.

The second mistake is a matter of usefulness. We are used to storing the trace of a command invocation, just in case of future problems, in order to analyze a hypothetical issue that perhaps should not have happened. So, log data is a kind of data that is persisted as simple text files, comma-separated-value files that are stored and probably never reused. When the issue happens, we need to find out what has happened in the middle of useless traces. Traces should be represented in a more functional way for faster and immediate usage, skipping useless data and emphasizing important data.

The third mistake is a matter of performance. In cloud computing, elasticity is one of the main issues. We can dynamically change the resource allocation accordingly, adding resources when the service is overloading, and releasing resources when it is underused. But how do we discover whether we need more or fewer resources?

We call them mistakes as we need to handle all the issues properly, somewhere in the code, strictly not in the command handling code. Every issue can be summarized by one assumption: something can happen after the command execution has been completed. There are many concepts here:

- *Has been completed*: Something has surely happened and it's the execution of the command.
- *After*: There is a time in the future when something will happen.
- *Can*: We cannot be sure (but is not the responsibility of this command) that something can happen. It is not mandatory; nothing can also happen.

The correct way to avoid these mistakes is by applying some coding patterns to decouple and distribute responsibility. Instead of handling multiple responsibilities in one piece of code, we need to notify other parts of the code (parties in the solution) that something has happened, giving them the opportunity to handle their own responsibilities. This notification cannot be represented as a line in a log file as it is a way to save and forget that it has happened. A better solution is to use an in-memory object, such as commands or entities, which can be used to communicate with other parts of the code, informing those parts that the command execution has been done. This object is called an *event*. There are two ways of handling events:

- Responding on a per-message basis
- Responding on a per-stream basis, which means you want to respond to a group of events because you have discovered that all the events together mean something for the application

Per-message event handling

After the basket has received the command to add a product in it, the web application will not yet be updated with the new basket information.

In terms of responsibility, it is correct that a command handler does not update the UI. Instead it has the responsibility of notifying that a product was added into the basket, and that the total and the content have changed.

This is an important concept for evolutional software. Events are a great way of decoupling, not only on actual features, but also with future, hypothetical features. If in future there is a need for another feature depending on how the basket updated, then none of the existing code would be affected as just another worker would be necessary to generate another answer to the event.

Because many (more than one) can be interested in an event, the service bus queue is not the correct solution, as it is designed around the idea that with competing consumers, only one receives the message. A variation on this kind of service is the publisher/subscriber messaging pattern. As a single actor, called a publisher, sends a message, this assumes the meaning of the topic as an argument of interest. There can be 0, 1, or many other actors, called subscribers, who can be interested in the topic. As any subscription is represented by a queue, for the publisher there is only one virtual queue and the system takes the role of replicating copies of the message to each subscriber queue.

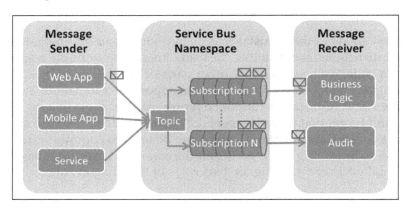

A topic is an event generated by something called a publisher. It defines a sort of virtual queue. It's virtual because the message received is copied n times in internal queues, where n is the number of subscriptions to the topic. The number of subscriptions depends on the number of consumers who are potentially interested in the event. "Potentially" means that each message copy is received by its subscriber, which should have its own business rule that discriminates between handling it and discarding it.

From the **Service Bus** tab in the classic portal, under a **Service Bus Namespace**, a **TOPIC** can be defined, like a queue, specifying a literal name, for example, **events**.

Under the selected topic, we can find one or more subscriptions. One rule can be a subscription for each role using the software solutions that need handling events. In our case, the web application needs to be updated on the basket update to give the UI interface information about the content change.

So, back in the worker, after the basket update on Azure Storage, an event must be raised. Azure WebJobs defines sending an event passing an argument that has two requirements:

- It's an `ICollector<T>` argument, which is an insert-only collection, instantiated by the caller, and the handler function can only append a new event in it. As for the command, our solution event will be a brokered message.

- The **Event collector** argument is decorated with `ServiceBusAttribute`, which associates the topic (or queue in general) when enqueuing the new events.

An event is, like our commands, described as an anonymous type serialized in the JSON format inside a brokered message.

There is no a general rule, but some advise that:

- An event must be a small object, so it cannot a lot of data

- The event producer should avoid making hypotheses about consumers, limiting the amount of information that can be contained in it

- An event should contain some data that describes what has happened; that is, it's the responsibility of each subscriber to retrieve more data after the event notification

- An event should be discriminated by a type or name that expresses what has happened in "past tense language" (the command is expressed in the present tense):

```
events.Add(new BrokeredMessage(
    JsonConvert.SerializeObject(new {
        UserId = command.UserId,
        LocalTime = DateTime.Now,
        Type = EventType.ProductAddedToBasket,
        ProductId = command.ProductId,
        ItemsInBasket = basket.Products.Count(),
        TotalPrice = basket.TotalPrice
    })
));
```

When the handler completes correctly without exceptions, incoming messages are marked as complete and output events are enqueued to the topic.

The web application can now function in its role as subscriber. Two things to note:

- Waiting for an event is a poll loop or a suspended task (depending on its implementation) that needs to be defined at the process level

- The only place to locate an ASP.NET application, which is mainly a stateless request/response application, is in a startup object level

We can define a class that helps describe the topic subscription:

```
public static void Subscribe(string topic,
  string subscription, Action<BrokeredMessage> handle)
{
    var client =
        SubscriptionClient.CreateFromConnectionString
            (ConfigurationManager.ConnectionStrings
              ["ServiceBus"].ConnectionString
            , topic, subscription);

    var options = new OnMessageOptions();
    options.AutoComplete = false;
    options.AutoRenewTimeout = TimeSpan.FromMinutes(1);

    client.OnMessage((message) =>
    {
        try
        {
            handle(message);
            // Remove message from subscription.
            message.Complete();
        }
        catch (Exception ex)
        {
            // Indicates a problem, unlock message in
              subscription.
            message.Abandon();
        }
    }, options);
}
```

The SubscriptionClient class in the Service Bus SDK is defined to handle message-receiving scenarios. It is configured by the Service Bus connection string: when generating it from the portal, we need to authorize it for listen and manage on the queue, as client needs retrieving and removing messages from it. With the construction, the topic and subscription name must be specific.

An `OnMessage` handler receives a callback, which in these scenarios can be generalized as:

- Decoupling outside the setup method specific handler code with a delegate.
- Wrapping the handler delegate call with an exception handler: the track message as `Complete` if the handler completes correctly and signal `Abandon` in the case of an exception. In this last case, subscribed messages will be retried for a defined number of times before being deleted or moved to the DeadLetterQueue if this is configured on the service.

The initialization task is called at the startup class level:

```
public void Configuration(IAppBuilder app)
{
    ConfigureAuth(app);

    // arguments to be saved in config file
    ServiceBusTopic.Subscribe("events", "WebApplication",
      message =>
    {
        var dto = JsonConvert.DeserializeObject<EventDto>(
            message.GetBody<string>());
        NotificationHub.Notify(dto);
    });

    // arguments to be saved in config file
    ServiceBusTopic.Subscribe("feedback", "WebApplication",
      message =>
    {
        var dto = JsonConvert.DeserializeObject<FeedbackDto>(
            message.GetBody<string>());
        if (dto.Message == $"UserId {dto.UserId} has failed login
          more than 3 times in the last 10 minutes")
        {
            var context = new ApplicationDbContext();
            var user = context.Users.Single(xx => xx.UserName ==
              dto.UserId);
            user.LockoutEnabled = true;
            context.SaveChanges();
        }
    });

    app.MapSignalR();
}
```

The handler specifies what to do with the message. As for commands, the brokered message contains a JSON object serialized as a string. We can deserialize it as a data transfer object and use it.

In our sample, we need to update the basket information that is visible on the page. For this purpose, we can use **SignalR**. This is an implementation of a two-way channel between client and server to complement the typical HTTP request/response scenario. This is important: request/response is a synchronous scenario, as it is triggered by the client. But we also need a server-triggered scenario for asynchronous, unattended executions in the server, which the client needs to know.

It works in two ways, depending on the configuration of the deployment server and on the client browser. If the two parties are modern enough to establish a connection with the **WebSocket** protocol, a real two-way channel is instantiated and SignalR can really push content to the client. If one of the two parties does not support WebSocket, the SignalR libraries simulate the channel with a client side long polling task implemented over the HTTP protocol.

A requirement for this to work is that authentication is done because it uses the username as the key to select the connected client and dispatch the message back to the correct user.

The SignalR infrastructure starts with the **Start** class on the Asp.Net project, where initialization is done in the `configuration` method with the following instruction:

```
app.MapSignalR();
```

These functions discover all classes known as *hubs* defined into the web projects that derive from a `Microsoft.AspNet.SignalR.Hub` class and create singletons. These instances are available through a `GlobalHost` object and are selected by typing the following code:

```
public class NotificationHub : Hub
{
    public static IHubContext Default
    {
        get
        {
            return
                Microsoft.AspNet.SignalR
                .GlobalHost
                .ConnectionManager
                .GetHubContext<NotificationHub>();
        }
    }
```

An `IHubContext` object is used to communicate with clients, handle HTTP and WebSocket requests, and create JavaScript code to prepare the communication from the client. In fact, in the HTML that needs to communicate with SignalR has to reference two JavaScript files via the `script` tag:

```
<script src="~/Scripts/jquery.signalR-2.2.0.js"></script>
<script src="~/signalr/hubs"></script>
```

The first one is the API library that extends the `jquery` library to use a consistent syntax; the second one contains the JavaScript proxy code that is automatically generated from the corresponding server hub classes: a method on the server object implies a method on the client proxy. For example, SignalR needs to be initialized on the page, and we use the user ID by which the user is logged (the username in our sample) and send it to the hub for the first time, allowing the `hub` class to associate our business key to the internal connection ID, which is strictly dependent on SignalR. The following code will help you to get through that:

```
$.connection.hub.start().done(function () {
    // register with my userId that comes from Server
      inside the view
    $.connection.notificationHub.server.
      RegisterUser('@ViewBag.UserId');
});
```

On the server side, our custom `RegisterUser` method saves the `userId` as a key in a collection to discover the `ConnectionId`:

```
[HubMethodName("RegisterUser")]
public void RegisterUser(string userId)
{
    __connections.Add(userId, Context.ConnectionId);
}
```

So, we started talking about the SignalR because of the need to notify UI, HTML pages with the events in the basket. The DTO we have received from the ServiceBus subscription can be sent to the client via SignalR:

```
public static void Notify(EventDto dto)
{
    foreach (var connectionId in __connections.GetConnections(dto.
UserId))
    {
        dynamic client = Default.Clients.Client(connectionId);
        client.handle_event(dto);
    }
}
```

The default property is required to access the server proxy to communicate with a client via a dynamic object. A dynamic object is required because there is no client-side, JavaScript typing information to know which methods are available on the client side. In our case, we invoke a client side member called `handle_event`. That method is defined as a prototype to the `$.connection.event.client` object:

```
$.connection.notificationHub.client.handle_event =
  function (event) {
    switch (event.Type) {
      case "ProductAddedToBasket", 0:
        ProductAddedToBasket(event.ProductId,
          event.ItemsInBasket, event.TotalPrice)
        break;
      default:
        // signal not handled
        break;
    }
  };
```

The `Basket` function will perform the correct operation to update the UI.

Per-stream event handling

We learned that an event is the notification of the execution of a command. In general, any action, not only a command execution with workers and queues, can notify events. The purpose is to react (or not) to the event with some tasks and this decision is completely decoupled from the task that has generated it. Note that in this way, we decide if and how by looking just at a single event.

There are some scenarios where we might take decisions because of a group of events that are raised in a period of time. Let's take the login process of a web application as an example.

A user types their username and password into the login form to perform authentication. Authentication fails. The effect of this action is to raise an invalid login event. We are used to locking out a username after three invalid login attempts. We typically implement this process, counting the number of login attempts and storing the counter into the username profile. When login fails and the counter is at 3, the account is locked out.

What is wrong in this process? Login and lockout are two different tasks, implemented together (coupled) because we implement lockout in the state of the account. We have also a third task: the failed attempt counter must be reset if the last failed login attempt was outside a predefined value of time. As we have already told you many times, coupling is bad. It is also bad using state to handle tasks because state can easily be corrupted (for example, by not resetting the failed attempt counter because a testing module might be missing).

What we can say is that we are solving the account lockout task in an imperative way: we implemented an algorithm that determines that the account needs to be locked out. Events are not useful to our objective: events are raised after task execution, so we have already implemented and changed state.

Talking in terms of an "imperative way" means, Can we express a lockout condition? Can we use events for this task? If we can do this, we can implement a login task that just determines if the username and password are correct or not and raises an event if they are not. Another independent task will determine whether we need to lockout the account. These two are distinct tasks, but simpler (applying the **Simple Responsibility Principle**) to implement and test.

We can express (or better "declare") the account lockout task with events: the user account needs to be locked out if we have three failed login attempt events in a period of 10 minutes. If this happens, an account lockout message must be sent to a system that can perform the lockout.

If we consider the **ASP.NET MVC** authentication process as it is implemented in the Visual Studio template with its form and controller implementation, we are led to a couple of considerations:

- It is not useful to change the classic authentication process to a command-based one. It is preferable to use something that is already wholly implemented and supported.

- If we generate an event that signals the authentication process has failed, we don't react to the single event because, again, the authentication process has already been implemented.

In general, there are many scenarios where we need to collect events but we don't need to process them one by one. For this kind of scenario there are different Azure services that are more focused on these objectives.

Collecting events with Azure Event Hubs

An Event Hub has similarities with Messaging in Service Bus, but it is structurally different. Event Hubs act as the "front door" for an event pipeline; once data is collected into an Event Hub, it can be transformed and stored using any real-time analytics provider or batching/storage adapter. Event Hubs decouple the production of a stream of events from the consumption of those events, so that event consumers can access the events on their own schedule.

The Azure Event Hubs service is a cost-effective reimplementation of a messaging queue as it has been designed with massive ingestion capacity in mind, in scenarios such as connected devices and the Internet of Things.

We create an Event Hub always under a ServiceBus namespace, in the same place and portal as Messaging. We start assigning a name to the hub and the specific type of messaging (EventHub). Then you can select (or leave the defaults in force) the following:

- The partition count, by which you can control the number of processors that scale out the service. This number cannot be changed afterwards so it is necessary to define the correct number in critical performance scenarios.

- The message retention, that is the number of days that messages can be retained without processing (this means: there is no processor running) before being discarded automatically.

Authentication in the Event Hub has the same rules as messaging: we can define an SAS for every subject relating to the Event Hub.

Now, we can go to the code and update the account controller that comes with the default Asp.Net template. We can send a message in a similar way to messaging. The API is already in the same assembly as the Service Bus SDK:

```
protected async Task SendEventHubAsync<T>(string name, T target)
{
    var eventHub = EventHubClient.CreateFromConnectionString(
        ConfigurationManager.ConnectionStrings["ServiceBus"].
          ConnectionString, name);
    var json = JsonConvert.SerializeObject(target);
    var bytes = Encoding.UTF8.GetBytes(json);
    var data = new EventData(bytes);
    await eventHub.SendAsync(data);
}
```

The code is similar to the queue code: the difference is just in the object to be enqueued; in this case, we have `EventData` that explicitly states its role. And it is known that for the producers (and consumers) of the messages, the serialization has to be done manually as we need to send a `byte` array (this is probably due to different teams developing SDKs).

This function can be called anywhere we need to track events in code. For example, in the login process, we can track it sending an event:

```
[HttpPost]
[AllowAnonymous]
[ValidateAntiForgeryToken]
public async Task<ActionResult>
  Login(LoginViewModel model, string returnUrl)
{
    //...code removed...
    var statusId = await SignInManager.PasswordSignInAsync(
        model.Email, model.Password, model.RememberMe,
          shouldLockout: false);
    await SendEventHubAsync("Accounts", new
    {
        Category = "Login",
        LocalTime = DateTime.Now.ToUniversalTime(),
        UserId = model.Email,
        ResultId = statusId
    });
```

It's interesting to notice that raising an event, that is, sending a message to Event Hub, is semantically equivalent to creating a log. The difference is essentially technical: we represent an event as an object in a queue in a more structured service, rather than in a plain text file for future reuse.

Processing event streams with Azure Stream Analytics

Azure Stream Analytics is a cost-effective event processing engine, built with data streams and Event Hubs in mind. It can perform real-time, mission-critical, scalable insights on data in motions. It abstracts the event processing from the API approach with an implementation of a SQL-like syntax, extended to handle specific features such as temporal, windowing, and scaling functionalities.

It works with heterogeneous data services in input and in output. This implies that data cannot be strongly typed, as input and output sources have no schema in general. Different data sources can share only a minimal type system, even if data sources have a stricter type system. The table that follows explains it in a concise manner:

Type	Description
bigint	Integers in the range of -2^{63} (-9,223,372,036,854,775,808) to 2^{63}-1 (9,223,372,036,854,775,807)
float	Floating point numbers in the range of -1.79E+308 to -2.23E-308, 0, and 2.23E-308 to 1.79E+308
nvarchar(max)	Text values, comprising unicode characters. Remember that a value other than max is not supported
datetime	Defines a date that is combined with a time of day (with fractional seconds) that is based on a 24-hour clock and relative to UTC (time zone offset 0).

> Azure Stream Analytics is available from the new Ibiza portal, but at the time of writing this, the implementation is not complete. So, we currently have a better development experience using the classic portal. There is no dev experience from Visual Studio.
>
> Be aware that the same service is accessible from the two portals at the same time. But if some v2 resources are used, such as Azure Storage v2 or DocumentDB, these will be visible only from the new portal.

To create a new stream from the classic portal, we need to select **New** | **Data Services** | **Stream Analytics** | **Quick Create**, and following information has to be filled in the respective fields:

- The name of the job under **JOB NAME**
- The region in the **REGION** field

- The storage account where the service stores log blobs, new or existing:

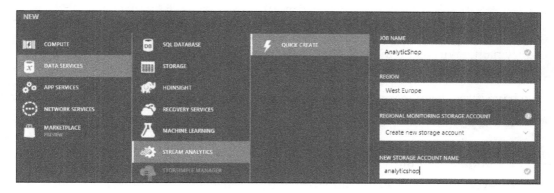

Stream Analytics is an Event Hub processor. It takes input streams, processes events, and generates new events on the output. To create a functional job, we need to define:

- Inputs, one or more
- Outputs, one or more
- Query, just one, simple or complex as needed

So, the first thing to do is create an input. We need to make two choices. The first one is between the data stream and reference data:

- The first one is a continuous sequence of events that will be consumed by the job and that is time-based.
- The second one is slow-changing data used for correlation and lookup. Reference data is only blobs inside a storage. Stream Analytics service is still evolving. There are many user requests for new input types for slow changing data, inside the service. But for now, any other scenario must be handled with some other services, like Azure Data Factory, that will generate blobs for us.

We can add three kinds of data streams:

- Event Hub, the original requirement
- IoT Hub, an extended version of Event Hub to be used in association with IoT and all device needs
- Blob Storage, to approach the original log files as streams of data

If we choose Event Hub and we refer to hubs from the same subscription, many of the parameters required are already automatically loaded, leaving blank just the name of the input. Remember that the name we use here will be used inside the query to reference the particular input. As always, we need to select the correct Event Hub policy name. We should avoid using **RootManageSharedAccesKey**, using this only for administrative purposes, and always create different policies for different processes.

We have three different event serialization formats:

- JSON, the typical serialization format to choose and implement in applications
- CSV, selecting the character value separator, for legacy sources that cannot update their output tasks
- Avro, a binary serialization format from Apache Foundation

The output choice is richer:

- SQL Database and Table Storage for table-structured data that can be used directly in applications.
- DocumentDB for JSON-structured data that can be used directly in applications.
- PowerBI for direct integration to data visualization. In this case, a business account in Office 365 is required. If there are issues using a business account in Azure, data can be stored in table-structured databases and then referenced by PowerBI.
- Blob Storage for long-term storage for future reference.
- Event Hub to connect another stream job organizing and distributing the workload.
- ServiceBus Queue and Topics to obtain per-message processing. The serialization settings are the same as input, with one more parameter in the case of JSON, named format: one event per row or a big JavaScript array

In our case, we need:

- A data stream input called `Accounts` that receives login attempts (remember it contains `Category`, `LocalTime`, `UserId` and `ResultId`)
- A reference data input stream called `LoginResults` to decode login attempts (containing `ResultId` and `Result`)
- A ServiceBus Queue output as we need to give feedback to the web application (or Topic if we need more than one subscriber)

Which is our objective? To notify the application that a user has failed the login more than three times in under 10 minutes. With this information, probably the application will disable the user account (but this is the responsibility of the application, not of the analytical process).

A query that satisfies our requirements with the defined input is as follows:

```
WITH FailedLogins AS (
    SELECT a.UserId, COUNT(*) AS Attempts
    FROM Accounts AS a TIMESTAMP BY a.LocalTime
    JOIN LoginResults AS lr ON a.ResultId = lr.ResultId
    WHERE a.Category = 'Login' and lr.Result <> 'Success'
    GROUP BY HoppingWindow(Second, 600,10), a.UserId
    HAVING COUNT(*)> 3
)
SELECT
    'Notification' AS Type,
    'Error' AS Severity,
    UserId,
    System.Timestamp AS LocalTime,
    ConCat('UserId ',
        CAST(UserId as nvarchar(max)),
        ' has failed login more than 3 times in the last 10 minutes') AS
Message
INTO Feedback
FROM FailedLogins
```

There are a lot of concepts inside it.

The first thing we see is that there are two queries, mixed together with the WITH keyword. From the T-SQL memory, WITH...AS is the **Common Table Expression (CTE)** construct, which is as a temporary result set that is defined within the execution scope of the outside select. Many CTEs can be associated to an external SELECT. In stream analytics they have the same role as temporary result sets, but supply more evidence about performance issues. CTE enables stream analytics to use **Streaming Units (SU)**. Many SUs can be allocated for a streaming job (up to 48), and building queries with the WITH keyword and the PARTITION BY keyword helps processes to span over more SU. The more you use, the more you pay; however, the more parallel the process is, the faster its processing.

The second thing we see is JOIN. In FailedLogins, we JOIN together DataStream and ReferenceData to decode the ResultId number with a literal and make a filter clearer. Inputs in SA normalize heterogeneous inputs of different nature in one consistent set-based syntax.

The third thing to note is the keyword TIMESTAMP BY. All data streams contain temporal data, so it important to define which is the timestamp associated to the event. We have two possibilities:

- **Arrival time**: Event Hub associates to the event time, calculated by the system, when an event gets into it

- **Custom time**: An explicit DateTime property on the event that can become the timestamp associated to the event with the keyword TIMESTAMP BY

The fourth thing to note is a windowing function used as a GROUP BY clause. This is one of the most important and complex concepts of ASA. Structurally, Event Hub does not retain events for more than seven days: this can be considered a *physical* time boundary for events. Even if ASA retained events indefinitely, what does grouping mean from the beginning of time? In temporal queries, time is always an explicit boundary. In our example, if a user logs on once a day and, for example, fails at least once a day, if we group login attempts for more than three days we will lock out every account. We say that there is an intrusion if there is a brute-force attack (an intense and repetitive username/password login attempt) more than three times in 10 minutes. HoppingWindow specifies to group events in a window-wide 600 seconds (10 minutes) and repeats that window moving over events every 10 seconds. So if in the Event Hub there are events distributed in an hour, for example, the query will be executed 3,600/10=360 times. ASA is smart enough to cache results if the events stream does not change in a determined window.

So we have the fifth and most theoretical concept. Writing a query doesn't express the imperative instructions needed to extract data (and we know that SQL DBMS create an execution plan for this from the SQL). The query expresses the requirements that data to be returned needs to satisfy. In fact, we say that SQL is a declarative language. The HoppingWindow function defines that from the starting time of the job, every 10 seconds, the query is executed over a window that is 600-seconds wide of the events in the past. That produces an intermediary result that is the result of the grouping clause, counting the number of events for every user in that window. The HAVING clause will limit the resulting rows only with what is considered a login attack, when the COUNT is greater that a specified threshold.

The temporary result is consumed by the outside query, and while it is being consumed, a subquery continues in parallel to perform the windowing work. This happens for all WITH subqueries.

The outside query composes a new row if there are corresponding rows in the internal subquery. If a window satisfies the filtering criteria (COUNT(*)>3) the row assumes the meaning of the event itself: UserId has failed login more that three times in the last 10 minutes.

The INTO clause in an external query tells the processor to insert the event row in the output target. In the case of a ServiceBus Queue, as configured, the set of data with its metadata (property names) will be used to compose a JSON message. And this will be used by a consumer.

Azure Stream Analytics defines three different windowing functions, with one condition in common: the window is always fixed in size:

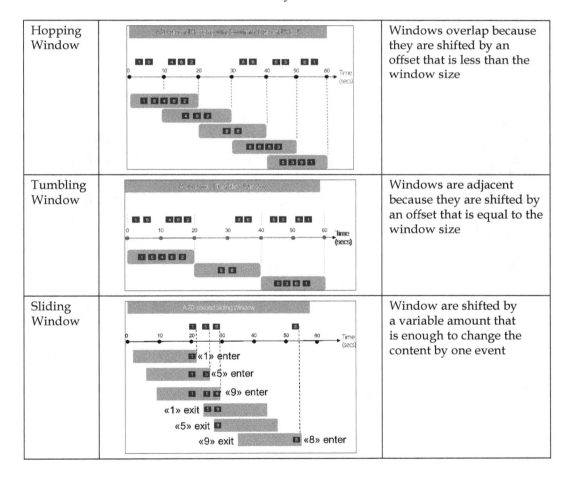

Hopping Window		Windows overlap because they are shifted by an offset that is less than the window size
Tumbling Window		Windows are adjacent because they are shifted by an offset that is equal to the window size
Sliding Window		Window are shifted by a variable amount that is enough to change the content by one event

On the web application, we can handle the receiving message on the queue and lock out the user. Refer to the following lines of code to implement it:

```
ServiceBusTopic.Subscribe("feedback", "WebApplication", message =>
{
    var dto = JsonConvert.DeserializeObject<FeedbackDto>(
        message.GetBody<string>());
    if (dto.Message == $"UserId {dto.UserId} has failed login more
      than 3 times in the last 10 minutes")
    {
        var context = new ApplicationDbContext();
        var user = context.Users.Single(xx => xx.UserName ==
          dto.UserId);
        user.LockoutEnabled = true;
        context.SaveChanges();
    }
});
```

Summary

In this chapter, we have learned what commands, events, and messages are. We have learned that we can write an application with commands and events, ensuring the correct responsibility for subdivisions between parties.

We have also learned how events can be used to discover patterns in data that mean something for the applications and that are impossible to discover by just looking at single events.

And we have covered ServiceBus, which supports the usage of messaging patterns.

In the next chapter, we will learn how we can formally describe a set of Azure services to deploy and manage a solution in a repeatable and reliable manner.

Deploying Solutions in Azure

8

We have already seen in the previous chapters that Azure is full of opportunities in terms of services available to be consumed in our solutions. The objective is developing code that is functional to solution objectives, more than non-functional aspects.

We have also told you that using Azure makes developers aware of the non-dev aspect of their work, which is called *operations*. We have spoken about networking and application lifecycle management, service management, and backup. It is always good that a developer knows about operations. However, there is something that is mandatory for dev about ops: deployment.

In the previous chapters, we used different ops tools, such as the PowerShell environment and APIs, the classic portal and new portal, and management APIs, to instantiate services when deploying our solution.

As we embrace the initial invitation to use Azure services as much as we can, we finally reach a complex solution made of different projects distributed over different instances of different services.

We might think that once a service is deployed and running, there are no benefits of using something different from what we have discovered in the course of this book, because they are one-time operations. Well, this is not correct.

There are many different motivations of developing and using a different way to deploy solution services. Here are some of them:

- **Environments**: Production in not the only environment we need to configure for our solutions. We have to take care of development, testing, and staging, which have the same roles and services instantiated but are used by different user groups.

- **Update and upgrade**: As we need to deploy a new version, it can affect all or part of the services.

- **Multi-tenancy**: We can deploy an entire production environment for each user and/or customer.

Disaster recovery (DR) and **business continuity (BC)** are, in general, not deployment issues, as we don't need to create an alternative DR or BC environment. This is because every single service in Azure refers to a Service Level Agreement, and each service implements its own DR or BC. We should take care in the case of accidental deletion of some services. We cannot discuss the business impact of this kind of incident, but technically speaking, we can have a solution to redeploy solution in minutes.

The Classic portal has highlighted some typical management issues that we now need to solve:

- Deploy all solution services as a batch
- Delete all solution services as a batch
- Identify the solution batch
- Search in the deployed services by batch

In this chapter, we'll cover only the first issue, but all other issues depend on the same concept. So, in this chapter, you will learn to:

- Understand Azure Resource Manager and ARM-based services
- Write an Azure Resource Manager template to deploy as a composite service solution
- Parameterize an Azure Resource Manager template with template functions

Azure Resource Manager

To solve the issues just exposed, Azure has implemented some concepts:

- A resource group is a batch of services that can be deployed in a single operation
- "Resource" is the generic term that refers to a service deployed in a subscription
- A resource group is described in a declarative way, with a JSON document called "resource template"
- All resources are managed by the **Azure Resource Manager (ARM)**
- ARM is accessible entirely via REST APIs in a single, consistent way, not specifically by service (it's the service that needs to expose an ARM-compatible interface)

The last topic is interesting for some issues:

- An Azure service needs to be rewritten or updated to be compatible with the ARM model.

- Not all services (at the time of writing this book) have already moved to the ARM mode, for example, the Service Bus service. These services are accessible only from the classic portal (in this case, we speak about ASM, Azure Service Mode).

- Some services coexist in two modes that are incompatible, for example, the virtual machines (V1 VMs are referred as classic VMs). This is one of the biggest issues (at the time of writing this book) as many support services (VLANs and backup) are not generally available, so V2 VMs are not completely production-ready.

- PowerShell has two distinct commandlet sets supporting the two modes (as we have seen in *Chapter 2, Enhancing the Hybrid Process*).

In general, we know that the ARM mode is the reference way to deploy resources, as all new services are available only in the ARM mode. All investments have to be done in the ARM mode.

We can have a view of Azure as resources for a special portal available to developers at https://resources.azure.com. It is authenticated with the same credentials and authentication as https://portal.azure.com/. It presents all resources organized by subscription and accessible by authenticated users.

On the left-hand side of the following screenshot, we can see a tree of resources, grouped by subscription at the first level and by resource groups at the second level, as an RG exists in only one subscription. RG names are local to the subscription.

A resource template is a declarative JSON text that describes how a resource has to be configured. JSON templates have to be considered as types of commands, as the template is not how a resource will look like when it is deployed, but how a resource should be configured once it is deployed.

Azure Resource Manager should be a standard way to deploy Azure resources, at least for developers, through an **Azure Resource Template**. The template is available in Visual Studio with Azure SDK installed. Visual Studio comes with an IDE experience, with **IntelliSense** that contains schema validation and creational wizards, which helps template creation. Wizards such as these offer some predefined template compositions for the most common deployment scenarios. To better understand how templates work, we will manually write a template.

We will use a classic three-tier web backed by a SQL Azure database as an example scenario. It needs:

- A web app plan to allocate server instances
- A web app for website deployment
- A slot for offline deployment, attached to a Git repository
- SQL Azure Server
- SQL database

Writing the template

From Visual Studio, when Azure SDK is installed (2.9 at the time of writing this book), you have cloud templates under the **Visual C#** templates tree, and the **Azure Resource Group** project is available:

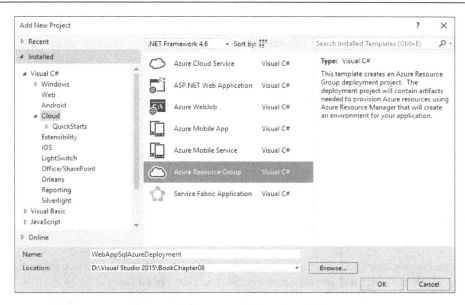

There are many predefined templates already available to handle some generic and common deployment scenarios with typical services deployed in combinations:

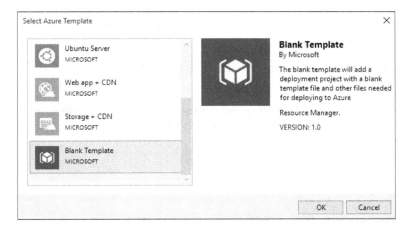

To better understand how it works, we start from a blank project template. The project constitution looks like this:

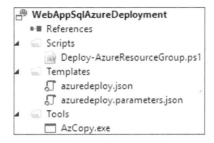

It contains:

- `azuredeploy.json`: This is the template itself.

- `azuredeploy.parameters.json`: This contains the persistence of initial values for defined parameters (we'll describe them later).

- `AzCopy.exe`: This is a common command-line utility to copy files from a local machine to an Azure storage account. This is useful if we want to deploy code from storage during this phase.

- `Deploy-AzureResourceGroup.ps1`: This is a PowerShell script that runs a template against the subscription and deploys code from the solution to the storage.

The empty template looks like this, made up of four JSON objects:

```
{
  "$schema": "https://schema.management.azure.com/schemas/
    2015-01-01/deploymentTemplate.json#",
  "contentVersion": "1.0.0.0",
  "parameters": {
  },
  "variables": {
      },
      "resources": [
  ],
  "outputs": {
  }
}
```

We will understand the parameters, variables, and outputs later in the chapter. For now, we will start with resources. Let's start with the **WebAppPlan**. It describes how the tenant has to be configured to run our web app. Take a look at the code that follows:

```
{
    "name": "WebAppFrontEndPlan",
    "type": "Microsoft.Web/serverfarms",
    "apiVersion": "2014-06-01",
    "location": "West Europe",
    "tags": { "displayName": "WebApp FrontEnd Plan" },
    "properties": {
        "sku": "Standard",
        "workerSize": "Small",
        "numberOfWorkers": 1
    }
}
```

It contains some properties:

- `name`: Refers to the resource inside the template
- `type`: The resource type inside the Resource Group
- `apiVersion`: Required to handle future version and template changes
- `location`: The region where the resource will be deployed
- `dependsOn`: As a template can contain many resources to be created, **dependsOn** allows the manager to order resource creation in the correct order
- `tags`: Allows the grouping of resources by description for future management search
- `properties`: The technical parameter to configure resources:
    - `sku`: Single value field that contains one of these values: `Free`, `Shared`, `Basic`, and `Standard`. It defines the tenants' capabilities.
    - `workerSize`: Single value field that has values such as `Small`, `Medium`, and `Large`. It defines the tenants' performance in terms of CPU, memory, and disk allocation.
    - `numberOfWorkers`: Number of instances that will be deployed of the same size.

Then, there is a web app template that looks like the following code block:

```
{
  "name": "WebAppFrontEnd",
  "type": "Microsoft.Web/sites",
  "location": "West Europe",
  "apiVersion": "2015-08-01",
  "dependsOn": [ "Microsoft.Web/serverfarms/WebAppPlan01" ],
  "properties": {
    "name": "WebApp",
    "serverFarmId": "/subscriptions/{your_subscription_id}/
      resourceGroup/WebAppSqlAzureGroup"
  }
}
```

There is a set of properties that are in common with the WebAppPlan. They are defined here:

- `type`: Specific for sites.
- `DependsOn`: A web app can be created only after the plan is already deployed and available. In general, a resource can depend on one or many other resources, so the property is an array that specifies all other resources already inside the template.
- `ServerFarmId`: Every resource has a globally unique ID that is used as a reference. This ID is typically a path (relative or absolute) inside the Azure subscription that is accessible by the logged-in user.
- `/subscription/<subscriptionId{guid}>`: The identification of the subscription, the owner of the resource.

These two resources are dependent resources, but they can live independently, as we can change the plan for the same web app.

There are other resources that cannot live without a *parent* resource.

We talked about slots in the web app in the previous chapter. There are many useful scenarios that have multiple versions of an app online at the same time. One usage of slots is deployments. We can deploy on a slot called `Stage`, for example, bringing live a new version. When the version is already tested and we have done a warm up (loading the code and web application), we can bring it live for all users with a `swap` operation. Slot is another web app, typically named `<WebApp(SlotName)>`, deployed as a resource inside the parent web app. The following code will help you get a clearer idea about it:

```
{
  "name": "WebAppFrontEnd",
  "resources": [
```

```
    {
      "name": "Stage",
      "type": "slots",
      "apiVersion": "2015-08-01",
      "location": "West Europe",
      "dependsOn": [ "Microsoft.web/sites/WebAppFrontEnd" ],
      "tags": {
        "displayName": "WebApp FronteEnd (Stage)"
      }
    }
  ],
  // code omitted
```

Here are the important points that you need to focus on:

- DependsOn as the slot depends by parent web app or the website
- And the resource inside the site (another resource)

The Stage slot is where we want to deploy code. There are many ways to deploy code. One way, which we described in previous chapters, is by connecting a deployment source, in this case, Visual Studio Team Service. For simplicity (but the way is the same), we will now configure a template using a GitHub public repository.

To proceed, it is important to do at least one manual configuration for this kind of deployment from the portal. This is because we need to preauthorize the Azure subscription accessing GitHub.

```
  {
    "name": "Stage",
    "resources": [
      {
        "name": "Web",
        "type": "sourcecontrols",
        "apiVersion": "2015-04-01",
        "dependsOn": [
          "Microsoft.Web/sites/WebAppFrontEnd/slots/Stage"
        ],
        "properties": {
          "repoUrl":
            "https://github.com/{your_github_account}/{your_repo}",
          "branch":  "master"
        }
      }
    ],
```

The way of adding SQL resources is the same and shows the value of PaaS, as the server is described by the few properties that are required to deploy a SQL Azure server:

```
{
  "name": "WebAppSql",
  "type": "Microsoft.Sql/servers",
  "location": "West Europe",
  "apiVersion": "2014-04-01-preview",
  "tags": {
    "displayName": "WebApp Sql"
  },
  "properties": {
    "administratorLogin": "{your_admin_username}",
    "administratorLoginPassword": "{your_admin_password}"
  }
}
```

In this case, the only notable properties are the administrator login and password. As a backend service for the particular web app in the front, it would be not useful if SQL did not allow the Azure services to accept connections from other Azure services (that is, common requests in the portal when we deploy the service manually). This can be done by adding a firewall policy as an embedded resource, allowing services to access SQL:

```
"resources": [
  {
    "name": "AllowAllWindowsAzureIps",
    "type": "firewallrules",
    "location": "West Europe",
    "apiVersion": "2014-04-01-preview",
    "dependsOn": [ "Microsoft.Sql/servers/WebAppSql" ],
    "properties": {
      "startIpAddress": "0.0.0.0",
      "endIpAddress": "0.0.0.0"
    }
  }
]
```

The SQL database is defined as another embedded resource in a server.

```
{
  "name": "WebAppDb",
  "type": "databases",
  "location": "West Europe",
  "apiVersion": "2014-04-01-preview",
  "dependsOn": [ "WebAppSql" ],
  "tags": { "displayName": "WebApp Db" },
  "properties": {
    "collation": "SQL_Latin1_General_Cp1_CI_AS_KI_WI",
    "edition": "Standard",
    "maxSizeBytes": "1073741824",
    "requestedServiceObjectiveName": "S0"
  }
}
```

The properties that need to be looked at are:

- `type`: `databases`: Set as the literal value for this field
- `edition`: A literal that has values from the set of `Basic`, `Standard`, and `Premium` for different levels of functionalities and calls of performances
- `requestedServiceObjectiveName`: The level of performance maintained inside `edition`
- `collation`: This chooses the right encoding and string handling

The template is almost complete, and it is time to deploy it. Visual Studio Experience is always integrated and supports us, as developers, on operational issues. Right-clicking on **Project** in **Solution Explorer** will show us a contextual menu with a **Deploy** action, different from **Publish**. This refers to a .NET code delivery to an Azure resource:

Clicking on **Deploy** will take us to a UI dialog, which allows us to execute a template:

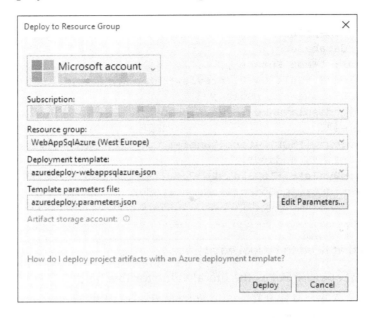

It defines:

- The Microsoft account to authenticate the user
- The subscriptions connected to the Microsoft account
- The resource group that will contain the resources described in the template; the **Resource Group** is selected live from the selected subscription or created with a specific dialog:

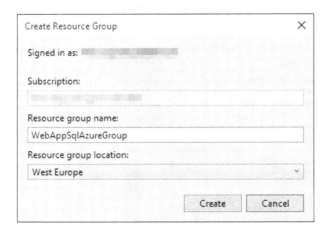

- The **Deployment Template**, as in the ARM project, many templates can be defined

- A template parameter file that we will describe later in the chapter

After clicking on **Deploy**, the process starts, which means, the PowerShell script inside the project is defined. We can customize the deployment process as we need. We have already mentioned that the Visual Studio template is mainly related to be added to a VS solution and that a web app project can be deployed using it. The PowerShell script is mainly devoted to supporting artifact upload from local machine to Azure Storage using the AzCopy command. Most of the code is used for this particular task. Remember that for VS integration, the IDE itself expects parameters to be wired by names as it needs to supply them via the dialog we showed earlier.

The core of the .ps1 file is the last two instructions that are specific to Resource Manager to deploy templates. The first one is required to create the Resource Group, if is does not exist:

```
New-AzureRmResourceGroup -Name $ResourceGroupName -Location
  $ResourceGroupLocation -Verbose -Force -ErrorAction Stop
```

The second is the effective deployment of the resources as described in the template:

```
New-AzureRmResourceGroupDeployment `
  -Name ((Get-ChildItem $TemplateFile).BaseName + '-' +
  ((Get-Date).ToUniversalTime()).ToString('MMdd-HHmm')) `
  -ResourceGroupName $ResourceGroupName `
  -TemplateFile $TemplateFile `
  -TemplateParameterFile $TemplateParametersFile `
  @OptionalParameters `
  -Force -Verbose
```

The execution of this script actually deploys the services into the selected Azure subscription. verbose parameter allows looking inside deployment process with detailed informations for diagnostic purposes, mainly if deployment fails. From Visual Studio, we can see it inside the output window.

Programming the template

In our template, we can discover two needs:

- There is a convention that is required to be followed while naming. All the resources share a common naming pattern, typically the project name.

- For multitenant projects, or projects that share the same architecture, the template is useful for more than one project and one requirement can be rewriting the template in such a way that we can reuse it with the minimal changes.

To support these needs, ARM templates implement two features. The first one is the presence of two other objects on the JSON ARM template: variables and parameters. Variables are specific key/value pairs to be referenced in other parts of the template. Parameters are key/value pair containers, like variables, with special features to be initialized from *outside* the template, using the `New-AzureRmResourceGroupDeployment` command, optional parameters, or the template parameter file that can be supplied with the template.

Variables and parameters are referenced inside the template with the second feature of the templates: programmability. Inside the template, JSON string values that start and end with a couple of square brackets are interpreted as a functional language that needs to be executed to generate effective JSON literals to be serialized and sent to the deploy action.

Two characteristics of this language are:

- **Object based**: All resources are represented by objects with properties from themselves, the contextual resources group, or the containing subscription

- **String manipulation**: As with previous properties and variables, the parameters can be combined to generate string values for the template

To start making the template more versatile, we can start with two parameters: `ProjectName` and `FriendlyName`. They are two strings that are used for reference in the template as the name and description in various resources:

```
"parameters": {
  "ProjectName": {
    "type": "string",
    "minLength": 1
  },
  "FriendlyName": {
    "type": "string",
    "minLength": 1
  },
```

The `type` property describes the validation type that you should apply for the parameter but is also helpful for an optional UI, such as Visual Studio. It can be selected among `string`, `securestring` (a password, captured in UI with asterisks), `array`, `object`, `int`, and `bool`. The `minLength` attribute and other attributes enhance the UI and validation experience for parameters.

With these two parameters, we can build up the name and description for references inside the template. We have two possibilities. The first one is using the parameter value inside a description, like a resource description, that is used once to describe the resource itself. So, to use parameters for this usage, we will use the following code:

```
"tags": {
  "displayName": "[concat(parameters('FriendlyName'),
    'FrontEnd Plan')]"
},
```

We first discover the elements of the string manipulation language:

- `"["` and `"]"` escape the template function language. All the text inside square brackets is evaluated as a function.

- The string literals are enclosed inside single-quote characters.

- `concat` is a string concatenation function that accepts one or more values. It is not an issue whether the value is a string or not as it will be automatically stringified.

- `parameters` is a function that accepts a literal containing the name of the parameter by which you read a value.

This friendly name generation is used once in templates. If the value is built and referenced more times inside the template, then a variable should be a valuable solution to reference the value more frequently:

```
"variables": {
  "WebAppPlanName": "[concat(parameters('ProjectName'),
    'FrontEndPlan')]",
  "WebAppName": "[concat(parameters('ProjectName'), 'FrontEnd')]",
},
```

The syntax is the same. The only difference is that variables are evaluated after accepting parameters, and they can be referenced in a similar manner as the parameters as shown in the following code:

```
"name": "[variables('WebAppPlanName')]",
```

The variables can be used as the name of a resource, as shown in the following code block:

```
"dependsOn": [
  "[concat('Microsoft.Web/serverfarms/',
variables('WebAppPlanName'))]"
],
```

The variables can be used as a resource reference.

Another value that repeats often inside the template is the deployment location. We can have a solution that is distributed geographically in many regions. However, inside a resource group, as it is relative to the region, we would like to deploy all resources inside the same region where RG is defined. We can use a variable to store the reference RG location:

```
"Location": "[resourceGroup().location]"
```

This shows us two new elements:

- `resourceGroup()`: A template language function that returns the RG object where the template is deployed
- It returns an object that is made up of properties that describe the RG and that can be individually referenced

So, every resource can be located by referencing the variable:

```
"location": "[variables('Location')]",
```

Built-in functions are very useful as we don't need to know many details, such as our Azure subscription ID, for example, when we need to reference resources by ID. As when referencing a WebAppPlan with the `serverFarmId` property to deploy a web app, we used subscriptionID to build up the ID. There is a function for this:

```
"serverFarmId": "[resourceId('Microsoft.Web/serverfarms',
  variables('WebAppPlanName'))]",
```

This function queries the live resource ID inside our resource group that is inside the subscription.

Back to parameters, there are two other situations with parameters.

When deploying a web app with a plan, we need to choose the size of the deployment among Free, Shared, Basic, and Standard. The parameter can be specified as a string literal that is more convenient as there are fewer significant integer values. There are two possibilities:

- The first one is a known property inside a resource. Possible values are already known because described by a schema. Visual Studio IntelliSense. For greater clarity, take a look at the following screenshot:

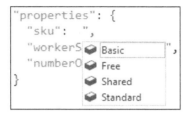

- The second one is value specified at parameter level. As the parameters are due to the choice of the developers and described by a generic type such as string, Visual Studio doesn't know which value literals are allowed. The developer should specify the set of literals via allowedValues property:

```
"WebAppSKU": {
  "type": "string",
  "allowedValues": [
    "Free",
    "Shared",
    "Basic",
    "Standard"
  ],
  "defaultValue": "Free"
},
```

For the Azure SQL Server, when we need to acquire the username and password, we can use a couple of parameters:

```
"administratorLogin": {
  "type": "string"
},
"administratorLoginPassword": {
  "type": "securestring"
}
```

Here, the password, typed in the UI, must be disclosed, with securestring (the UI will show asterisks as characters).

The template is now correctly parameterized. When we deploy the project by selecting our template, we can now access the **Edit Parameters** button. It will show a simple dialog that contains a grid with all the parameters we have defined in our template:

Parameters will be supplied by the `@OptionalParameters args` object in the `new-AzureRmResourceGroupDeployment` PowerShell command.

 Now that you have learned how a template looks and how we can customize it with parameters and template functions, we can take advantage of the Visual Studio deployment projects by adding more resources using the correct wizards. They automatically add the principal properties, useful variables, and required parameters and also solve resource dependency issues directly.

Be aware that template code can bloat rapidly. The wizard is useful to start, but then a manual fine-tuning is preferred.

Organizing deployment tasks with the Deploy to Azure button

IT professionals love PowerShell. Fine-tuned `.ps1` scripts will be the first choice of experienced professionals to deploy resources. Company governance, instead, will require specific, vertical template to deploy and manage Azure IT resources.

The developers will find useful handling resources via Visual Studio integration for portal-aware tasks.

On GitHub, in the Azure Team account (`http://github.com/azure`), there is a great ARM quickstart template repository (`https://github.com/Azure/azure-quickstart-templates`) that solves many specific resource-deployment scenarios. They are described in a very detailed way, so they are useful and provide knowledge too.

If we look inside these templates, we find a nice feature, presented as a button, called **Deploy to Azure**. From the specific template web page, where template objectives are described, by clicking on the button, we can deploy the template on Azure. The button redirects you to the Azure portal, presenting a form that is built up from parameter description inside the template itself. This is a functionality that is equivalent to the deploy task we have used inside Visual Studio. In this case, it is executed directly by the Azure portal. This can be useful for two scenarios:

- **Community or educational purposes**: As we share Azure-specific solution code on GitHub, it simplifies distributing and deploying Azure service configurations. We can deploy the template directly in the Azure portal, without using a deployment project inside the Visual Studio. This can be useful for deployment not on Windows platform also.
- **Company operations**: These are performed to organize and share preconfigured templates to help daily cloud operations.

We can try to do this as a custom web portal. From Visual Studio, we create a website project, as we don't need any backend logic to reach this objective. We include Bootstrap and jQuery as NuGet packages, as we need to do some client-side logic and layout in our HTML page.

In the project, we will create a folder named `Templates` where we can copy our ARM templates, like the one we have developed in this chapter:

We will create a file called `index.json` that is the list of templates inside the folder, with the name and description:

```
[
  {
    "name": "Web App Sql Azure",
    "description": "Create a Web App configured accessing a Sql Azure
database",
    "template": "azuredeploy-WebAppSqlAzure.json"
  }
]
```

In an `index.html` page, which will be the main page for the website, we will type an HTML table that will contain the list of templates that we can deploy:

```
<table class="table table-striped templates">
    <thead>
        <tr>
            <th class="col-lg-2">Template</th>
            <th>Description</th>
            <th class="col-lg-1"></th>
        </tr>
    </thead>
    <tbody></tbody>
</table>
```

With some JavaScript code, we can read the `index.json` file and fill the table dynamically. We can add templates to the file and update the index, and the website will update automatically.

The **Deploy to Azure** button works in a simple manner. We need to redirect the user who clicks on the button to https://portal.azure.com/#create/Microsoft. Template/uri/<templateurl>.

This can be used inside an HTML anchor tag. The reference to a specific template is done via the <templateurl> part of the URL. Our templates must be publicly accessible from our website, and <templateurl> is a properly escaped template URL (as special characters such as slash and colon are not to be considered part of the portal URL, but only a parameter). We can do this via JavaScript:

```
var azureDeployButtonImgUrl =
  "http://azuredeploy.net/deploybutton.png";
var azureDeployUrl =
  "https://portal.azure.com/#create/Microsoft.Template/uri/";

var urlBase = window.location.href;

$.getJSON("Templates/index.json", function (templates) {
    $.each(templates, function (i, item) {
        var templateUrl = urlBase + "Templates/" + item.template;
        $("table.templates > tbody").append(
            "<tr>"
            + "<td>" + item.name + "</td>"
            + "<td>" + item.description + "</td>"
            + "<td><a href='"
            + azureDeployUrl + encodeURIComponent(templateUrl)
            + "'><img src='" + azureDeployButtonImgUrl +
            "'/></a></td>"
            + "</tr>");
    });
});
```

We need to escape the templateUrl URL with the encodeURIComponent JavaScript function to be included inside another URL, avoiding URL misunderstanding. Button image can be directly referenced from Azure Deploy site.

This code creates a page like the one shown here:

If the website is properly deployed to a public endpoint, when we click on the **Deploy to Azure** button, the result is a redirection to the new Azure portal. Some observations are listed as follows:

- The template is identified as **Custom Deployment** and redirected to a specific blade
- We need to specify **Subscription** and **Resource Group**
- It retrieves our template and uses the parameter description to build up the input **Parameters** blade

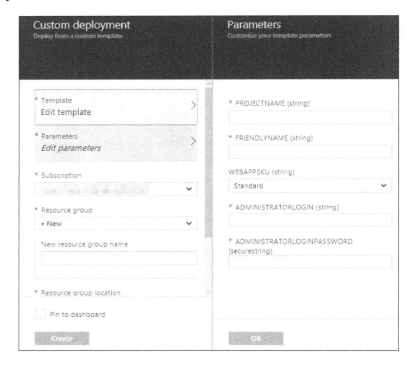

After clicking on **OK**, the deployment will proceed as a standard template available from the Azure portal.

Now that the template has run and services are deployed, we have two situations:

- Template deployment has executed parameters over the template function, so when you look in the JSON file, the functions will have been replaced with value literals
- Template deployment has done most of the work but DevOps now have to do some fine-tuning by updating some parameters

The two situations raise two specific issues:

- In the first case, when it comes to the resource group redeployment, do we need to re-execute the template by setting the parameters again?
- Manually updating to the services makes template deployment unrepeatable, as we have no knowledge of how to repeat manual updates

We could add a third situation. We have manually deployed services inside a resource group and we want to make it a Resource Manager template to make it repeatable.

All these situations have one solution in common, which is, exporting the template. From the portal, go to **Resource Group** and open **Settings**. There is a function of **Export template** that looks like this:

This opens a new blade that transforms the resource group's JSON description into a template replacing typical properties (for example, the name property) and dependencies with the corresponding parameters:

It also automatically generates template invocation code from PowerShell, the Bash command line, or .NET. We can make three things with it:

- **Redeploy**: This is used to immediately deploy another resource group.

- **Download**: Obtain a ZIP file containing all the script necessary to rerun the template, so we can use it in future or import it in a deployment solution in Visual Studio and make it more general.

- **Save template**: You open up a dialog to acquire a name and a description of the specific template. This template is saved on a new Azure service that is a **Template** repository.

The **Template** repository allows us to manage templates directly from the Azure portal, from creation to editing and then deployment:

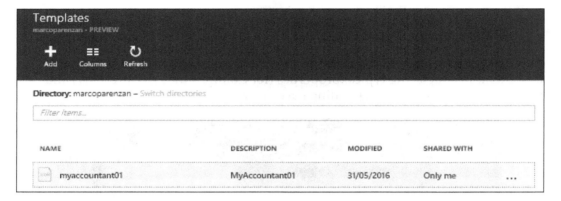

Summary

In this chapter, you learned the principles of Azure Resource Management and the notions of resource template and resource group.

You learned how a template should look in order to deploy services and how we can make it dynamic with template programmability features.

Finally, you saw an overview of how we can organize all our templates in a website to deploy them directly to Azure Portal.

As deployment closes the development phase, with Azure resource group deployment, we end our journey with this book. Moving through the eight chapters, you should have understood the features of the many Azure services available and learned how to use them in a solution. You also learned how to move your skills from a monolithic, three-tier, SQL-based, on-premise, web-only development to a distributed, service-based, public cloud solution, backed by different data storage methods and usable from devices rather than just the browser.

Through this book, we have covered as many services as possible to describe as many possibilities as we can. Now, it's your time to discover your specific service usage with your own projects, being aware that every project is different and has its specific requirements and services selection.

The cloud and Azure are a point of no return. Software complexity is increasing over time and you need to concentrate on the domain problem. So you need to code your domain logic and presentation, reusing as many services as you can for common patterns, as this will lower your **Total Cost of Ownership (TCO)** of the solution in the long term.

Learning Azure service usage throughout this book, you will discover that the services have probably evolved since we wrote these chapters, but the principles are here to stay. Azure is a major player in the cloud game and its fast and increasing adoption means Microsoft is continuously investing more and more in the development of new services and features over time.

Happy Azure coding!

Index

Symbols

.NET 4.6 MVC 102

A

Access Azure Service Management 257
access restriction policies
  about 251
  caller IPs, restricting 252
  call rate, limiting 252
  HTTP header, checking 251
  JWT, validating 252
  usage quota, setting 252
advanced policies
  control flow 252
  EventHub, logging 253
  one-way request, sending 253
  request, forwarding 253
  request, sending 254
  response, returning 253
AdventureWorks Cycles (AWC)
  about 84
  scenario 84-87
Aggregate Root (AR) 279
Apache Cordova
  mobile applications, building with Visual
    Studio Tools 190-200
API
  API Gateway 245, 246
  App Service 238, 239
  ASP.NET Web API, using 229-232
  building 228, 229
  deploying 237, 238
  documenting, with Swagger/OpenAPI 235

  importing, with Swagger 248
  ServiceStack 233
API Gateway 245, 246
app
  defining, as single page application 198
  defining, as web site application 198
  publishing, into Azure web apps 131-133
application deployments
  Production 135
  Testing 135
  User Acceptance 135
application development
  general scenarios 200, 201
  mobile development scenario 201
  prototyping scenario 201
  short-term application scenario 201
**Application Lifecycle Management
    (ALM) 4, 17**
app models
  API apps 136
  Logic apps 136
  Mobile apps 136
  Web apps 136
App Service
  application logs 243, 244
  App Settings management 239, 240
  backup 244
  continuous deployment 241
  debugging, with remote
    debugging 259, 260
  features 238, 239
  hybrid connections 242
  restore 244
  slots 240, 241
  traffic routing 240, 241

ARM Explorer
URL 14
ARM quickstart template repository
reference link 317
ARM Virtual Network
Windows Azure Virtual Machine,
deploying 61-64
ASP.NET MVC application scenario 269
ASP.NET MVC authentication process 289
ASP.NET Web API
using 229-232
Assets folder, resources
Certificates 35
Credentials 35
Modules 35
Schedules 35
Variables 35
Atomicity-Consistency-Isolation-Durability
(ACID) 146
authentication policies
basic authorization 254
certificate authentication 254
Azure
and Node.js 217-222
reference link 301
Azure Active Directory
used, for provisioning development
environment 27, 28
Azure Active Directory B2C
about 176-180
URL 178
Azure AD 174-176
Azure AD tenant
URL 28
Azure API Management (APIM)
about 246-248
Access Management 255
advanced APIM Management 256, 257
Echo API, creating 248-250
Identity Management 255
policies, using 251-255
using 246
Azure Automation
used, for automating repetitive
operations 34-40

Azure Data Factory (ADF)
about 160
DataSet 160
Linked Service 160
Pipeline 160
Azure DocumentDB
catalog, writing 87-101
Azure Event Hubs
used, for collecting events 290, 291
Azure Portal
URL 85, 178
Azure Redis
used, for speeding up data access 123-125
Azure RemoteApp
about 33
used, for provisioning development
environment 29-32
Azure Resource Manager (ARM)
about 44, 300-302
features 45
issues 301
Azure Resource Template 302
Azure Scheduler
used, for automating repetitive
operations 40, 41
Azure Search service
creating 107-114
Azure SQL Database
versus Azure SQL Data Warehouse 158
Azure SQL Data Warehouse
about 157
URL 157
Azure Storage
unstructured data, storing 115-123
Azure Stream Analytics
used, for processing event streams 291-298
Azure Stream AnalyticsDealing
used, for processing messages 266, 267
Azure Table Storage
used, for persisting shopping cart 126-130
Azure Team account
reference link 317
Azure web apps
application, publishing 131-137
web application, configuring with Custom
Domain Name 138, 139

B

backend servers
Service mode (classic) Virtual Network, configuring 52-55
Bootstrap
URL 195
Bower
URL 191
Bower Package Manager (BPM) 191
brokered messaging
about 268
advantages 268
business continuity (BC) 300

C

caching
used, for speeding up data access 123-125
camera shoot, parameters
destinationType 215
encodingType 215
mediaType 215
sourceType 215
claims-based authentication 174-176
Classic Manager
versus Resource Manager 30
classic portal
management issues 300
Classic Storage Account 31
classification 165
CloudMakersClassic 56
CloudMakers (CM) 56, 142
CloudMakers.XYZ
about 2, 43, 44
API infrastructure, creating 226-228
bootstrapping 3
e-commerce software platform, creating 142, 143
CM GeoService
implementing 234
RequestDTO, implementing 233
command messages 267
Commands ApiController 273
Common Table Expression (CTE) 295

complex API workflows
App Service, debugging with remote debugging 259, 260
debugging 257, 258
Service Bus relay, using 260-262
ConnectionStrings 272
consistency 80, 81
Consistency-Availability-Partitioning (CAP) 80
consistency level
BOUNDED STALENESS 92
EVENTUAL 92
SESSION 92
STRONG 92
Content Delivery Network (CDN) 8, 120
Continuous Integration (CI) 23, 136
Create-Read-Update-Delete (CRUD) 80, 201
Cross-origin resource sharing (CORS)
about 182
URL 182
Custom Domain Name
web application, configuring 138, 139
customer solution
issues 45
Custom Image 31

D

data access
speeding up, via caching 123-126
speeding up, with Azure Redis 123-126
data center
setting up 7, 8
data transfer
reference link 55
Data Transfer Object (DTO)
reference link 88
DefinitelyTyped
URL 194
deployment tasks
organizing, with Deploy to Azure button 317-322
Deploy to Azure button
reference link 319
used, for organizing deployment tasks 317-322

Developer Command Prompt 60
development environment
    data center 7, 8
    development machine, building 8-12
    provisioning, for mobility 25, 26
    provisioning, with Azure Active
        Directory 27, 28
    provisioning, with Azure
        RemoteApp 29-33
    setting up 4-7
    VM, generalizing 13-16
development process
    implementing 17
    third-party services, integrating 23, 24
    Visual Studio, integrating 21, 22
    VSO environment, creating 18-20
DevEnv 25
disaster recovery (DR) 300
DocumentDB
    reference link 91
Domain-driven Design (DDD) 279
Domain Name System (DNS) 138

E

Easy tables (ET) 202
Echo API
    about 247
    creating 248-250
e-commerce software platform
    creating 142, 143
    orders, handling 144, 145
    prerequisites 143
Entity Framework DbContext 87
event collector 283
EventHub
    messages, sending 266, 267
events
    used, for dealing with past 280, 281

F

Facebook
    URL 181
First-In-First-Out (FIFO) 147, 268
frontend servers
    Resource mode Virtual Network,
        configuring 47-52

G

GitHub
    reference link 90
global mobile app events
    deviceready 195
    pause 195
    resume 195
GoDaddy.com 138

H

hosting requisites, worker code
    Azure WebJob 276
    Cloud Services V1 276
    Service Fabric (Cloud Services V2) 276
    virtual machine 276
HTML UI customization
    reference link 182

I

id
    idempotency feature 273
    tracing feature 273
Identity Access Management (IAM)
    about 20, 28, 142
    advanced features 181-184
    Azure Active Directory B2C 176-180
    Azure AD 174-176
    claims-based authentication 174-176
    outsourcing 172, 173
Identity Provider (IdP) 175
index, actions
    Facetable 110
    Filterable 110
    Key 110
    Retrievable 110
    Searchable 110
    Sortable 110
Index.html
    URL 183
Infrastructure-as-a-Service (IaaS) 1
IntelliSense 302
IP addresses
    reference link 62

iris dataset
  about 166
  URL 166
ITableEntity interface, entity
  ETag 128
  PartitionKey 127
  RowKey 128
  Timestamp 128

K

Kudu environment 217, 218

L

latency 8
LinkedIn
  URL 181

M

machine learning
  about 165
  classification 165
  regression 165
  supervised learning 165
  unsupervised learning 165
  URL, for standard workspace 166
machine learning algorithm cheat sheet
  URL 171
Makecert.exe 60
Malware Assessment 76, 78
Manage schema functionality 207
markup metadata
  class attribute 189
  ID attribute 188
  name attribute 189
  tag 188
messages
  about 267
  processing, with workers 275-279
  sending, with queues 270-274
messaging patterns, Azure Service Bus
  brokered messaging 268
  notification hub 268
  relay messaging 268

Microsoft ASP.NET MVC
  used, for building up web frontend 102-106
Microsoft Azure
  URL 9
Microsoft Thin PC
  about 25
  reference link 25
mobile applications
  building, with Visual Studio Tools for
      Apache Cordova 190-200
  capability 187
  touch and gestures 187
  views 187
  visibility 187
  writing 187-190
mobile apps
  about 202
  building 203-209
  data, obtaining from service 209-212
  data, sending to service 213-217
mobile apps, access options
  Allow anonymous access 206
  Disabled 207
Monaco 218
Multiclass Neural Network 168

N

namespace 45
Network Interface (NI) 62
Network Security Group (NSG) 9, 51
Node.js
  and Azure 217-222
  considerations 218
  URL 217
NuGet
  reference link 90

O

Office connectivity
  configuring, with point-to-site VPN 59-61
Online Transaction Processing (OLTP) 145
OpenWeatherMap API
  URL 227

Operational Insight
  key features 67
  Malware Assessment 76-78
  SQL Assessment 73-76
  System Update Assessment 71-73
  used, for managing virtual network 65-71
operations 299
orders, e-commerce software platform
  data, extracting into data
    warehouse 155-164
  data, loading into data warehouse 155-164
  data, transforming into data
    warehouse 155-164
  denormalized data, producing for
    analysis 152-155
  handling 144, 145
  Pull approach 144
  Push approach 144
  user actions, decoupling from SQL
    sinking 145-151
  valuable information, predicting with
    machine learning 164-171
organizational containers
  data server 50
  gateway 50
  web server 50

P

Package Manager 272
Package search tool 191
partitioning 81
per-message event handling 281-288
per-stream event handling
  about 288, 289
  arrival time 296
  custom time 296
  events, collecting with Azure Event
    Hubs 290, 291
  event streams, processing with Azure
    Stream Analytics 291-298
Platform-as-a-Service (PaaS)
  about 1
  maintenance 17

point-to-site VPN
  about 56
  used, for configuring office
    connectivity 59-61
policies, Azure API Management (APIM)
  access restriction policies 251
  advanced policies 252
  API level 251
  authentication policies 254
  operation level 251
  product level 251
  transformation policies 254, 255
  using 251, 255
Polyglot Persistence 82-84
Premium Storage 11
Preshared key (PSK) 256
production slot 137
Project Column block 171
Pull approach
  advantages 144
  disadvantages 145
Push approach
  advantages 144
  disadvantages 145

Q

queues 267

R

redundancy 80
regression 165
**Relational Database Management System
  (RDBMS)**
  comparing, with partitioning 81, 82
remote debugging
  App Service, debugging with 259, 260
Remote Desktop Protocol (RDP) 4
remote VM, user administrator
  advantage 27
  disadvantage 27
repetitive operations
  automating 33, 34
  automating, with Azure Automation 34-40
  automating, with Azure Scheduler 40, 41

resource group 45
Resource Manager
   about 10
   versus Classic Manager 30
   versus Service Manager (classic)
      mode 44-46
Resource mode Virtual Network
   configuring, for frontend servers 47-52
REST services
   debugging, with Service Bus relay 260-262
RootManageSharedAccesKey 294
runbook
   executing 40

S

scenarios, OMS
   automation 67
   availability 67
   log analytics 67
   security 67
SDK
   reference link 277
Service Bus relay
   using, to debug REST services 260-262
Service Level Agreement (SLA) 276
Service Manager (classic) mode
   versus Resource Manager mode 44-46
Service mode (classic) Virtual Network
   configuring, for backend servers 52-55
Service Providers (SP) 235
ServiceStack 233
Shared Access Secret (SAS) 91, 272
shopping cart
   persisting, with Azure Table
      Storage 126-130
SignalR 286
Simple Object Access Protocol (SOAP) 235
Simple Responsibility Principle 289
single page application 198
site-to-site connection
   used, for connecting two virtual
      networks 56-59
site-to-site VPN 56
Software-as-a-Service (SaaS)
   about 5
   maintenance 17

solution services, deploying ways
   environments 299
   multi-tenancy 300
   update and upgrade 299
SQL Assessment 73-76
SQL databases 80
SQL Data Warehouse (SQLDW) database
   about 157
   URL 157
StackExchange Redis 125
Start class 286
storage account 9
Streaming Units (SU) 295
subscription
   storage, reference link 75
supervised learning 165
Swagger Editor 236
Swagger/OpenAPI
   API, documenting 235, 236
   API, importing 248
Swagger UI
   about 236
   URL 236
System Update Assessment 71-73

T

Team Foundation Server (TFS) 4, 16
team project
   reference link 18
technical community case study 185, 186
template
   object based programming 312
   programming 312-317
   string manipulation 312
   writing 302-311
Test/Prod Deployment Environment 4
third-party services
   Azure Service Bus 23
   Azure Storage 23
   integrating 23, 24
   Jenkins 23
   MyGet 23
   Slack 23
   ZenDesk 23
Traffic Manager 271

transformation policies
  about 254
  backend service, setting 254
  URL, rewriting 255
  URLs, masking 254

U

unstructured data
  storing, in Azure Storage 115-123
unsupervised learning 165
User eXperience (UX) 187

V

Virtual Hard Disks (VHDs) 13
virtual networks
  managing, with Operational Insight 65-67
Virtual Network (VN) 46 9
Visual Studio
  integrating 21, 22
Visual Studio Online (VSO) 17
Visual Studio Tools
  mobile applications, building with 190-200
VM
  generalizing 13-16
VPN
  point-to-site VPN 56
  site-to-site VPN 56
VPN gateway configurations
  reference link 55
VSO environment
  creating 18-20
  events 23
  project collections 18
  Team Projects 18
  URL 18
VSO environment, configuration settings
  Process Template 19
  version control 19

W

web application
  configuring, with Custom Domain
    Name 138, 139
WebAppPlan 305
web frontend
  building, up with Microsoft ASP.NET
    MVC 102-106
**Web Services Description Language
  (WSDL) 235**
web site application 198
WebSocket protocol 286
Windows Azure Virtual Machine
  deploying, in ARM Virtual Network 61-65
Windows Phone device accessory
  URL 26
worker code
  hosting, requisites 276
workers
  used, for processing messages 275-280

Z

Zapier
  about 24
  URL 24